After Foucault

꞊ AFTER ꞊
FOUCAULT
Humanistic Knowledge,
Postmodern Challenges

꞊ EDITED BY ꞊

Jonathan Arac

꞊ Rutgers University Press ꞊
New Brunswick and London

Library of Congress Cataloging-in-Publication Data

After Foucault.

   Includes index.
   1. Foucault, Michel.   I. Arac, Jonathan, 1945–
B2430.F724A64   1988   194   88-6455
ISBN 0-8135-1329-4
ISBN 0-8135-1330-8 (pbk.)

British Cataloging-in-Publication information available

CONTENTS

INTRODUCTION

Jonathan Arac

These essays address the conditions of disciplinary knowledge in humanistic studies after the work of Michel Foucault. They cover a wide range of fundamental concerns within the humanities: from philosophy of knowledge in both theoretical and applied forms, to philology, stylistics, history, psychoanalysis, and politics. In some cases, Foucault's work is severely criticized as an obstacle to effective understanding or action; in other cases, Foucault's work offers a resource with which the author attempts to displace received disciplinary self-conceptions. But whether they would be tabulated as "for" or "against" Foucault, all of the authors show that their understanding has been altered by the challenges his work has posed; even to defend a subject against Foucault requires redefining the subject.

By its use of historical (archaeological, genealogical) research as the means for revising the premises of our current philosophical understanding, through its powerful claims that both truth and the human subject that knows truth are not unchanging givens but are systematic, differential productions within a network of power relations, Foucault's work has changed the basis for the work of all scholars. To specify its particular force, the contributors locate Foucault's work in its relations of resemblance and difference to the critical theory of the Frankfurt school, the philosophical deconstruction of Jacques Derrida, the wider rethinking of the human sciences called "poststructuralism," and the horizon of our contemporaneity that figures so different as Fredric Jameson, Jean-François Lyotard, and Jürgen Habermas define as the "postmodern."

Edward W. Said's remarkably compressed and forceful memorial notice mentions all the most important motifs in the essays that follow; yet this collection, precisely because of its collective character, does more than any single author could to explore the ramifications of Foucault's work. Our undertaking is Foucaldian insofar as it correlates essays by a number of specific intellectuals, rather than hoping for the magisterial synthesis that might have been achieved by a general intellectual of the old school. Even those chapters that are boldest in sweep remain located in specific groups or disciplines, rather than claiming to speak for all humanity or all knowledge.

In finding the practice of writing in Foucault's work an instance of the postmodern, Said strikes the note for David Couzens Hoy's extraordinary meditation on Foucault, postmodernity, and the conditions of knowledge, the status of the "unthought." Yet for all its philosophical precision, Hoy's essay ranges into social theory, such as the debates provoked by the Critical Legal Studies movement. Epistemology can no longer stand alone as a master discourse; postmodern knowledges "are trivial until they are used in a way that could make a difference."

Said raises several telling points of comparison between Foucault's work and that of Theodor W. Adorno, and Paul A. Bové views the work of Adorno and his collaborator Max Horkheimer in tandem with that of Foucault as a means of criticizing the extremely influential work of Stephen Toulmin on the basis of disciplinary knowledge. Although the issues he raises in his chapter are of extremely wide sweep, Bové maintains a local focus on the profession and discipline of literary study, that in which he is most deeply involved and himself most knowledgeable.

"The greatest of Nietzsche's modern disciples" is one of Said's first formulations of Foucault's identity, and this thread guides Daniel T. O'Hara's path through the labyrinth of postmodern stylistic practice as he tracks down an answer to "What Was Foucault?" Echoing and almost mocking the title of one of Foucault's most famous and influential essays ("What Is an Author?"), O'Hara himself practices the mode of radical parody which he finds Foucault taught our age and learned from Nietzsche: "the exaggerated imitation" of a style or position that the parodist "shares with others by virtue of a network of ideological and professional identifications and associations."

No one could miss the force of Foucault's erudition, which Said emphasizes, but the discipline of history has been reluctant to put that erudition to use, for Foucault's work usually deployed historical materials counterdisciplinarily. Marie-Rose Logan argues that Foucault's interpretation of the relationship between words and things in the Renaissance defines his divergence from the continuing tradition of scientific history, in the name of which Anglo-American historians have tended to judge him. Yet Foucault's work also resists that textualism which has offered the primary alternative to scientific history in contemporary Renaissance studies. The result is heterotropic, like Magritte's *Les Deux Mystères,* a painting to which Foucault devoted important commentary.

Said notes with regret the Eurocentric provinciality of Foucault's major arguments and has himself done much to remedy that in his pathbreaking work *Orientalism* and elsewhere. Against the grain of Foucault's own insistent opposition to hermeneutics, H. D. Harootunian suggests a use of Foucault which combines with the dialogism of the Soviet scholar Mikhail Bakhtin to help us understand the Other: in this case, to help make possible a Western reconception of a crucial moment in Japanese history. The question at stake throughout Harootunian's essay is crucial to the responsible practice of sociology and anthropology, as well as history, namely is there some nondominative form of knowledge of an Other?

The questions that feminism poses further indicate an Other, as Said notes, that Foucault's work failed to address. The paired essays by Isaac D. Balbus and Jana Sawicki explore the possibility of a Foucaldian feminism. As an advocate of insurgencies that speak for particular groups rather than for humanity, Foucault might seem very useful to feminists, who have come to understand the ways in which the "human" has occluded "woman." Balbus thinks otherwise, however, arguing that Foucault's critique of true discourse undermines the basis on which a feminist transformation of our society might occur. Sawicki, in contrast, finds Foucault useful not only for feminism but also for criticizing Balbus's arguments. Balbus's concern with the object-relations theory of mothering leads him to find in coparenting the means to break through our cycle of psychological and social malformations, yet in addition to other objections Sawicki asks why feminism should in the end come down to childrearing.

Finally, Sheldon S. Wolin addresses head-on the question of Foucault's use for political renewal, a matter on which Said also touches, and which in differing ways traverses most of the other essays. Wolin questions Foucault's neglect of the major institutions of organized power in our world—the economy, the state, the law—and he finds Foucault still surprisingly under the spell of the so-called hard sciences. Most important, however, Wolin tries to redefine the position of the critical intellectual, from Moses and Plato, through Marx, to the present. He insists that against Foucault's emphasis on the notion of practice, we must restore a sense of action, an emphasis that Said shares in his own critique of Foucault in *Orientalism*. The challenge of Foucault's work may renew as well as dissolve humanism, yet, as witnessed by the Renaissance, what is reborn is never the same.

This volume takes its beginning from a conference held in 1985, sponsored by the Institute for the Humanities of the University of Illinois at Chicago, at which the essays by Hoy, Logan, Harootunian, Balbus, and Wolin were first presented. These contributors join me in thanking Robert V. Remini, Director of the Institute, and the others at the University of Illinois who made the conference possible, including Donald N. Langenberg; Richard M. Johnson, John Curtis Johnson, and Lawrence W. Poston; Philip Dwinger and Jay Levine; and Penelope Maddy. *Raritan* is also gratefully acknowledged for permission to reprint Edward Said's essay; as is Basil Blackwell, who published a slightly different version of Isaac Balbus's essay. I warmly appreciate both the contributors' patience through the process of publication and the support of Leslie Mitchner of Rutgers University Press, who made this process possible. Eleni Coundouriotis of Columbia University has given valuable assistance in preparing the final manuscript and index.

After Foucault

MICHEL FOUCAULT, 1926–1984

Edward W. Said

According to the medical bulletin published in *Le Monde* (June 27, 1984) Michel Foucault died at 1:15 p.m. on June 25 in Paris's Hopîtâl de la Salpetrière of neurological complications following acute septicemia. Framing the announcement was an extraordinary array of tributes grouped under a page one, two-column headline, "La mort du philosophe Michel Foucault." The lead article was by Pierre Bourdieu, Foucault's distinguished colleague at the Collège de France. It is difficult to imagine so concentrated and estimable a degree of attention paid to any other contemporary philosopher's death, except in France and in Foucault's case, which despite the difficulty and intransigence of his philosophical and historical work even drew a memorial tribute from the prime minister. Why this was so explains the enormous loss Foucault's death represented, just as it says something about the startling yet sustained force and influence of his thought.

He is best understood, I think, as perhaps the greatest of Nietzsche's modern disciples and, simultaneously, as a central figure in the most noteworthy flowering of oppositional intellectual life in the twentieth-century West. Along with Jean-Paul Sartre and Maurice Merleau-Ponty, Georges Canguilhem, Jean-Pierre Vernant, Lucien Goldmann, Louis Althusser, Jacques Derrida, Claude Lévi-Strauss, Roland Barthes, Gilles Deleuze, and Bourdieu himself, Foucault emerged out of a strange revolutionary concatenation of Parisian

Reprinted by permission from *Raritan: A Quarterly Review* 4, no. 2 (Fall 1984). Copyright ©1984 by *Raritan*, 165 College Avenue, New Brunswick, New Jersey 08903.

aesthetic and political currents which for about thirty years produced such a concentration of brilliant work as we are not likely to see again for generations. In what amounted to a genuine upheaval in modern thought, the barriers between disciplines and indeed languages were broken, then the fields separated by these barriers were reshaped from beneath the surface to their most complex superstructures. Theory, images of astonishing fecundity, and vast formal systems—to say nothing of idioms that seemed barbarous at first but soon became fashionable—poured out from these figures, whose ancestry was a contradictory amalgam of the academic and the insurrectionary. All seemed to have been deeply affected by Marx and individually to a greater or lesser degree by Freud; most were rhetorical tacticians and obsessed by language as a way of seeing, if not actually constituting, reality; many were influenced by university courses and almost legendary teachers—the names of Gaston Bachelard, Georges Dumézil, Emile Benveniste, Jean Hyppolite, and Alexandre Kojève (whose famous lectures and seminars on Hegel seem to have formed an entire generation) recur with frequency—as much as they were influenced by surrealist poets and novelists like André Breton and Raymond Roussel, as well as by the maverick writer-philosophers Georges Bataille and Maurice Blanchot. Yet all of these Parisian intellectuals were deeply rooted in the political actualities of French life, the great milestones of which were World War II, the response to European communism, the Vietnamese and Algerian colonial wars, May 1968. Beyond France, it was Germany and German thought that mattered most, rarely the work of British or American writers.

Even in this unprecedently exceptional company, Foucault stood out. For one, he was the most wide-ranging in his learning: at once the most concrete and historical, he was as well the most radical in theoretical investigation. For another, he seemed the most committed to study for its own sake ("le plaisir de savoir" in Bourdieu's phrase about him) and hence the least Parisian, the least modish, fashionable, or backbiting. Even more interesting, he covered huge expanses of social and intellectual history, read both the conventional and unconventional texts with equal thoroughness, and still seemed never to say routine or unoriginal things, even during the final stage of his career when he had a tendency to venture comically general observations. He was neither simply a historian, nor a philosopher, nor a literary critic, but all of those things together, and then more still. Like Theodor Adorno, he was rigorous, uncompromising, and ascetic in his attitudes, although unlike Adorno his obscurities had less to do with his style, which was brilliant, than with the grippingly large, often obscure, theoretical and imaginative suggestions about culture, society, and power toward which his entire oeuvre tended.

In short, Foucault was a hybrid writer, dependent on—but in his writing going beyond—the genres of fiction, history, sociology, political science, and philosophy. He therefore imparts a certain deliberate extraterritoriality to his work, which is for that reason both Nietzschean and postmodern: ironic, skeptical, savage in its radicalism, comic and amoral in its overturning of orthodoxies, idols, and myths. Yet in Foucault's most impersonal prose, one can still hear a distinctive voice; it is not accidental that he was a master of the interview as a cultural form. Thus the old acceptable demarcations between criticism and creation do not apply to what Foucault wrote or said, just as they do not apply to Nietzsche's treatises, or to Gramsci's *Prison Notebooks,* Barthes's writing generally, Glenn Gould's piano and verbal performances, Adorno's theoretical or autobiographical fragments, the work of John Berger, Pierre Boulez, Luchino Visconti, or Jean-Luc Godard. This is by no means to say that Foucault's histories, for example, have no historical validity or accuracy, but it is to say that—like the others works I have mentioned—the form and concern of these histories as artifacts require principal attention as self-aware, mixed-genre performances in the present, full of learning, quotation, and invention.

Although there are at least three distinct phases to his intellectual career, a number of themes recur in Foucault's work from inception to end. These themes are better grasped as constellations of ideas, rather than as inert objects. An insistently durable chain of conflicts marks everything Foucault studied and wrote about, and is the focus of his famous archaeologies and Nietzschean genealogies. In the beginning he seems to understand European social life as a struggle between, on the one hand, the marginal, the transgressive, the different, and, on the other, the acceptable, the normal, the generally social, or same. Out of this struggle are born (and the metaphors

4
EDWARD W. SAID

of parturition and biological sequence are important to Foucault's conception of things) various attitudes that later develop into institutions of discipline and confinement which are constitutive of knowledge. Hence, we get the birth of the clinic, prison, or the asylum, the institutions of medical practice, penal science, or normative jurisprudence. These in turn produce resistance to and consequently changes in the very same institutions, until—and this is a grim insight formulated by the later Foucault—prisons and hospitals are seen as factories for delinquency and illness respectively. Thereafter Foucault argues that power insinuates itself on both sides of the sequence, within institutions and sciences, and eruptively and as a form of attractive but usually coopted insurrectionary pressure, in the collectivities and individuals doomed to confinement and the production of knowledge—the mad, the visionary, the delinquent, the prophets, poets, outcasts, and fools.

Another major constellation of ideas present from start to finish in Foucault's work is knowledge (*savoir*) itself. He studied its origins, its formation, its organization, its modes of change and stability, always responsive to its massive material presence, its reticulated complexity, its epistemological status, as well as to its minutest detail. His archaeologies were purposely intended not to resemble studies in the sociology of knowledge. Instead he was, in his words, attempting to turn history against itself, to "sever its connection to memory, its metaphysical and anthropological model, and construct a counter-memory—a transformation of history into a totally different form of time." ("Nietzsche, Genealogy, History").

Between himself and knowledge, Foucault therefore developed an evolvingly complex and ambivalent attitude, and here I want to make quick reference to the three phases of his career. In his earliest large works—*Madness and Civilization (Histoire de la folie)* (1961; English translation, 1965) and *The Order of Things (Les mots et les choses)* (1966; 1970) (the rather approximate relationship between the translations and their French originals, titles as well as texts, is an index of how erratic were Foucault's English translations)—is the enthusiastic, relentlessly erudite researcher, digging up documents, raiding archives, rereading and demystifying canonical texts. Later, in the second period, in *The Archaeology of Knowledge* (1969; 1972) and "The Discourse on Language" (*L'Ordre du discours*) (1970; 1971), he

stands away from knowledge, spinning out a whole systematic apparatus so as to do to knowledge what knowledge does to *its* material.
During this period knowledge is, so to speak, taken apart and redisposed into Foucault's terminology: this is when words like *archive,
discourse, statement, ennunciative function* fill his prose as a way not so
much of signaling a French obsession with precise classification, as of
controlling, making productive his emerging hostility toward knowledge as a kind of transparent mental prison. Yet, paradoxically, the
overall bias of Foucault's work remains rational, dispassionate, calm.
But with *Discipline and Punish* (1975; 1977), which emerges directly
from Foucault's work on behalf of prisoners, and *The History of
Sexuality* (1976; 1978), whose basis in the vicissitudes of Foucault's
own sexual identity is notable, knowledge has clearly been transformed into an antagonist. To it he pessimistically attaches power, as
well as the ceaseless, but regularly defeated, resistance to which it
gives rise.

At the heart of Foucault's work is, finally, the variously embodied idea that always conveys the sentiment of otherness. For
Foucault, otherness is both a force and a feeling *in itself*, something
whose seemingly endless metamorphoses his work reflects and shapes.
On a manifest level, as I said, Foucault wrote about deviation and
deviants in conflict with society. More interesting, however, was his
fascination with everything excessive, all those things that stand over
and above ideas, description, imitation, or precedent. This fascination was back of his anti-Platonism as well as his unwillingness to tilt
with critics (except for occasional sardonic forays against critics—
George Steiner comes to mind—who insisted on calling him a structuralist). What he was interested in, he said in the *Archaeology,* was
"the more" that can be discovered lurking in signs and discourses but
that is irreducible to language and speech; "it is this 'more,'" he said,
"that we must reveal and describe." Such a concern appears to be
both devious and obscure, yet it accounts for a lot that is specially
unsettling in Foucault's writing. There is no such thing as being at
home in his writing, neither for reader nor for writer. Dislocations, a
dizzying and physically powerful prose (for example, the description
of torture that opens *Discipline and Punish,* or the quieter but more
insidiously effective pages on the death of man in *The Order of
Things),* the uncanny ability to invent whole fields of investigation:

these come from Foucault's everlasting effort to formulate otherness and heterodoxy without domesticating them or turning them into doctrine.

This is Nietzsche's legacy operating at a deep level in the work of a major twentieth-century thinker. All that is specific and special is preferable to what is general and universal. Thus, in a memorable interview, Foucault showed his preference for the specific as opposed to the universal intellectual, for the thinker who like himself worked at the concrete intersection of disciplines rather than for the great pontificators (perhaps Sartre and Aron were intended) who presumed to command the whole culture. However alienated, estranged, or "commodified" it may have been then, the present and its concerns dictated the imperatives of study and its ethics to Foucault. Neither identity in the object nor the author's identity, neither object nor subject, were as important to him as the fugitive energies making up human, or even institutional, performances in the process of taking place. Hence the almost terrifying stalemate one feels in his work between the anonymity of discourse and discursive regularity on one side, and, on the other side, the pressures of infamous egos, including Foucault's own, whose will to powerful knowledge challenges the formidable establishment of impersonal rules, authorless statements, disciplined enunciations. At the same time that he was immersed, perhaps even immured, in archives, dossiers, and manuscripts, Foucault seems paradoxically to have stimulated himself and his audience to a greater degree of sovereign authority, as if to illustrate his own thesis that power produces resistance, and resistance, new forms of power.

The middle phase of his career was, I think, energized by the events of May 1968; for the first time, Foucault was impelled to serious methodological reflection. This is also when he gave his first interviews, using them to advance ideas that he would later elaborate in *The Archaeology of Knowledge*. His philosophy of power also originated in the late sixties as he seemed to begin to understand both the limits of insurrectionary rebellion and the extent of the domains regulated imperceptibly by the laws of discourse. Curiously, although Foucault was already tending to the almost Schopenhaurian pessimism and determinism of his late work, his essays during the sixties and early seventies can be read as an expression of pleasure in variety, the density and energy, of aesthetic and intellectual projects. The pieces on Bataille, Flaubert, Deleuze, Hölderlin, Magritte, and Nietzsche which date from this period (some were collected and sensitively annotated by Donald Bouchard in *Language, Counter-Memory, Practice*) are to some readers his finest work, essays in the truest sense of the word, brilliant without being overbearing.

The pivotal work, however, was an inaugural lecture at the Collège de France, *L'Ordre du discours* (translated as *The Discourse on Language*) given in the spring of 1970. Here he set forth his program of research and lectures at France's premier academic institution. In typical fashion he addressed his audience across the centuries, as it were, outlining projects on nothing less than truth, rationality, and normality in a voice that was simultaneously Beckettian in its gnomic ellipses and Renanian in its portentous sonority. At roughly the same time he took on Derrida, whom he must have viewed as his major domestic competitor for intellectual ascendancy. Even allowing for Foucault's clearly genuine fear that the school of deconstruction was licensing an ahistorical laissez-faire attitude, there is an edge and a derisive scorn to his words about Derrida that were not typical of him, as if in striking he had to strike definitively at the man who was otherwise affiliated with him by virtue of a common antimythological, anticonservative project. To the best of my knowledge Derrida did not respond to Foucault, a mark of compunction and restraint which led, I believe, to a gradual healing of the rift between them.

It is too early to disentangle the numerous threads of Foucault's interests, antinomian, often violent, always provocative and political, which proliferated during the seventies. He became a celebrated author and a lecturer much in demand all over the world. His courses at the Collège de France drew large audiences, to whom he returned the compliment by actually preparing his lectures, always researching them exhaustively, delivering them with appropriate formality and respect in the best tradition of the *cours magistrale*. His work on behalf of prisoners and penal reform matured and was completed during this period, as were his related—highly eccentric—attitudes toward psychiatry and revolution. These, naturally enough for an intellectual with his sociopsychological trajectory, were embodied in the hostility he frequently evinced for the work of Freud and Marx,. authors without whom Foucault himself would have been unthinkable. But it is a fact that his socially anomalous personality and his immense gifts made Foucault suspicious of his own genealogy. He was therefore a self-born man, choosing his predecessors carefully, like Borges's Kafka, effacing some of his life's biological, intellectual, and social traces with great care and effort. He was even more careful with his contemporaries, distancing himself in the course of time from both the Maoist currents of the sixties and the worst excesses of the *nouveaux philosophes*, who were generally respectful of him as they were not of the other great Parisian idols.

In the last phase of his career Foucault's interests narrowed from investigations of the social aspects of confinement, as reflected in the microphysics of power, to ruminative histories of sexual identity. In other words, he shifted his attention from the constitution of the human as a social subject, knowable through the detail of disciplines and discourses, to human sexuality, knowable through desire, pleasure, and solicitude. Even so, his very last project changed considerably from what he had said it would be in the first volume of his *History of Sexuality*. By the time the next two volumes (*The Use of Pleasure* and *The Care of the Self*) appeared after a hiatus of eight years, in the year of his death, he had completely reconceived the project, returning to classical Greece and Rome to discover how "individuals were led to focus their attention on themselves, to decipher, recognize, and acknowledge themselves as subjects of desire, bringing into play between themselves and themselves a certain relationship that allows them to discover, in desire, the truth of their being, be it natural or fallen" (*The Use of Pleasure*, p. 5).

What caused this particular and overdetermined shift from the political to the personal was, among other things, some disenchantment with the public sphere, more particularly perhaps because he felt that there was little he could do to affect it. Perhaps also his fame had allowed a considerable relaxation in the formidable, and the formidably public, regimen of erudition, production, and performance he had imposed on himself. He was noticeably committed to exploring, if not indulging, his appetite for travel, for different kinds of pleasure (symbolized by his frequent sojourns in California), for less and less frequent political positions. It was nevertheless sad to think of him as yet another progressive who had succumbed to the blandishments of often hackneyed pronouncements against the Gulag and on behalf of Soviet and Cuban dissidents, given that he had in the past so distanced himself from any such easy political formulas.

Yet we can also speculate that Foucault's shift had come about —characteristically—via an unusual experience of excess, the Iranian revolution. He had been one of the first Westerners to look into what he called the "spiritual politics" of the Shi'ite opposition to the Shah. He discovered in it just that entirely collective, involuntary excessiveness which could not be herded under conventional rubrics like class contradictions or economic oppression. The ferociously murmuring and protracted energy he discerned in the Iranian revolution attracted him to it for a while, until he saw that its victory had brought to power a regime of exceptionally retrograde cruelty. It was as if for the first time Foucault's theories of impersonal, authorless activity had been visibly realized and he recoiled with understandable disillusion.

A truly intelligent man, Foucault had a world reputation at the time of his death. What all his readers will surely remember is how in reading him for the first time they felt a particular shock at encountering so incisive and egregiously interesting a mind which, with one electrical burst after another, staged ideas with a stylistic flair no other writer of Foucault's depth and difficulty possessed. In so productive and exhaustive a researcher, it was remarkable that his books— even the very long ones—tended always to the aphoristic, and his mastery of the art of making crisp negative distinctions in series of threes and fours (e.g., "archaeology" is neither the history of ideas, nor intellectual history, nor the history of mind) rarely tired one out: on the contrary, they exhilarated and stirred the reader. Yet in the English-speaking world he was most influential among literary theorists who, alas, dissected and redissected his methodologies and paid little attention to his histories.

On the other hand, his weaknesses were quite marked even though, I think, they did not seriously mar the quality and power of his fundamental points. The most striking of his blind spots was, for example, his insouciance about the discrepancies between his basically limited French evidence and his ostensibly universal conclusions. Moreover, he showed no real interest in the relationships his work had with feminist or postcolonial writers facing problems of exclusion, confinement, and domination. Indeed his Eurocentrism was almost total, as if history itself took place only among a group of French and German thinkers. And as the goals of his later work became more private and esoteric, his generalizations appeared even more unrestrained, seeming by implication to scoff at the fussy work done by historians and theorists in fields he had disengaged from their grasp.

But whether Foucault is read and benefited from as a philosopher or as a superb intelligence riskily deploying language and learning to various, often contradictory ends, his work will retain its unsettling anti-utopian influence for generations to come. His major positive contribution was that he researched and revealed technologies of knowledge and self which beset society, made it governable, controllable, normal, even as these technologies developed their own uncontrollable drives, without limit or rationale. His great critical contribution was to dissolve the anthropological models of identity and subjecthood underlying research in the humanistic and social sciences. Instead of seeing everything in culture and society as ultimately emanating from either a sort of unchanging Cartesian ego or a heroic solitary artist, Foucault proposed the much juster notion that all work, like social life itself, is collective. The principal task therefore is to circumvent or break down the ideological biases that prevent us from saying that what enables a doctor to practice medicine or a historian to write history is not mainly a set of individual gifts, but an ability to follow rules that are taken for granted as an unconscious a priori by all professionals. More than anyone before him Foucault specified rules for those rules, and even more impressively, he showed how over long periods of time the rules became epistemological enforcers of what (as well as of how) people thought, lived, and spoke. If he was less interested in how the rules could be changed, it was perhaps because as a first discoverer of their enormously detailed power he wanted everyone to be aware of what disciplines, discourses, epistemes, and statements were *really* all about, without illusion.

It is almost too neat an irony, however, that Foucault died in the very hospital, originally a mental institution, now a hospital for neurological disorders, he had researched for his *Madness and Civilization*. This is eerie and depressing, as if his death confirmed Foucault's theses on the symbiotic parallelism between what was normal and what was pathological, rational and irrational, benign and malignant. A more striking irony is that "the philosopher of the death of man," as Foucault was sometimes called, should seem to be, at the time of his own death, the very example of what a truly remarkable, unmistakably eccentric, and individual thing a human life really is. Much more than a French public figure, Foucault was an intellectual with a transnational vocation. Instead of easy denunciation, he brought to the job of exposing the secret complicities between power and knowledge the patient skepticism and energetic fortitude of philosophic seriousness. And he was stylish and brilliant to boot.

FOUCAULT
Modern or Postmodern?

David Couzens Hoy

The question about where we are now in philosophy is not a new one. Michel Foucault thinks that Kant begins the modern tradition of making this a central question for philosophy, although only in what was for Kant an occasional, minor essay entitled "What Is Enlightenment?" Recently the assumption that philosophy has contributed to a growth in enlightenment and to the progress of reason has been contested by critics whom Kant could not have foreseen. The debate is now no longer between ancients and moderns, but between moderns and postmoderns. The issue is whether modern philosophy, which starts around the time of Descartes, has ended. "Ended" may be too strong a word, since of course philosophers can continue to work on the problems of modern philosophy. But the question is whether an alternative conception of philosophy emerges at some point in the nineteenth century, perhaps at the precise moment on January 3, 1889, when Nietzsche collapses into insanity. By leaving us a fragmentary, aphoristic collection of philosophical writings, Nietzsche provides a model for philosophy which is so different from the model of Kant and other moderns that we are forced to call it postmodern.

Is the distinction between modern and postmodern philosophy simply a polemical one? Even if it is, once the distinction is drawn, philosophers will have to worry about it. Once philosophers start taking the idea of the paradigm shift (which may itself be a postmodern idea) seriously, the thought that philosophy would be a more likely candidate than physics for such a shift is not far behind. What may worry philosophers today, then, is that somehow a paradigm shift is occurring which will leave some behind. We who are involved with contemporary philosophy will want to consider seriously the question of whether our stance is modern or postmodern. If neither label fits, we can nevertheless try to assess whether there are reasons for postmodernism, however disquieting it may seem, which will make us dissatisfied with the modern tradition as well.

The question of whether we are at a juncture between two conflicting conceptions of philosophy, the modern and the postmodern, has been formulated most explicitly in books by Jürgen Habermas and Jean-François Lyotard.[1] In this chapter I shall ask whether Michel Foucault should be read as a modern or a postmodern thinker, given the Habermas-Lyotard debate. Of course, Foucault does not address the question of postmodernity in detail, although I think he would have had to do so had he lived longer. Reflecting on his own relationship to Kant's conception of the task of modern philosophy in his own late essay entitled "What Is Enlightenment?" he does suggest that we should not think of modernity only as an era coming between a premodern and a postmodern one. Instead, we are to consider modernity more as an attitude, one that is always accompanied by a contrasting countermodern attitude: "consequently, rather than seeking to distinguish the 'modern era' from the 'premodern' or 'postmodern,' I think it would be more useful to try to find out how the attitude of modernity, ever since its formation, has found itself struggling with attitudes of 'countermodernity.'"[2]

Periodization, I must add, is itself a modernist tool. As Heidegger remarks in "The Age of the World Picture," the modern age defines itself as the latest period, but it does not yet know what period it is. The term *modern* thus functions as a placeholder in the absence of a more definite description. Any period that does not understand itself as a period would not accept its periodization. To be able to delineate the characteristics of a period is already to be beyond it. The time beyond does not yet seem to have defining characteristics and thus is apparently not a period itself. Periods are always past, and the present cannot understand itself as a period, even if, qua modern, it has a metabelief that it too is yet another period. The postmodern thinker challenges this metabelief by disrupting the modernist assumption that periods are self-contained unities or coherent wholes which can be clearly individuated from one another. The modernist may wish to rejoin that in using the prefix *post,* postmoderns are themselves invoking periodization. The postmoderns could reply, however, that they are doing so simply because they are speaking to moderns. If postmoderns use the tools of modernity, they may do so rhetorically to subvert the progressivist assumption that modernity is the unequivocal telos of history.

If Foucault is undoubtedly correct in saying that modernity is more significantly an attitude than an era, he still must consider differences between various countermodern attitudes. Habermas has accused the French poststructuralists of adopting a postmodern stance that conceals a deeply conservative desire to return to the premodern. Lyotard contests this strategy of lumping together the premodern and the postmodern. Foucault's own development, I shall argue, shows how at least one thinker evolves from a modern stance to one that, for lack of a better word, could be called postmodern rather than premodern because his resistance to the modern is not nostalgic. Foucault's work is a good case study, not only because it is not decided in advance about the modern-postmodern contrast, but because it too takes seriously the possibility of paradigm shifts in philosophical knowledge.

Foucault does not, of course, have a fully worked-out theory of knowledge in the Kantian sense, and he offers no account of how knowledge *in general* is possible, or how it must be acquired and communicated.[3] However, his books on the history of medicine, the human sciences, the disciplinary pseudosciences, and sexuality certainly seem to tell us something about the acquisition and communication of some forms of knowledge. We learn how forms of knowledge develop gradually and spread to cover neighboring areas of inquiry, and we are also told that there are abrupt, discontinuous changes in what counts as knowledge from one moment to another. The point of these claims about knowledge is sometimes wrongly thought to be that there is no knowledge, that truth is relative, or that there is no truth that needs to be taken seriously. What the stories really tell us is that conceptions of what counts as true or false are complex and multileveled. Cognitive disciplines do not progress by fine-tuning an already correct representation of an independent domain of objects. Instead, the objects are themselves functions of the conceptions of what sorts of things we could desire to know about. The increase of knowledge is not the progressive discovery of the nature of the things themselves, but the spinning of ever more subtle webs of beliefs and practices.

The moral of this story about the spinning of webs is surprising, however. Foucault does not celebrate the transcendental capacity of the spidery human mind to spin the web of its world, as Kant did. For Kant knowledge looks empirically like a function of the world rather than of the mind, but transcendentally it turns out to be intrinsic not to the things themselves but to the cognitive apparatus. Empirically, the spider might appear to be dependent on or even caught in its own web, but transcendentally the web is possible only because it is the creation of the spider. If the web includes not only facts but also values, particularly moral values, then for Kant the web is indeed a sign of the spider's transcendental freedom.

Foucault's version of the story is notoriously different. Empirically the web may appear to the spider to be a freely created device that it spins to capture its victims. From a transcendental point of view, however, the web is seen to be most effectively the prison not of the spider's victims, the largest and smallest of which can escape it. The prison most effectively entraps the spider itself, who cannot live without it or even perceive whether anything lies beyond the ethereal substance of its spatio-temporal, causally connected strands. Of course, unlike Kant, Foucault does not posit further a redeeming, noumenal standpoint.

The Unthought and How to Think It

The contrast between the transcendental and empirical standpoints is one of three doubles that Foucault sees in the attempts of modern thought to inquire into the conditions for the acquisition and communication of knowledge. I select these pages of *The Order of Things* as an exemplary instance of Foucault's description of modernity, and of the conditions for the possibility of the acquisition and communication of modern knowledge. Modern thought turns from the world to ask about the being to whom the world appears, and the being thus posited is called man. The other two doubles that go along with the transcendental turn reflecting on man, as depicted in *The Order of Things*, are the double of the cogito and the unthought, and that of the retreat and return of the origin.

Doubles are not like distinctions, dichotomies, or dualisms, because both sides of the double are in effect in cognitive inquiry and give it a dynamic quality. All three of these doubles result when inquiry turns from directly investigating the world and asks how it is *possible* for the world to be investigated. Thought tries to think what had remained unthought, namely, not how the world appears to thought, but how thought could itself be something to which the world could appear. Thought is at first its own unthought. Gradually, however, it becomes a feature of the modern to inquire into thought. Descartes first takes the cogito as completely transparent to itself, but for later empiricism the metaphor for thought is a blank slate or a black box. The mind will be a black box from the empirical point of view because it cannot be empirically perceived, but Kant, the precursor of contemporary cognitive science, then constructs a transcendental method for reconstructing how the mind functions. However, Kant's enterprise tells us only enough about what can be thought to explain how knowledge of the world is possible. More than that he believes we cannot know, and ultimately the mind is not only unthought, but also unthinkable. Genuine self-knowledge is in a sense impossible, since the self that we make appear to ourselves as an object of knowledge will never be identical to the self that is constructing that object.

The third double, that concerning the retreat and return of the origin, results from this inability of self-knowledge to capture the activity rather than the possibility of knowledge. "We have seen," says Foucault toward the end of *The Order of Things*, "how labour, life, and language acquired their own historicity, in which they were embedded; they could never, therefore, truly express their origin, even though, from the inside, their whole history is, as it were, directed towards it. It is no longer origin that gives rise to historicity; it is historicity that, in its very fabric, makes possible the necessity of an origin which must be both internal and foreign to it."[4] From within a particular field of knowledge the horizon of the field stretches out indefinitely. Just as the limits of any perceptual horizon can never be seen insofar as they lie just beyond what is visible, so the origin of the horizon, the standpoint that makes a horizon possible, is itself not in the visual field, but prior to it in both a logical and a phenomenological sense. So although we can date the beginnings of our own preferred forms of knowledge and thus recognize that people did not always think in our terms, nevertheless from within our perspectives, thinking of the world and ourselves in the ways we do seems inescapable. "Inescapable" may well be the wrong word, since our modes of knowledge do not feel restrictive but rather, enabling. To *desire* to think differently seems whimsical, irrational, and perhaps crazy if the desire is an impossible one to want to have.

According to *The Order of Things*, we have come to think of ourselves and our world through categories like labor, life, and language, and although it was recognized that historically other people had not experienced the world through these categories, nevertheless the categories are invariably presupposed in the disciplines studying these peoples:

> [F]rom the moment the first object is manipulated, the simplest need expressed, the most neutral word emitted, what man is reviving, without knowing it, is all the intermediaries of a time that governs him almost to infinity. Without knowing it, and yet it must be known, in a certain way, since it is by this means that men enter into communication and find themselves in the already constructed network of comprehension. Nevertheless, this knowledge is limited, diagonal, partial, since it is surrounded on all sides by an immense region of shadow in which labour, life, and language conceal their truth (and their origin) from those very beings who speak, who exist, and who are at work. (*OT*, p. 331)

Knowledge is no longer a result of an individual Cartesian privately examining the certainty of the contents of thought. Instead, it is produced socially, and the individual must be educated into an ongoing discourse, the original questions and motivations of which are either remote and tacit or else themselves the subject of controversy. Furthermore, the Cartesian methods of introspection, self-examination, and self-study will no longer work because we are not transparent to ourselves, as the Cartesian cogito was supposed to be. On the contrary, for the most part we do not know how we know what we know. Our beliefs about how and why we have come to believe what we do are unlikely to be right, or at least not the whole story, since we always presuppose ideas and practices that we do not and perhaps could not articulate to ourselves.

Modern thought cannot leave the unthought alone, however. Because it is investigating itself, it cannot rest content with the thought that there is more about itself that it does not know and that might threaten the soundness of what it believes it knows. The drive of modern thought is expressed differently by different philosophers: "the whole of modern thought is imbued with the necessity of think-ing the unthought—of reflecting the contents of the *In-itself* in the form of the *For-itself*, of ending man's alienation by reconciling him with his own essence, of making explicit the horizon that provides experience with its background of immediate and disarmed proof, of lifting the veil of the Unconscious" (*OT*, p. 327). Hegel, Sartre, Husserl, and Freud cannot leave the unthought unsaid but must try to eliminate its alienness by thinking it.

Although Foucault is not explicit about those to whom he is referring, he seems to think that Heidegger is also caught in the modern double. Heidegger calls for an attitude of *Gelassenheit*, of letting beings be, so that we shall get beyond the modern technologi-cal concern with making everything clear and distinct. In contrast to modern technology, Heidegger, the prophet of the postmodern, is reconciled to the inevitability of the unthought. Nevertheless, in the very act of describing his attitude as one of waiting for the call of Being, Heidegger seems to Foucault to be unclear about whether his concern for the unthought should be described in terms either, in Foucault's words, "of becoming absorbed in its silence, or of straining to catch its endless murmur" (*OT*, p. 327).

All modern thinkers believe that man's reflection on himself will change man. Success in revealing some previously unthought features that have been operative in or constitutive of thinking is itself what makes thinkers modern:

> In modern experience, the possibility of establishing man within knowledge and the mere emergence of this new figure in the field of the *episteme* imply an imperative that haunts thought from within. . . . What is essential is that thought, both for itself and in the density of its workings, should be both knowl-

edge and a modification of what it knows, reflection and a transformation of the mode of being of that on which it reflects. Whatever it touches it immediately causes to move: it cannot discover the unthought, or at least move towards it, without immediately bringing the unthought nearer to itself—or even, perhaps, without pushing it further away, and in any case without causing man's own being to undergo a change by that very fact, since it is deployed in the distance between them. (*OT*, p. 327).

Since thinking the hitherto unthought changes man, Foucault believes that modern thought is unable to formulate a morality for itself. In contrast to the Stoic and Epicurean moralities modeled on a conception of the order of the world, modern thought is always both obscure about its own nature and in the process of changing that nature. So any order it would consider accepting is always tentative and tenuous. But even though Foucault believes that "for modern thought, no morality is possible," he is not suggesting that modern thought generates no values. "As soon as it functions," Foucault insists, modern thought "offends or reconciles, attracts or repels, breaks, dissociates, unites or reunites; it cannot help but liberate and enslave" (*OT*, p. 328). Modern thought is itself a form of action, and thus Foucault believes it to be a truism that "knowledge of man, unlike the sciences of nature, is always linked, even in its vaguest form, to ethics or politics" (*OT*, p. 328).

Notice that Foucault says modern thought will both liberate and enslave. I take it he means that both of these happen at once. Knowledge (of man, though not necessarily of nature) is tied to politics, that is, to power, since knowledge is not only put to use, but the uses we have for gathering knowledge will themselves determine what sorts of knowledge we acquire. Knowledge is not gained independently of its uses, but the facts gathered will be functionally related to the uses to which they can be put.

The Controversy about Postmodernity

In *The Order of Things* Foucault has identified the attempt to think the unthought behind man's attempt at both knowledge and self-knowledge as the distinctive feature of *modern* thought. These reflections raise the question of whether Foucault is himself a modern, one who continues to try to think the unthought. Or by having exposed the dialectical illusion of the attempt to think the unthought, has Foucault moved beyond the aims of modern philosophy? Should we think of Foucault as a postmodern philosopher?

Derrida and other postmoderns aspire to a break with modernity by breaking up modernity and showing its self-delusions. Similarly, Foucault in *The Order of Things* talks about the end of "man," the paradigmatic object for modern thought. So in that book he is not a modern insofar as he brackets belief in the object that modern thought is concerned to investigate. Furthermore, only a few years later in his inaugural lecture in which he describes his planned research program, he insists that "[w]e must not imagine that there is a great unsaid or a great unthought which runs throughout the world and intertwines with all its forms and all its events, and which we would have to articulate and think at last."[5] Yet what is striking about his portrayal of the problem of thinking about the unthought is that he seems to be describing something much like what he is doing in his later works on power and on sexuality. Power permeates knowledge as the latter's unthought, since the acquisition of knowledge is traditionally assumed to be undistorted by power relations, even when the knowledge is about the social sphere. Insofar as Foucault seems to show power to be the modern unthought, is Foucault then still a *modern* thinker? Is he unable or unwilling to break with the effort of modern thinking to penetrate its own origins even when he knows that the origin will invariably retreat and hang just beyond the limits of his inquiry, returning only when he looks away?

Defenders of modernity, enlightenment, and reason will see Foucault as a postmodern and imply thereby that he is advocating irrationality. Foucault himself denies that he is an enemy of reason, and he never accepted the label of postmodernism. But I want to look beyond his own self-interpretation and ask whether he can usefully be seen as evolving toward a postmodernism that is not adversarial toward reason and enlightenment. Much of the current debate depends on a confused picture of exactly what the postmodern attitude is. Postmoderns are often characterized as those who think they are already beyond the modern. Habermas, however, maintains that postmodernism is linked more to a nostalgic desire to return to the archaic or premodern. For him the postmodern critique of modernism is largely the same as the antimodernism that accompanied the initial rise of modernism. Lyotard contests Habermas's conception of the postmodern as premodern nostalgia, but even Lyotard does not think postmodernism really transcends modernism. He sees postmodernism not as a repetition of the premodern but as a moment within modernism itself. Lyotard stresses that modernism has always included those who try to go beyond it, but who thereby merely generate yet another development within modernism itself. Modernism and postmodernism are thus linked, and for Lyotard they can be found in other ages than our own.

When asked in a late interview explicitly about postmodernism and the Habermas-Lyotard debate, Foucault refuses to side with either. He rejects Habermas's description of him as a conservative who is nostalgic for an archaic past.[6] Foucault does not side with Lyotard, though, because Foucault does not want to be cast as an enemy of reason and enlightenment. But in contrast to Habermas, Foucault thinks the task today is not to defend reason or the ideals of the enlightenment tradition so much as to bring to awareness the dangers that have resulted from attempts to put these ideals into practice in social institutions that have had different historical effects than were intended.

I want to pursue the question of whether critics of Foucault like Habermas are correct in suspecting a cynicism and conservatism in his apparent refusal of any normative or constructive socio-political position. These criticisms require a decision both about whether Foucault's voice is modern or postmodern and about the relation of the postmodern to the modern. To explore the issue I shall sketch a line of interpretation of Foucault's development that will suggest he evolved into a postmodern thinker, although I shall suggest that Foucault's postmodern attitude differs from and even undermines Lyotard's conception of the postmodern condition.

The Modern/Postmodern Distinction

I start with the hypothesis that both the modern and the postmodern ways of thinking can be described as thinking the unthought. The difference between them is in *how* to think it. I shall continue to focus on the particular problem of knowledge rather than on art or culture, but I am making claims about the acquisition of knowledge not in the natural sciences (as Lyotard does), but only in the social and human sciences (which are Foucault's concerns). Let me differentiate modern from postmodern ways of thinking the unthought in four ways.

The first difference between the modern and the postmodern is a willingness of postmoderns to accept rather than to lament the inevitable inability to think the "great unthought." Instead of believing with the Cartesian and Enlightenment tradition that thinking must self-validate itself and leave nothing that could be known unknown, the postmodern denies that thinking is completely lucid, and that it works by illuminating everything about the world and itself. Avoiding the metaphorics of light, the postmodern sees thinking as generating further complexity and complications, not as being self-transparent. Of course, this way of thinking is prepared by other moderns. Kant, for instance, destroys the idea of empirical scientific inquiry coming to an end, and he does so by rejecting the Cartesian notion of the mind as having privileged access to itself and to its self-validating ideas. Heidegger goes beyond neo-Kantianism, and particularly beyond Husserl's version of it, by denying that we should think of the mind as being able to represent discretely all that can be known and believed. For Heidegger we should not think of our understanding of the world as consisting of beliefs and rules that are in principle completely articulatable. We cannot talk about *all* our true beliefs representing the world, or *most* of our beliefs being true, simply because beliefs are not discrete things that can be counted. Understanding is a holistic phenomenon for Heidegger, which means that to have discrete, articulatable beliefs about the world I must first already be in a world. My beliefs emerge from a background of shared practices with which I am already familiar, and indeed, this background is required for me to be what I am.

Heidegger's theory is not holistic in the sense that Hegel's is, however. There is no claim that the truth is the whole, or that to know anything we must know everything. For Heidegger understanding is relative to context, and contexts are multiple and diverse. Lyotard speaks in more Wittgensteinian terms of language games, which Lyotard asserts are heteromorphous, such that there is no metagame or metacontext from which to identify rules common to any and every language game.[7] In general, the poststructuralists infer that we should always be suspicious of any totalizing discourse. Lyotard thinks that even science is less of a totalizing discourse than it used to be. Citing examples ranging from quantum theory to catastrophe theory to studies of schizophrenics, he believes that modern science is increasingly interested in studying not general regularities but singularities, incommensurabilities, and unstable rather than stable systems. Postmodern science is described as going the way of postmodern art and architecture: "Postmodern science—by concerning itself with such things as undecidables, the limits of precise control, conflicts characterized by incomplete information, 'fracta,' catastrophes, and pragmatic paradoxes—is theorizing its own evolution as discontinuous, catastrophic, nonrectifiable, and paradoxical. It is changing the meaning of the word *knowledge*, while expressing how such a change can take place. It is producing not the known, but the unknown."[8]

However dramatic this claim sounds, it is a much stronger thesis than would be needed to reject totalizing discourse at the level of social theory and the human sciences. Foucault's enterprise is less one of offering an alternative epistemology, as Lyotard seems to be doing, than of showing empirically that the social, medical, and human sciences did not improve the human condition in the way that was theoretically intended. If Foucault is anywhere near the historical truth, the humanitarian intentions behind the development of some modern social institutions and their accompanying social sciences were instead undermined by the supposedly just practices constructed to acquire the supposedly objective knowledge. When Foucault's empirical studies are also intended to undermine comparable Marxist studies (as in *Discipline and Punish*), the point is to show that larger, more speculative theories of the social totality are not needed to criticize the present. Foucault thus finds himself forced to oppose the progressivist rhetoric of Marxism and sexual liberation movements, however much he might welcome their practical politics. His plight is understandable, however, and the poststructuralists are not alone in finding themselves unable to believe theories of world history, or claims to absolute knowledge, or utopian social theories.[9]

The second feature captures better what makes the postmodern seem like a more radical break from the tradition, even though whether it represents a radical break from antitraditional modernism is another matter. The problem at this point is, granting the first point (the postmodern sense that elements and conditions of our thinking will inevitably remain unthought), should postmoderns continue to try to think the unthought? Heidegger's enterprise certainly implies that they should, and indeed must. So the second feature has to do with the way postmoderns continue to try to think the unthought. The question they struggle with is how to do so given the paradoxes that they see in the efforts of moderns to reveal the unthought as a whole.

Heidegger exemplifies the problem. Sometimes his notion of *Gelassenheit*, or letting beings be, is taken to imply that we cannot ever think our own unthought. We can only await the call of Being. This point is often taken to imply a reactionary politics. Allan Megill, for instance, states in his recent book, *Prophets of Extremity*, that Heidegger's philosophy is "an acceptance—indeed, a confirmation—of the existing social and political order."[10] However, this interpretation is hard to square with Heidegger's criticism of the modern age for being so essentially technological. Heidegger's claim is that only by understanding what technology leaves unthought—namely, the essence of technology (how it transforms the world into discrete objects and human beings into functional resources) —is there any chance of getting around the dangers of modern technology.

Heidegger's strategy is not so different from that of the French poststructuralists. In response to the question of whether we should continue to try to think the unthought, they would say in common against the tradition that it all depends on what is meant by "trying to think." If by that is meant forcing the unthought out of the darkness into the light, or formulating the implicit ideas clearly and distinctly, or deducing the unthought conditions for experience (transcendentally or otherwise), we must give up trying to think the unthought. But that does not mean we can fail to be claimed by the unthought and interested in revealing it. An alternative approach is suggested by Heidegger's metaphor of the unthought as like a clearing (*Lichtung*) in the forest. The unthought is not hidden from us in the depths and darkness of the forest, but is instead the openness that allows discrete objects to be seen, although the openness itself is not seen (at least, not in the same sense that a discrete object within the clearing is seen). Anticipating the poststructuralist turn away from Freudian and Marxian attempts to explain surface events by deeper causal forces, Heidegger maintains that the modern era has misconceived the unthought, and it has done so by trying to conceive it as a discrete form either of objectivity (e.g., economic forces) or, more typically in philosophy, of subjectivity (e.g., Hegel's spirit, Schopenhauer's will, Nietzsche's will-to-power, Freud's libido, Husserl's intentionality). Since there will always be conditions of understanding which remain unarticulated, the point is not to continue to try to articulate them all but to let them appear when, in the effort to expand our understanding of ourselves and the world, they emerge indirectly. They will emerge when anomalies force changes in normal science, that is, when we encounter problems that force into the foreground the background practices and standard assumptions that previously had functioned imperceptibly as the clearing in which discrete observations and arguments made sense.

For the French poststructuralists, however, the unthought behind the acquisition and communication of knowledge is not some single a priori of communication, such as Habermas posits in his theory of the ideal speech situation as the counterfactual condition of truth assumed in any and every discourse. Instead, for the later Foucault the unthought that conditions knowledge is power. The tradition assumes that knowledge is logically independent of power, since to be known seems to mean to be acquired in conditions free from distortion and coercion. In the history of the acquisition and communication of knowledge, however, Foucault thinks that the interconnection between increasing social organization and the growth of certain forms of knowledge becomes apparent, and makes the idea of interest-free knowledge appear to be the anomaly instead of the rule. Or rather, what appears anomalous is the modern tendency, which is inherited from Kant, to believe in the narrative of Enlightenment and to hold paradoxically the two premises, namely that social progress must accompany the growth of knowledge, and that knowledge is logically independent of the social conditions of its acquisition and communication.

The Frankfurt School critical theorists explain the failure to perceive the anomaly as a self-deception forced on individuals by massively repressive social institutions. They thereby presuppose a way of thinking which is free from such distortion. More radically, Foucault does not continue to posit the ideal of knowledge free from power relations, even for his own knowledge of the history of the interrelations of knowledge and power. I think this is why Foucault finally abandons his efforts to formulate his theory of power, and of the relation of power and knowledge. As the modern unthought, power cannot be thought in the modern way by being completely represented in a theory. It resists theory, not because it is mysterious, but because it is not a single thing. Power is the unthought that is linked to every mode of knowledge, but since there are different modes of knowledge, there will be different power relations conditioning the different disciplines.

So the unthought is not merely another particular thought that we can learn to think and represent adequately in a theory. Instead, the unthought includes the background conditions and the general style of organization of a way of thinking rather than particular objects, contents, or thoughts. Furthermore, if the different ways of thinking have only a vague family resemblance, then there is no single form of organization which characterizes all possible ways of thinking. This is not to say that there are different categorical frameworks in the Kantian sense of the term, but only that we are no longer in the grip of the Kantian idea that there can be a single world only if there is a single categorical framework. Or as Foucault said in the passage from "The Order of Discourse" cited earlier, we learn to give up the belief in the reality of the great unthought running throughout the world in all its forms and events.

The third feature of the postmodern is to hold that (a) there is no single, privileged way to think the unthought. Corollary claims are (b) there is no reason to believe that there is only one unthought, and (c) no unthought is a single thing, capable of only one description or level of analysis. Foucault suggests these points when he says that he is a nominalist about power and a perspectivist about knowledge. According to my interpretation of Foucault he becomes a postmodern only when he comes to full recognition of these points. Accepting the consequences and giving up any pretensions to epistemology (in the traditional sense of the privileged discourse about the conditions for the possibility of any and every form of knowledge) results in a significant shift of emphasis in Foucault's thought between *The Archaeology of Knowledge* and *Discipline and Punish*.

The shift may have something to do with a move away from a belief in the autonomy of language to a concern with the social practices that contextualize language, as Hubert Dreyfus and Paul Rabinow claim.[11] Following their influential interpretation, *The Order of Things* is now generally classified in Foucault's quasi-structuralist phase. *The Archaeology of Knowledge*, which Allan Megill cleverly shows to be a parody of Descartes's *Discourse on Method*,[12] is the methodological treatise summing up this phase. Then after some more or less silent years he produces *Discipline and Punish*, and calls his method not archaeology but genealogy.

If, however, his project in his later works is still to think the unthought, then there is at one level a continuity to his work despite the discontinuities in his attempts at theoretical self-understanding and methodological self-justification. During the archaeological phase his own remarks suggest that he is describing how linguistic structures are the conditions for the possibility of what can be known. In the genealogical phase his focus is less on language alone than on the connection between discursive disciplines and social power. In his last writings he says that neither language nor power was ever his true concern, but instead, that his interest all along has been in how human subjects and their historically variant subjectivities are constituted either by unthought social practices and discourses or by not completely thought-out ethical self-fashionings.

But these revised self-interpretations should not obscure underlying, continuous interests. On the apparent shift from language to power Megill notes that Foucault continues to be concerned more with discourse about social and sexual practices in the later works than with the social practices per se.[13] Foucault's own later denial that power is his main concern suggests further that there is a continuity in his thinking manifested in his earliest and last works by his concern for experience and subjectivity. His belief throughout is that subjective experience is socially and historically constituted by factors that individuals learn to internalize without being consciously forced to do so. This interest in subjectivity seems to go against the usual claim that the structuralists and poststructuralists no longer believe in man and subjectivity, but substitute language and systems instead. But there need not be an issue here. The interest in systems is compatible with the interest in subjectivity if subjectivity is a function of systems, such that the system conditions the subjectivity that emerges, and the subjectivity serves in turn to maintain and further the system.

The postmodern attitude toward subjectivity is that it is not a deep philosophical reality underlying the surface manifestations studied by sciences like psychology and sociology. We do not need a transcendental deduction of it because it is itself a surface phenomenon with no deep structures or underlying causal forces that need to be explained. The postmodern concern with surfaces rather than with deep explanations implies that instead of explaining, postmoderns are interpreting. I mean by this that instead of taking themselves to be discovering an independently given reality governed by lawlike regularities, they see themselves as doing something more like interpreting texts. Moreover, instead of assuming that every text has a single unifying structure, they think that texts are almost infinitely complex. The postmodern paradigm is not profundity but complexity. Foucault's development is consistent with this paradigm shift, but instead of tracking this development through the content of what he studies at various times, I shall focus on his move from a modernist, quasi-Kantian conception to a more hermeneutical, genealogical understanding of how to justify his interpretive practices.

Beyond Nostalgia: Foucault's Path to Postmodern Genealogy

The fourth, and most characteristic feature of the postmodern attitude is the way it has moved beyond not only the rhetoric of progress but also the rhetoric of nostalgia. Both rhetorics involve taking oneself too seriously, perhaps even so seriously as to make "man" (or at least our modern, enlightened selves) the center of philosophical investigation (as in Kant's "Copernican revolution," which seems really to reverse the scientific revolution started by Copernicus).

A typical postmodern ploy for disabusing us of our modern self-seriousness and showing us that profundity is just an appearance produced by complexity is pastiche. As Fredric Jameson points out, postmodern architectural pastiche recapitulates "a whole range of traditional Western aesthetic strategies" so that "we therefore have a mannerist postmodernism (Michael Graves), a baroque postmodernism (the Japanese), a rococo postmodernism (Charles Moore), a neoclassicist postmodernism (the French, particularly Christian de Portzamparc), and probably even a 'high modernist' postmodernism in which modernism is itself the object of the postmodernist pastiche."[14]

Pastiche is not the same as parody,[15] but it can be used by a social critic, I believe, to satirize and challenge common social assumptions. Both parody and pastiche can undermine a previous cultural statement. But pastiche manages to appear to be committed to an aesthetic vocabulary at the same time that it does not take that vocabulary as rigid and fixed. It manages to make its statements without making them directly in any representable style but rather indirectly through the vocabulary of previous styles, which it enjoys and about which it does not seem to be cynical. Unlike pastiche, parody is ironic and attempts to show a particular cultural statement to be false. Parody therefore implies either that there are cultural statements that could be true, or, if it wants to be more radical and even paradoxical, that all cultural statements are absurd. If parody implies this more extreme view, it must avoid making any positive cultural statements of its own. This paradox can transform irony into cultural cynicism.

Irony is paradigmatic of modernism, and the tone of postmodernism is less ponderous and not at all cynical. Postmodern architectural pastiche enjoys itself and succeeds because it is not anxious about whether it is a lasting cultural statement. Perhaps it has been cured of the anxiety of influence, which is the central obsession of modernism. More lighthearted in a Nietzschean manner and less self-important, it openly displays influences that it transcends in the same gesture. It also transcends the obsessiveness of the modernist concern with itself as the culmination of cultural progess. I do not know if there can be a postmodern postmodernism, but I doubt that the possibility would worry the postmodern to the degree that the possibility of the postmodern worries the modernist. Whether the present represents progress over the past, or whether it will itself be displaced in the future, are not questions that worry postmoderns. For the postmodern interest in complexity rather than in modernist functional simplicity, the narrative of progress, which preoccupies modernism, appears to be simply a story, or at least too simple a story.

If the metanarrative of progress inherited from the Enlightenment falls away, postmodern art and thought should feel no nostalgia and should not regret the lack of a new metanarrative to put in its place. Nostalgia only makes sense in contrast to the hope for progress, and abandoning the trope of enlightened progress makes wistful longing for an age of innocence pointless as well. The ability to act without nostalgia is what carries the French postmoderns beyond Heidegger, whose tone remains one of regret over the historical withdrawal of Being, and who seems unable to free himself from the desire for an anchoring in Being. As Lyotard portrays the postmodern attitude, it has freed itself from nostalgia for the lost narratives that the modern tradition used to justify itself and no longer feels the need to recapture an underlying continuity with the past: "Postmodern knowledge is not simply a tool of the authorities; it refines our sensitivity to differences and reinforces our ability to tolerate the incommensurable."[16]

This statement is excessive, however, since strictly speaking, no rational inquiry could tolerate the incommensurable, if that means to believe relativistically that there are no grounds for adjudicating between one way of understanding some phenomena and another, competing one. When Foucault was writing *The Order of Things* and *The Archaeology of Knowledge*, he was charting historical discontinuities to make us more tolerant of discourses that seem incommensurable with ours. Later, however, he focuses as much on continuities as on discontinuities, perhaps because he recognizes that there are philosophical problems with identifying a language as incommensurable with ours. Some philosophers of language have argued that an apparent language that is not commensurable with ours, in the sense of not being translatable into ours, could not really be considered a language at all, let alone tolerated or treated as if it were really making sense of a totally different kind. So in his last writings on sexuality Foucault would probably settle for the more plausible description of his task as refining our sensitivity to differences.

Not to be a tool of the authorities is also a basic desire of Foucault's, but he does not think that the only way to avoid being a tool
is to give up the desire to legitimate one's own discourse and practices, at least to some degree. Lyotard's suggestion that postmodern
thinkers will experience incredulity at the ideal of self-legitimation
through metanarratives does not entail that other forms of legitimation are not viable.[17] Philosophical self-legitimation is traditionally achieved by a metanarrative, for instance, about the necessary
progress of knowledge and freedom. Foucault never subscribed to this
metanarrative, but *The Archaeology of Knowledge* looks much like an
attempt at a self-justification which would put his own philosophy, in
Kantian fashion, on the secure path of science. Even if he later gave
up on this attempt, he never freed himself entirely from his philosophical background and thus from the temptation to try to justify his
own method and position. The *Archaeology* is his most notable attempt at self-legitimation, but despite later disclaimers to the effect
that he is not interested in his own legitimacy, his interviews and
lectures evidence a continual effort on his part to interpret and
understand himself. This frequently repeated search for a narrative
about his own development to explain his present stance is not
inconsistent with his genealogical method, however, since there is
nothing impossible about studying oneself genealogically.

Where there is a methodological difficulty is with the quasi-
epistemological theory stated in the *Archaeology*, where Foucault
strikes me as being guilty of what he himself calls "transcendental
narcissism."[18] Previous philosophies are said to be guilty of taking
themselves to be the only discourse that can justify the right of any
other discourse to speak with authority and to have a legitimate
claim to count as knowledgeable. But Foucault himself claims a
comparable privilege for archaeology itself. Archaeology in his sense
studies archives, that is, the historically differentiatable kinds of
assumptions about what could count as a body of knowledge. Much
like the epistemes he describes in *The Order of Things*, an archive is
the "historical *a priori*" that gives the conditions of the possibility to
"what we can say—and to itself, the object of discourse" (*AK*, p.
130). Archives remain unthought at the time they are operant, and
no archive can be grasped in its totality. So our archive is our own
unthought: "it is not possible for us to describe our own archive,

since it is from within these rules that we speak" (*AK*, p. 130). Does archaeology itself have an archive? Yes. Can it describe that archive? Only "obliquely," by studying "the very discourses that have just ceased to be ours" and that separate us "from what we can no longer say" (*AK*, p. 130).

Archaeology starts looking like Kantian transcendental philosophy when it posits an a priori that can be deduced or at least indirectly inferred only by this one particular method. Although archaeology is not a theory of knowledge in the standard philosophical sense, it sounds suspiciously narcissistic when it appears to think of itself as the only method we can use to understand our own assumptions about what we count as knowledge. "The analysis of the archive," Foucault says, "involves a privileged region: at once close to us, and different from our present existence, it is the border of time that surrounds our presence, which overhangs it, and which indicates it in its otherness; it is that which, outside ourselves, delimits us" (*AK*, p. 130).

By the time of *Discipline and Punish* Foucault's pastiche emulates Nietzsche more than Kant. Archaeology is just a strategic moment of a more general method called genealogy. And like Nietzsche Foucault does not believe that genealogy is a privileged way to think the unthought, but merely one way of doing so. Not claiming to be objective and value-free, its advantage is precisely that it recognizes the possibility of alternative ways of letting the unthought reveal itself, since the unthought is not single but plural, not an archive but multileveled complexity. Genealogy does not need to think of itself as digging down to the foundations of thought, since if thought is always interpretation, there is no uninterpreted foundation containing the conditions for the possibility of any and every way of thinking or discoursing.

Once Foucault moves from a modernist, quasi-transcendental neo-Kantian stance to a postmodern, neo-Nietzschean stance, he has further reason to stop insisting on the radical incommensurabilities of various cognitive discourses and to give up his earlier tendency to see historical discontinuities occurring holistically. In his early works on the medical and clinical practices, and to some extent in *The Order of Things*, he describes conceptual revolutions as if they occurred in all sciences and all aspects of society at roughly the same time (e.g., a ten- or twenty-year period starting with the French Revolution). In the last writings on the history of sexuality there are still discontinuities, for instance, between Greek sexuality and Christian sexuality, and between both of those and modern sexuality, and between all of those and Chinese sexuality. There is a shared *concept* of sexuality since all have a common core consisting of three central components: acts, pleasure, and desire. But each has a different *conception* of the relation and relative importance of the three.[19] These conceptions are not incommensurable, since the later ones may include elements of the earlier ones. If there is change, the change is not total since only some elements of the ethical substance (the shared assumptions of what it is to be a member of a community and thus to aspire to being a certain kind of person or here, more specifically, what it is to be a sexual subject) change while others persist. I take Foucault's view to be that sexual ethics could be changed without necessarily altering at the same time all the political and economic structures that are contemporaneous with a particular formation of sexual practices.

Foucault and the Habermas-Lyotard Debate

Given this reading of Foucault's trajectory toward a genealogical rather than an epistemological self-legitimation, how should we now view Foucault in the light of the debate between Habermas and Lyotard on modernity and postmodernity? Habermas is only one of many critics who charge Foucault with failing to admit to the modern political and moral values of liberty and justice, when these same values seem to be presupposed by his critique of modern institutions like prisons, asylums, and schools.[20] Many of Foucault's critics assume that critical principles can only be developed from a standpoint independent of the social one being criticized. Anyone sharing this modernist assumption will tend to see Foucault as a nihilistic, fatalistic functionalist. As a functionalist Foucault would seem to presuppose that society is a social whole governed by an invisible hand rather than by an accountable, legitimate state power and a rational rule of law. As an anarchist/nihilist, Foucault would be read as disavowing not only any political structure but also any human nature that could persist without social systems. So Foucault would apparently believe that, short of abolishing modern society altogether,

social improvement is impossible. He would seem to be condemning
the modern period in wholesale fashion at the same time that he fails
to suggest alternatives to present institutions because he thinks that
there are no criteria for judging societies as being better or worse than
one another.

What can be said in Foucault's defense? I suggest that these
criticisms all reflect a misunderstanding of Foucault's enterprise,
caused perhaps by Foucault's own rhetoric in his political interviews.
Principally, the objections overestimate what it is he is intending to
do because they take him as a modern when he is finally a postmodern. I have been trying to show that postmodern views of knowledge need not deny that there is social knowledge or that there are
truths. But truths are trivial until they are used in a way that could
make a difference or that could lead to controversy and dissent. If
Lyotard is right, a central characteristic of postmodern thinkers is
that when the question is one about social theory and social science,
they are incredulous about the idea of holding state power rationally
accountable for a complex modern society: "Even if we accept that
society is a system, complete control over it, which would necessitate
an exact definition of its initial state, is impossible because no such
definition could ever be effected."[21]

This claim does not deny the domain of discussion of political
theory, but it does doubt its efficacy. Postmoderns need not go so
far as to deny that all social institutions are legitimate, a denial that
may seem to follow, for instance, from Lyotard's incredulity about
legitimation through rational consensus.[22] Lyotard could settle for
arguing against the Habermasian insistence that social institutions are
legitimate only to the extent they permit the rational formation of
consensus. There would be no need for postmoderns to suggest the
more extreme counterassertion that institutions should maximize dissent.[23] To view the debate as being between moderns like Habermas
who espouse consensus and postmoderns who promote dissent is to
oversimplify. Consensus and dissent are not contradictory values.
The consensus theorist does not believe that people should be forced
to consent or even that they are likely to reach consent in the real
world; the argument is only that communication presupposes, perhaps counterfactually, that those who disagree with one another still
presuppose the possibility of reaching consensus insofar as they con-

tinue to communicate and to believe that truths are at stake in the discussion. The dissensus theorist could not rationally assert both that any degree of consensus is an evil and that anyone who disagrees with this claim is wrong. To oppose consensus by stressing dissent as an alternative ideal is misguided, since the defender of dissent is thereby put in the awkward position of arguing against dissenters. What any defender of dissent probably believes is that dissent should never be suppressed, and that a society lacking signs of dissent would not be ideal but, on the contrary, could thereby be suspected of being massively repressive. The postmodern might thus think that the test of social justice is whether the social structures allow things other than what would normally be agreed on to be said and thought. Of course, if I am right that this position is crucial to postmodernism, then its major task is to consider whether there are limits to how much dissent and difference can be socially and politically tolerated. [24]

Foucault himself noticed the difficulty in appearing to defend dissensus over consensus. In a late interview where he was questioned about his reaction to Habermas's consensus model, he remarked, "The farthest I would go is to say that perhaps one must not be for consensuality, but one must be against nonconsensuality."[25] He thereby demurs from the Habermasian argument that rational discourse not only presupposes the possibility of reaching consensus but also identifies consensus and correctness. Although this conclusion strikes him as too strong, he does not thereby disagree with the kernel of truth behind the argument, which is that when we find others who appear to be rational and who nevertheless do not agree with our basic beliefs, we must investigate what this lack of agreement signifies. Perhaps there will be such significant differences in social practices that we could not expect to reach consensus, but nevertheless we will benefit from becoming more fully aware of how our practices are conditioning our perceptions, attitudes, and beliefs.

If my interpretation of Foucault's remark is correct, it would confirm the interpretation of his later writings which I have been offering. On this reading Foucault is not, and perhaps never was, a functionalist who believes that society is a single system in which no part can be changed or improved without a complete change in the entire system. He is also not a fatalist who believes that power is always dysfunctional or that there is no point in attempting to change our social practices. The late works on sexual ethics are not nihilistic since they are trying to show that mores and morals have a substantive cultural basis and role. These works are not fatalistic since they can have a corrective value, although in an indirect way. The earlier sexual formations are not genuine alternatives for us both because we cannot go back to them and because we can see that they were as problematic then as ours are now, although in different ways. But they do at least show us that our understanding of sexuality is not the way sexuality has always been understood and practiced. Therefore, sexuality as we understand it is not biologically and eternally fixed, but socially induced. If the modern understanding of sexuality is experienced as oppressive and inhibiting, thinking about historically different understandings may give us yet another understanding.

Of course, Foucault is not pointing toward the emergence of a postmodern sexuality that would be more natural than the modern one, since he rejects the idea that we have natural selves that could be liberated from social distortions. But he is suggesting that we ourselves recognize that we would be better off without the modern obsession with classifying people according to their sexual preferences and using distinctions such as that between normal and deviant sexual practices. The claim to be better off need not entail, however, an appeal to a sexual utopia.

What Foucault does in these last works is show us how to think the unthought without presupposing that what remains unthought is a metaphysical entity named man. If there is no such thing as man, there is no single thing that sex must always or most naturally be. The unthought consists of historically variable conceptions of what it is to be a sexual subject. These conceptions are hard to excavate. However, if we sift archaeologically through older texts that at first seem alien to our own experience, we can gradually re-create a conception of experience that will not conflate the previous conception and our own, but will allow the distinctiveness of ours to emerge in contrast to the distinctively different ones out of which ours was formed.

So in thinking the unthought we are no longer engaged in the modern enterprise with its metaphysical assumptions about the nature of man and its epistemological assumptions about a priori and invariant categories. The postmodern method is critical, genealogical history.[26] What genealogy describes is simply how we have come to be what we are. But in the very act of giving a successful genealogy we become different, or postmodern, in that we understand ourselves differently. Even if the task of becoming different seems uncertain and unclear, the postmodern self-understanding is "incredulous," as Lyotard would say, that it left unquestioned certain assumptions about itself for so long and suffered under the self-imposed illusion that a certain mode of experience or existence was necessary and unalterable.

Thinking the unthought in the postmodern, genealogical way thus counts as a genuine form of knowledge, since it comprehends some of what was left unthought. But it may not count as self-knowledge except in a partial and indirect way, since the successful genealogy reveals an implicit self-conception and thereby weakens the iron grip that conception had exercised precisely by remaining unthought. If the postmodern genealogy counts at all as self-knowledge, then the self that is thereby known turns out to be not single, unified, complete, and whole, but complex, disseminated, fractious, and fragile.

Conclusion

If I am reading Foucault's last writings correctly, he cannot be classified as either a modern or an antimodern. On his own terms he is not a modern since he no longer believes that our central unthought is the nature of man. He is also not nostalgic for the premodern since he has no neo-Rousseauian desire to return to a golden age of innocence. For Foucault there never was or will be such an age.

What about Lyotard's idea that the postmodern is always a moment of the modern? This suggestion does capture the way Foucault uses the modern interpretive project of thinking the unthought while simultaneously abandoning the modern metanarrative of social and epistemological progress. What remains to be seen is whether Foucault is coopted by the style of thinking he was attempting both to exploit and to invalidate. So finally the postmodern position must face a historical question, namely, whether its attempt to be posthistorical will either succeed or be succeeded. What makes me distinguish the postmodern from the modern more sharply than Lyotard does is that whereas both conceive themselves as facing this question, the postmodern attitude can face whatever is to come next without nostalgia. The modern attitude, in contrast, remains troubled both by anxious looks over its shoulder and by stern demands that the future be predictably better than the past. If this description is right, Foucault's attitude is neither modern nor antimodern but postmodern.

According to the view of postmodernism I have been advancing, a less extreme view than Lyotard's, calling Foucault a postmodern thinker does not entail, however, that his contemporaries and survivors either are or must become postmoderns as well. Historical breaks do not occur for everyone everywhere at the same time. The same person, discipline, or institution can be traditional in some respects, modern in others, and postmodern in yet others. Furthermore, since there is no necessary progress, no forward movement in history, and perhaps no such thing as history (in the absence of a convincing metanarrative), the postmodern cannot imply that there is any normative advantage that comes from being either later in time or a sign of the future. Postmodernism cannot and should not claim to be better, more advanced, or more clever than whatever preceded it. That modernism does assume this superiority is what distinguishes it from postmodernism, and what postmodern pastiche disruptively reveals. So a postmodern cannot argue that those who are traditional or modern must eventually follow the path to postmodernism. In contrast to Lyotard's stance, a Foucaldian postmodern would not need to be an advocate of postmodernism. I think that Foucault was a consistent postmodern in that he would never have called himself a postmodern. Moreover, he is the paradigmatic postmodern in that he never seemed to expect that his own incredulity about modern social knowledge would be reciprocated with anything other than a corresponding incredulity.

Notes

1. See Jean-François Lyotard, *The Postmodern Condition: A Report on Knowledge*, trans. Geoff Bennington and Brian Massumi (Minneapolis:

University of Minnesota Press, 1984); and Jürgen Habermas, *The Philosophical Discourse of Modernity: Twelve Lectures*, trans. Frederick Lawrence (Cambridge, Mass.: MIT Press, 1987). See also Habermas's essay, "Modernity versus Postmodernity," *New German Critique*, no. 22 (Winter 1981), p. 13, where he writes:

> The *Young Conservatives* recapitulate the basic experience of aesthetic modernity. They claim as their own the revelations of a decentered subjectivity, emancipated from the imperatives of work and usefulness, and with this experience they step outside the modern world. On the basis of modernistic attitudes, they justify an irreconcilable anti-modernism. They remove into the sphere of the far away and the archaic the spontaneous powers of imagination, of self-experience and of emotionality. To instrumental reason, they juxtapose in manichean fashion a principle only accessible through evocation, be it the will to power or sovereignty, Being or the Dionysiac force of the poetical. In France this line leads from Bataille via Foucault to Derrida.

2. Michel Foucault, "What Is Enlightenment?" in *The Foucault Reader*, ed. Paul Rabinow (New York: Pantheon, 1984), p. 39.

3. "Knowledge: Its Acquisition and Communication" was the title of Jonathan Arac's conference on Foucault at the University of Illinois at Chicago, May 10–11, 1985, for which this chapter was first written.

4. Michel Foucault, *The Order of Things: An Archaeology of the Human Sciences* (New York: Random House, 1970), p. 329. Hereafter cited as OT.

5. Michel Foucault, "The Order of Discourse" (December 2, 1970), trans. by Robert Young in his *Untying the Text: A Post-Structuralist Reader* (London: Routledge and Kegan Paul, 1981), p. 67. In context Foucault's remark suggests that historical discontinuity is the methodological consequence of disavowing the reality of any "great unthought" that would provide the ontological substratum for historical continuity.

6. Michel Foucault, "Space, Knowledge, and Power," in Rabinow, *The Foucault Reader*, pp. 248–250.

7. Lyotard, *The Postmodern Condition*, p. 65.

8. Ibid., p. 60.

9. Martin Jay charts the history of the devolution of the concept of totality in *Marxism and Totality: The Adventures of a Concept from Lukács to Habermas* (Berkeley and Los Angeles: University of California Press, 1984).

10. Allan Megill, *Prophets of Extremity: Nietzsche, Heidegger, Foucault, Derrida* (Berkeley and Los Angeles: University of California Press, 1985), pp. 194–195.

11. Hubert L. Dreyfus and Paul Rabinow, *Michel Foucault: Beyond Structuralism and Hermeneutics* (Chicago: University of Chicago Press, 1982), pp. 101, viii.

12. Megill, *Prophets of Extremity*, p. 228.

13. Ibid., p. 237.

14. Fredric Jameson, Foreword to Lyotard, *The Postmodern Condition*, p. xviii.

15. In another article ("Postmodernism, or, The Cultural Logic of Late Capitalism," *New Left Review* 147 [Summer 1984]) Fredric Jameson makes the convincing argument that parody "finds itself without a vocation" in the absence of dominant social and cultural metanarratives. Parody is eclipsed by pastiche in the move from modernist styles to postmodernist codes: "Pastiche is, like parody, the imitation of a peculiar mask, speech in a dead language: but it is a neutral practice of such mimicry, without any of parody's ulterior motives, amputated of the satiric impulse, devoid of laughter and of any conviction that alongside the abnormal tongue you have momentarily borrowed, some healthy linguistic normality still exists" (p. 65). Jameson remarks aptly that nostalgia is not "an altogether satisfactory word" to describe the "increasing primacy of the 'neo'" in postmodernism because there is no sign of "the pain of a properly modernist nostalgia with a past beyond all but aesthetic retrieval" (p. 66).

16. Lyotard, *The Postmodern Condition*, p. xxv.

17. See ibid., p. xxiv.

18. Michel Foucault, *The Archaeology of Knowledge*, trans. A. M. Sheridan Smith (New York: Pantheon, 1972), p. 203. Hereafter cited as *AK*.

19. Rabinow, *The Foucault Reader*, pp. 340–350. A concept, in this usage, consists of defining characteristics that are then interpreted or applied variously in its different conceptions. John Rawls employs this distinction in *A Theory of Justice* (Cambridge, Mass.: Harvard University Press, 1971; see p. 10).

20. I include many of these critics in my anthology, *Foucault: A Critical Reader* (Oxford and New York: Basil Blackwell, 1986), describing and discussing their criticisms in the Introduction.

21. Lyotard, *The Postmodern Condition*, p. 56.

22. See ibid., pp. 60–67.

23. "Consensus is a horizon that is never reached," says Lyotard, and he concludes that "it is now dissension that must be emphasized" (ibid., p. 61).

24. As an example consider recent debates about the rule of law. For the postmodern the rule of law need not be either objectionable or uncriticizable in practice. An example of an explicit attempt to come to terms with

the issue of the rule of law is the Critical Legal Studies Movement. I would label as postmodern, for instance, Roberto Unger's claim that the point of interpreting law is neither to preserve existing social institutions at whatever cost, nor to destroy them at whatever cost. Instead, he urges an active judiciary to use legal interpretation to keep social institutions from becoming too rigid and restrictive. See Roberto Mangabeira Unger, *The Critical Legal Studies Movement* (Cambridge, Mass.: Harvard University Press, 1986), and my discussion in "Interpreting the Law: Hermeneutical and Poststructuralist Perspectives," *Southern California Law Review* 58 (January 1985), pp. 136–176.

25. Michel Foucault, "Politics and Ethics: An Interview," in Rabinow, *The Foucault Reader*, p. 379.

26. For further discussion of methodological issues about genealogy and critical history, see my article, "Nietzsche, Hume, and the Genealogical Method," in the anthology *Nietzsche as Affirmative Thinker*, ed. Yirmiyahu Yovel (Dordrecht, Holland: Martinus Nijhoff, 1986), pp. 20–38. On the connections between Nietzsche's postmodern style and poststructuralist philosophy, see my essay, "Philosophy as Rigorous Philology? Nietzsche and Poststructuralism," in *Fragments: Incompletion and Discontinuity, New York Literary Forum* 8 and 9 (1981), pp. 171–185.

THE RATIONALITY OF DISCIPLINES
The Abstract Understanding of Stephen Toulmin

Paul A. Bové

Stephen Toulmin's *Human Understanding*[1] is roughly contemporary with the beginning of Michel Foucault's explicit preoccupation with disciplines and power.[2] Yet the differences between Toulmin and Foucault are so great that a limited comparison of their approaches to examining the relationship of the past to the present, especially in terms of disciplinary institutions and discourses, points up the main distinction between the legitimating activity of Toulmin's evolutionary model of history and philosophy of science, and Foucault's genealogical critique of post-Enlightenment forms of reason.

As Toulmin sees it, his task is to account for the advances reason makes in solving the problems that human needs discover in our (often technologically) modified environment. He aims to redefine reason, to free disciplinary knowledge from the traditional need to be logically systematic, and to correct philosophy's repeated error of identifying reason with logic (understood as a system of internal self-consistency). (I will return to the problematics of error in a discussion of Georges Canguilhem.) Toulmin's disciplinary project is quite clear: to reconstruct history and the philosophy of science as a general model of collective understanding, as an account of disciplinary rationality which would make it immune to critique by either, as he puts it, the followers of Plato, such as Bertrand Russell and Gottlob Frege, or the "radical relativisers," such as R. G. Collingwood and Paul Feyerabend.

Toulmin insists that Philosophers[3] must find a way around the consequences of these two positions, because both threaten the truth-producing abilities of science and its legitimacy. In other words, for Toulmin the problem is that science and the practical activity of scientists do not and cannot conform to the rationalist model of the Platonists; yet, science cannot be as anarchic as Feyerabend suggests and must be saved from charges of relativism to ensure the social efficacy and truth-value of disciplinary knowledge. The effect of Toulmin's project, however, extends beyond these two specific objectives and results in a general theory aimed at legitimizing and universalizing the social role of instrumental reason. Max Horkheimer, in the foreword to a late selection of his essays, *Critique of Instrumental Reason*, offers brief remarks on how this notion should be understood:

> Today . . . it is the . . . essential work of reason to find means for the goals one adopts at any given time. And it is considered superstitious to think that goals once achieved are not in turn to become means to some new goals. . . . When stripped of its theological garb, "Be reasonable" means: "Observe the rules, without which neither the individual nor society as a whole can survive; do not think only of the present moment."[4]

Horkheimer's critique bears on Toulmin's project. Although Toulmin claims a revolutionary potential for his conception of reason as practical,[5] ecological problem-solving (in contrast to the normal philosophical equation of reason with logical systematicity), the ideological effect of his scheme is to justify scientific and nonscientific discourses and disciplines without considering their position within the complex of affiliated social relations that make up and support the production of knowledge and value in postmodern societies. Toulmin seems to want to escape the dilemma he thinks follows from Locke's concept of reason; he hopes to show that disciplinary and professional structures ensure that the ends of reason are for human benefit, if not in every case, then in their institutionalized completion.

But Horkheimer, along with Theodor Adorno and many others, has struggled to drive home the historical implications of Locke's thought, that is, the concept of reason in a capitalist, instrumentalist society:

> The definition of reason in terms of individual self-preservation apparently contradicts Locke's prototypical definition, according

to which reason designates the direction of intellectual activity regardless of its intellectual goal. But Locke's definition still holds true. It does not liberate reason from the atomic self-interest of the individual. It rather defines procedures which more readily suit whatever goal self-interest may require.[6]

I submit that the ideological weight of Toulmin's project is to depoliticize thinking about reason and knowledge by detaching them from the sphere of self-interest, so that the entire cultural structure in which self-interest is inscribed can, in turn, be naturalized. In effect, Toulmin's writings exemplify how the Philosophy of Science is the high intellectual discourse of political obscurantism; it becomes, as Toulmin would put it, the only discourse that can speak unerringly of how complex matters are: it alone can address a "professionalized," state-funded audience of scientists and other professionals to explain how and why things must work as they do. As I shall try to show, Toulmin's populational and neo-evolutionary theories obscure the political functions of what he calls "irrational self-interest" in institutionalized, professional disciplines and their regulative discourses. In other words, it is the ineluctable and unavoidable linkage of error and truth in reason which *Human Understanding* tries to deny.

Although Toulmin's talk of knowledge as human activity recalls certain moments in Marxist theory and seems to correct more dominant modes of abstract or idealist History and the Philosophy of Science, his own sense of reason is very abstract, without content, formalist, and ahistorical. Moreover, despite the attention he gives to such professional institutions as journals, organizations, promotions, and grants, he provides little analysis of the specific place of particular professions and disciplines within the concrete and specifiable structures and functions of social material organization. In other words, he treats these professional social structures in a vacuum, as if they had internal rules and existed unaffected by any other aspects of the larger culture. His treatment of the various practices within the concept of self-interest is, as a result, undertheorized and undercontextualized; its lack of reflexiveness is common among high-powered technical academics in a society that is ideologically committed, as Toulmin himself argues, to technological or practical forms of rationalism.

Toulmin's adaptation of Darwin is ideologically and culturally

bound by his own place within this technologized academic culture. [7]
This is clear if we contrast *Human Understanding* with Canguilhem's
On the Normal and the Pathological, which works out a powerful Dar-
winian model for the Philosophy of Science. This model influenced
Foucault in his development of Nietzsche's genealogical method for
investigating the cultural role of reason in modernity. [8]

The issues that Toulmin addresses are, in many ways, the essential ones for a study of intellectual disciplines: institutional authority, the transmission of authority within disciplines, the response of
reason to social problems, the effects of professionalization upon intellectual disciplines, and so on. His fundamental response to these
complex matters is the populational model of disciplinary reason
evoked by a reading of Darwin. [9] As Toulmin sees it, the importance
of this model lies not only in its revision of Platonic and Kantian
models of logical systematicity, but also in its applicability to social as
well as intellectual change. At points the populational model seems
to converge with Foucault's interest in historical discontinuities. For
example, Toulmin claims that "an entire science comprises an 'historical population' of logically independent concepts and theories,
each with its own separate history, structure, and implications" (*HU*,
p. 130). This recalls Foucault's notions of the episteme and discourse.
But although this line of thinking corrects concepts of science which
insist upon total logical systematicity and so total conceptual inter-
dependence, in its insistence upon the discrete histories of various
concepts and theories—unlike Foucault's notions—it effectively
isolates these from each other, from other discourses, and from nondiscursive social practices. Toulmin's correction results in atomistic,
empirical history in which one can only study the evolution of particular concepts as individual responses to socially or naturally given
contexts.

Foucault learned from Canguilhem that just this sort of history
of science was neither necessary nor needed:

> If I have wanted to apply an identical method to discourses
> completely different from legendary and mythical narratives, it is
> undoubtedly because the idea came to me from the works of the
> historians of science that were open before me, especially those
> of M. Canguilhem. I owe him my understanding that the his-

tory of science is not tightly caught in this alternative: on the one hand, to chronicle discoveries or, on the other, to describe the ideas and opinions that border science either from the side of its indecisive origins or from the side of its external consequences [my translation; original is *retombées extérieures*]. But rather that one could—that one should—do the philosophy of science as an ensemble of theoretical models and conceptual instruments that is at one and the same time coherent and transformable.[10]

The contrast with Foucault on this point lets us see some of the contradictions that reduce Toulmin's position to absurdity: although the very idea of a populational model implies a family resemblance that contradicts such isolated discussion of conceptual developments; and although Toulmin discusses how the ripeness of a problem often determines the direction of research (and not the money allocated for political and military purposes, such as "Star Wars"), his own analyses suggest that the proper mode of disciplinary study need not examine the way in which one concept or discourse comes to mean, to have authority. How problems come to be ripe and solvable in certain ways—these questions are not theorized. Toulmin gives no thought, for example, to how the inscription of a problem within an entire network of institutions and practices (many of them explicitly elements of the extended state which produce and sustain its knowledge and norms) might effect or modify practice within a discipline.

The populational model unduly restricts the politically motivated genealogist of the modern and postmodern "regime(s) of truth" in two ways. First, it prevents the critique of reason in its complicity with dehumanization, especially when enfigured as a commodity fetishism. (This complicity I call "error"—what Toulmin assumes shall be corrected and eliminated by rational practice.) Second, this model itself reifies the various disciplines and in the process blocks theorizing the estranged relationship between disciplines and their practitioners. A full critique of the limits of Toulmin's model, and hence of a great deal of neohumanist rhetoric that relies on post-Wittgensteinian models of Anglo-American ethics and the Philosophy of Science, would require at least two lines of thought: first, an application of the basic terms of the Frankfurt School to display the irrationality, reification, and authoritarianism implicit in these self-confident procedures; and second, a consideration of Toulmin's normalizing of values, practices, and discursive institutions within the context of the post-Nietzschean work carried out by Gaston Bachelard, Canguilhem, and Foucault. Furthermore, since intellectuals concerned with this entire set of issues have noticed the value of bringing Antonio Gramsci to bear, with Foucault, on a critique of intellectual practice, the full analysis I envision would also require a study of science in relation to the extended state within the terms of hegemony Gramsci has elaborated. But before this could be done, a theory of the relationship between Gramsci's fundamental analysis of the constitutive and oppositional roles played by intellectuals vis-à-vis hegemony and Foucault's analysis of the regime of truth would have to be formulated.

For Toulmin, the paradigm case of the rationally continuous development of a discipline is the displacement of the authority of mechanics by quantum physics. His discussion of this example is important because it illustrates the problems of his commitment to a common-law model as a means of understanding changes in the fundamental assumptions and practices of a discipline. Toulmin's summary of this example must be quoted at length:

Our own task, here, is to make the implications of this switch from "codified" to "common-law" argument absolutely explicit. Before it, the argument over quantum mechanics had run into barren cross-purposes, just because both parties still assumed that some formal procedure or pattern of argument could be found, on whose authority they could jointly agree. (Given this, they could simply have agreed to "calculate" and accept the result.) After the switch, they no longer appealed to formal arguments since, as they now saw, there were no longer any formal arguments carrying conviction to both parties. Now, all the solid arguments were informal, consequential ones: designed, not to invoke or apply particular calculative procedures, but rather to come to terms with their strengths and weaknesses, their range and limitations. This meant appealing to considerations of an essentially historical kind: using the theoretical experiences of earlier physicists as a precedent, in estimating the most promising lines for future theoretical development. By this switch from formal (or codified) to historical (or common-law) arguments, the true character of the issues in debate was brought out into the open. The question now became at just what point it was legitimate to challenge claims to sovereign intellectual authority on behalf of existing standards of scientific judgment, and to begin looking for a Young Pretender to take over the throne. Such a question must certainly be resolved in a rational manner; but that could be done only by setting aside the formal demands of all theoretical principles, and treating the matter in broader, disciplinary terms. (HU, pp. 238–239)

Although in this example we see both the strengths and weaknesses of Toulmin's method, his strengths are finally rather banal. He usefully reminds us that the history of disciplines is the history of changing guards and that guards change in accord with shifts in ruling paradigms. But despite this reminder, Toulmin tells us little more than Thomas Kuhn does. Toulmin would claim that by employing the populational and common-law models he is better able than Kuhn to account for changes within and from one paradigm to another. He feels he has discovered a model that describes the shift as a rational appeal to precedent and to the persistent ideals of a changing discipline. Common law, in other words, exemplifies the appeal to precedent and shared ideals which he feels not only regulates a discipline but ensures it legitimacy. Just as in common law, a judge "reanalyses the social functions of the law in its application to some novel historical situation" (HU, p. 239), so the physicist when confronted by novelty must reconsider the accepted authority of sovereign rules and procedures to determine the best direction in which physics should develop.

Toulmin's argument by analogy is just as unsatisfactory because it has the appeal of common sense. We need only recall Gramsci's warning that common sense is fragmented folklore, that is, ideology, to be wary of the attractions an English-speaking audience might find in Toulmin's work.[11]

The fetish character of intellectual disciplines in Toulmin is perhaps clearest in the way he asserts their self-regulating functions. At once this notion recalls Max Weber's theory of rationalization and Georg Lukács's counterpointed idea of reification. Toulmin's conception condenses the disciplines into merely formal regulations for producing knowledge which bracket the effects of other social relations on those regulations. Although Toulmin seems to propose a theory describing the practical interdependencies of persons and their discourses, his insistence on abstracting the ruling principles of organized attempts to produce knowledge into the rarefied model of common law and the instrumentality of practical reason results in a displacement of human interactions by formalist procedures that, in turn, further displace considerations of the social into reified schemas that acquire independence and objective status. The common-law model has the opposite effect to what it seems meant to have: it closes off any consideration of the ideological component of these procedures.

At the strongest moments in the text, this model appears very attractive, offering a guarantee of commonsense practicality at the heart of an enlightened society able successfully to guard against incursions of the prophetic and irrational. The common-law model comforts Toulmin and his followers because they find in it instances of the success they desire: judges, for example, understand that they often come up against what Toulmin calls "rational frontiers" (HU, p. 241), that is, the points at which the established and up-to-that-moment efficacious rules generated and applied by tradition and the discipline of law are no longer applicable to the case at hand; judges must then decide on new directions for the law and their practice.

Toulmin concludes from this that when faced with novel situations, that is, when confronting possibilities for action in the present in light of their desires for the future, professionals steeped in the history of their discipline make the best informed and best intentioned judgments possible. Indeed, this is often just what does happen when individuals and their disciplines confront novel circumstances. Yet the problems with this attractive and humanistic commonsensical rationality appear on the surface of Toulmin's own rhetoric. In the following passage, Toulmin is speaking of the law but makes clear that the law is only the purest example of the process he has in mind, that is, it is the space in which the ideal comes to a certain amount of self-consciousness and so makes itself available for figuration and foregrounding:

Pound and Holmes put their fingers, very precisely, on the point at which legal reasoning ceases to be a formal or tactical matter—of applying established rules and principles to new situations—and becomes concerned with strategic issues: the point (that is) at which the "just" way ahead can be determined, only by reappraising the fundamental purposes of the law in a new historical context. Over such strategic issues, they insisted, judicial decisions can no longer be treated clearly and definitively, as "right" or "correct"; yet such decisions are, in their own way, none the less rational for all that.[12]

Toulmin insists over and again that at these boundary lines, at these rational frontiers, when "strategic issues" arise in a discipline, the actions and decisions of humans are rational despite the failure or inapplicability of the established rules of the discipline to the problems created by the discipline's own crisis. In other words, for Toulmin, a discipline's efforts at revision and renewal are, in themselves, the highest examples of social rationality.

Toulmin, we should notice, has shifted rationality into the space of reappraisal and, with one stroke, legitimated all already established institutions intent on maintaining themselves and their social role through a process of reform and readjustment. Should a discipline continue? Should it alter entirely its organization? Can it do this from within, as it were? (It is worth noting that Toulmin pays no attention to the problematic of inside/outside in his discussion of the internal practices of disciplines.) Can it realign the complex relationships between disciplines and the largest of cultural and political organizations, for example, the state? Can it ever initiate relationships? Must it always only react to already given circumstances and changes? Can it even ask, let alone theorize answers to, these and other more fundamental questions?

Rather than approach any of these matters directly, that is, rather than offer a political analysis or justification for the expressly liberal ideology of his Philosophy, Toulmin falls back upon the populational model to ground his conclusions about the common-law model. But as if he implicitly understood the weakness of this form of argument, he often simply appeals to the essentiality of reason that is reflected in and guaranteed by the history of disciplines as rationally evolving practices. What this appeal to historical evidence amounts to, however, is nothing less than a confusion of categories as Toulmin transforms the rational into reason and vice versa.

It is not accidental that Toulmin wants to renew the Hegelian commitment to the rationality of reason (the title of his last chapter, "The Cunning of Reason," is borrowed from Hegel), "simply," as Toulmin says, stripped of its progressive and providentialist aspects.[13] In the process of this act of disciplinary renewal, that is, the "anti-metaphysicalizing" revision of Hegel, Toulmin is forced to abstract from human history a guarantee of rationality and inscribe it within the evolutionary, or revisionary, enterprises of professionalized disciplines—all despite his asserted belief in the social activity of human beings as the agency and subject of history. That is to say, Toulmin has an even less material and less adequate theory of human activity than does Hegel.

The effect of these contradictions, and especially of the inscription of the rational in disciplines, is an overly abstract and therefore self-legitimating conception of the disciplinary practices of modern social organization. Necessarily occluded in this doubling and self-revising model are the effects of interest and conflict (that is, error) located within disciplines as essential features of their survival and their roles within larger complexes of power and knowledge in modern societies dominated by extended states and the international order of capital. Put crudely the questions are these: Who determines the new just way? Who sets out the strategic problems? Who puts in place the new terms and how do they acquire the power and position to do so? Marx taught us the dangers of Hegel's abstractions. But Toulmin, like many of his colleagues, abstracts even from Hegel.

His account of human action at the frontiers of reason fails to theorize any form of ideology. He has not considered the notions of mystification and self-interest which can be found in Marx's *The German Ideology*, to say nothing about more complex formulations developed, for instance, by Louis Althusser and Gramsci. Toulmin's ideological and conceptual inability to consider the complexity of the factors that make up the decisions of intellectuals is a mark of both the disciplinary illiteracy of Philosophy in the United States and of the self-confirming representation of intellectuals which implicitly underlies his work. For who will read this text? Only those willing and able to accept affirmation of the rationality of the intellectual and the state institutions that they justify. Whatever interests professional intellectuals have, Toulmin narrowly circumscribes. In other words, he carries out a radical ascesis to maintain his theory:

> At such points, a Supreme Court Justice can no longer speak for the law as it is; instead, he must pass judgment in the light of a longer-term vision, both of what the law has been and is, and of what it should become. . . . Cases of this kind take us to the "rational frontier" at which fallible individuals, acting in the name of the human enterprise that they represent, have to deal with novel and unforeseen problems by opening up new possibilities; and, at this frontier, we can no longer separate the rational procedures of law from the judicial purposes of the men who are reshaping them, or from the historical situations in which these men find themselves. (*HU*, p. 240)

In the best construction that can be put on the matter, these intellectuals accept their responsibility to bet on the future, to risk being wrong despite their best-educated (here we deal with *Bildung*, not just professional training) judgments, and escape the risks of quietism and defeat. There are weak and strong objections to be made to this position. One could easily argue that representative intellectuals have no expertise that can guarantee the accuracy of their judgments or the priority of their values and decisions. But Toulmin already has an answer to this: rationality offers no such guarantees, only the best possible chance. In fact, such objections are uninteresting not only generally but also particularly because Toulmin has developed models to preempt any critique calling for either absolute standards of reason or any commitment to relativism.

But five stronger objections, I think, can be made: first, Toulmin ignores the role that ideology plays in the cultural sphere—general talk about historical situations won't do it; second, his atomistic genealogical evolutionary model ignores the importance nondiscursive contexts have upon the regulative development of any one institution or discourse; third, he rarely reflects on his own reasons for vaporizing individuals and their uniquely informed, rational decisions as the basis for the deeper rationality of disciplines—a rationality that must be thought of as social, especially given the legal and populational models; fourth, nowhere does Toulmin reflect on what I will call the underlying humanism that is the self-confirming condition for the possibility of his project; and fifth, nowhere does he consider that jurists act, even in the law, on the basis of more than their judicial purposes. Even insofar as they are judges, factors other than their position within the law, no matter how broadly this is taken (unless it is so broadly taken as to be absurd), modify, indeed constitute, their judicial purposes.

Human enterprises exist within larger contexts of economic and social life than Toulmin grants. Even highly professionalized individuals, acting as experts, occupy positions crossed by many social, intellectual, political, and cultural vectors. Toulmin, like those who make much of interpretive communities, undertheorizes the complexity of what used to be called "context." If we take the case of academic literary study, the issue becomes clearer: its emergence was not simply the result of decisions made by representative intellectuals; rather, at least in the United States, it must be seen within the context of larger discursive formations as they produced and altered the subject, imagination, and "aesthetic autonomy."[14] Of course, the academic study of literature is part of the general professionalization of middle-class life and social dominance.[15] It is also part of the rise of functionalism to ideological prominence in the United States.[16] Furthermore, within the disciplines themselves much more consideration must be given to the effects that instrumentalism and self-interest have upon the revisionary decisions made by these intellectuals. Toulmin does admit (but does not theorize) the fact that older generations, as he puts it, always resist the changing of the guard, but that finally the disciplinary appeal to reason, proof, expertise, and public argument guarantees the success of the better ideas— even if not at the time of their first conception, when, for a variety of reasons, their time might not be ripe.[17]

One can only conclude that Toulmin is a weak reader of Darwin. At no point does he begin to think the relationship between instrumental reason and self-interest, on the one hand, and what we might call "self-preservation," on the other. But Toulmin is not only a weak reader of Darwin; he is also a weak theorist of modernity, as a contrast with Horkheimer and the Frankfurt School suggests. In modernity, Horkheimer argued, reason placed itself at the disposal of the powerful.[18] Foucault revises this to say (and Adorno would agree in part) that instrumentalized, disciplinary reason provides power and is one crucial site of power. Following Nietzsche, these critics of modernity discover there the collectivization of the Lockean notion of reason as the satisfier of self-interest. Horkheimer's material analysis leads him to conclude in part that those who enjoy what he calls a "life of abundance" are free to choose.[19] But, in effect, their freedom is hollow. This is a point Adorno pursued in his critiques of mass culture.[20] More important, however, is Horkheimer's demonstration that this ability to choose is purely abstract, always conditioned by the need to survive as a group (or class):

> For them [those who enjoy a life of abundance] it was possible to select among the so-called cultural goods, always provided that these goods were in harmony with their interests of domin-ion. This was the only pluralism of values that materialized. . . . The perpetuation of privileges was the only rational criterion which determined whether one should fight against or collude with other interests and groups. . . . The great historic decisions differed from one another in being farsighted or nearsighted, not in the nature of their ends.[21]

It is not necessary to recapitulate the Frankfurt School's complex judgment on the totalitarianism of the Enlightenment to concede the cogency of this remark about the bourgeois's self-interested consumption and production of cultural alternatives. The virtue of Horkheimer's analysis for our purposes is that it does not demarcate as rigidly as does Toulmin's practice distinct political, intellectual, and social spaces for cultural and disciplinary production. As a result, Horkheimer's comment seems apropos on at least two levels: Toulmin talks of his disciplinary analysis as an analogue for an analysis of all society—he operates as if we were still living in a classically liberal social order—especially in his discussion of the common law and the competition among ruling ideas (note: not ruling classes or groups) in a society; furthermore, even though Toulmin fails to consider or acknowledge it, the global operations of rationality in a culture inscribe all disciplines so these cannot, except arbitrarily and with great violence, be treated individually or internally, as it were. Without tracing the marks of this inscription across the institution and through the culture itself, any analysis must be reductive. Above all, this tracing must have a material component. Ideas do not come to the field of battle disembodied, unarticulated, and undisseminated. How they progress, why some do not, and how they take hold must be re-marked.

In effect, then, Toulmin reverses the necessary procedures for studying the role of reason in society. He postulates the rationality and veridicality of concepts and the institutionalized procedures that produce them by virtue of their pragmatic efficacy. He does not examine how these concepts become established within regulative structures of discourse, nor, more important, how these regulative structures themselves come to be except, implicitly, as the result of the rational activities within already given institutions and discourses. Furthermore, Toulmin's move reasserts the traditional intellectual's claim to superiority over others. Specifically, it transfers from sociology into Philosophy the classic abstract formulations of sociology of knowledge which first emerged in Karl Mannheim. [22]

In his trenchant critique of Mannheim's work, Adorno demonstrates that attention to the material foundations of reason and its modern forms of practice requires that the commonsensical model of rational efficacy be suspended and brought itself under examination:

> The thesis of the primacy of being over consciousness [this is a reassertion of the thesis of The German Ideology] includes the methodological imperative to express the dynamic tendencies of reality in the formation and movement of concepts in accordance with the demand that they have pragmatic and expedient features. The sociology of knowledge has closed its eyes to this imperative. Its abstractions are arbitrary as long as they merely harmonize with an experience which proceeds by differentiating and correcting. [23]

Toulmin's common-law model attempts to rationalize this process of differentiation and correction. In his hands, History and the Philosophy of Science itself become an instance of instrumental reason as it legitimates the processes of struggle which take place within disciplines: the controls and intentions that circumscribe those struggles both guarantee and mark their rationality.

We are, after Feyerabend, accustomed to charges that the Philosophy of Science has as its major institutional purpose the legitimation of capitalist science and technology.[24] What we are perhaps not quite so used to hearing, however, is the charge that the sort of model Toulmin proposes also legitimates disciplinary elites and their social and professional privileges as institutions of the extended state. Yet this is precisely Toulmin's function in high intellectual culture: to obscure the irrationalities of social life by ensuring the rationality of strategic thinking; and to occlude the difficulty societies and institutions face in preserving themselves within contradictory social orders.

Equally essential to an understanding of Toulmin's function are the intellectual elites whose gifts, training, and social position make them the supports of the reason of not only their own disciplines but also the social order as a whole. Such an attitude is itself an echo of Mannheim's mistaken insistence upon the free-floating nature of intellectuals as well as a prolepsis of Alvin Gouldner's lapse into pre-Gramscian categories: Gouldner came to believe that traditional elite intellectuals provide the best hope for rational social life in late capitalist society.[25] Toulmin's failure to consider how these intellectual elites come into being, in relation to which other social groups, and to perform which social functions typifies his refusal to come to grips with the material problems of power and privilege in society. In place of critical and historical thinking about these questions, Toulmin replicates the worst of liberal thinking, offering us only a neohumanist explanation of the goodwill and values of the elites. He reduces matters of normativity and social reproduction to the following scene of bureaucratic benevolence, to trust in the "men" who, properly trained and connected, know what to do:

> strategic uncertainties take us to a "rational frontier," where men must deal with novel types of problems by developing whole new methods of thought; and, at these frontiers, we can no longer separate entirely the rational processes of a science from the intellectual purposes of the men who are reshaping them, or from the historical situation in which they find themselves. . . . Any profound redirection in the strategy of a discipline thus has to be justified by appeal, not to any previously established patterns of argument, but to the overall experience

of men in the entire history of the rational enterprise concerned. (*HU*, p. 241)

The very grounds for appeal which justify the rationality of disciplines and their society have material workings, but Toulmin does not pursue them. What this quotation offers is an idealizing reification and fetishization of the intellect and of the value of social memory and tradition as the guarantee of rationality beyond the reach of already known procedures. (For Toulmin, no rational professional ever wagers on the future.) In contrast, Adorno remarks about elites in capitalist societies that "whoever does not fit in is kept out. Even the differences of conviction which reflect those of real interests serve primarily to obscure the underlying unity which prevails in decisive matters."[26]

After Nietzsche, Foucault helps us see that Toulmin's fetishization of disciplined, humanistic reason not only prevents the intellectuals' examination of the real social and material interests at work in the struggles within disciplines (and over the positions they occupy in society) but also blocks all critical reflection upon the nature of intellectual agency: above all, the agents of these rationalized structures are themselves functional elements in discursive and nondiscursive structures which deny autonomy to the agent and may well be said to have emptied out in advance of any deconstruction the concept of the autonomous subject in a postmodern society.

Toulmin's liberal model implies a harmony between individual agents as autonomous subjects and the discourses and institutions that inscribe them as intellectuals. Toulmin's concept could not withstand a Gramscian critique of the intellectual when he argues that this harmony itself depends upon the continuity of human experience as internalized and preserved (as canon and tradition) by the leaders of a culture. In other words, this continuous experience (in a otherwise amnesic society) belongs only to Philosophers and other professionals. When we recall such early modern texts as Nietzsche's *On the Genealogy of Morals*, which is a demonstration of the dissolution of the liberal subject, and Baudelaire's elaborate salon celebration of Delacroix as the sole aesthetic appropriator of the great tradition in modernity, then we must marvel at the dispassionately self-assured ease with which Toulmin and other neohumanists assert that

this appropriation—the ground of intellectual assurance and legitimacy—is always already there for us in the given institutions of our
culture. As Jake says to Brett in *The Sun Also Rises:* "Yes. Isn't it
pretty to think so?"

Unlike Toulmin, Foucault begins with the very question of the
cultural and political status of both knowledge and reason, on the
one hand, and of the institutions, discourses, and empowered elites
that deploy and embody them, on the other. Foucault follows Canguilhem in questioning the "normativizing" moves of the Philosophy
of Science and expands his research to examine the disciplined society itself. The result of this approach is to trace the irrationality of
practice in professions and among institutionalized intellectuals.

In *On the Normal and the Pathological,* for example (a text introduced by Foucault), Canguilhem analyzes how the very existence of
physiology as a science depends upon the phenomenological experience of sick men which is itself rationalized into a high intellectual
discourse that comes to be disseminated and institutionalized in society. Of course, this study can be read as prefiguring Foucault's work
on prisons, clinics, and sexuality, and as a useful point of entry into
the contrast between Toulmin's legitimating practice and Foucault's and Canguilhem's critical genealogical approach.

Canguilhem focuses his analysis upon the question of the norm
in scientific discourse and how it comes into being: "*Normative,* in
Philosophy, means every judgment which evaluates or qualifies a fact
in relation to a norm, but this mode of judgment is essentially subor-
dinate to that which establishes norms. Normative, in the fullest
sense of the word, is that which establishes norms."[27]

Canguilhem and Foucault have a different approach to the rational and discursive than does Toulmin. A reader of Foucault, for
example, will recognize that this move in Canguilhem prefigures
Foucault's entire theorizing about "power/knowledge" which is the
controversial center of his work. In addition, though, Canguilhem's
move indicates that both of these writers, like Nietzsche, are interested in the irrationality of the moves made by intellectual and
cultural discourses as these are written over and around the phenomenal everyday experience of human beings in society. Furthermore,

they focus this interest on the ways in which this experience comes into being, acquires cognitive and cultural status by virtue of being taken up within already existing objective categories and processes of disciplinary practice. We can see, after Foucault and Canguilhem, that discourses constitute and emerge from new experience just insofar as within them this experience becomes sensible.[28] In other words, it is possible (but inexact) to say that new experiences change institutions only because this constitutive power of discourses has the institutional power to make ontic whatever experiences they represent. Above all they prevent noninstitutionalized, nonprofessional, nontraditional figurations from gaining access to the cultural means of communication and reproduction. This structuring of knowledge has brought about a permanently institutionalized society; it would be merely naive or utopian to imagine as an alternative a noninstitutionalized or nonprofessionalized apparatus for producing knowledge; rather, what needs to be thought through more clearly is the relationship between any apparatus and the hegemonic forces in a particular society: this, after all, is the central focus of Foucault's notion of the regime of truth.

What Foucault finds in Canguilhem to develop his Nietzschean critique is a relentless assault on positivism. Canguilhem directs his attack against Comte's insistence that the priority of science as a means to truth (based on laboratory experimental procedures) justified therapeutic interventions into the sickness of men who had already identified themselves as sick. But the attack on positivism is itself only a way into the critique of the fetishization of science as the reification of reason. Canguilhem's analysis is an ideological critique that exemplifies how one should study the relationships between knowledge and (in the broadest sense) political institutions. For our purposes here, it is the second aspect of Canguilhem's work which is of the greatest interest both because it sharpens our sense of Toulmin's inadequacies as a Philosopher of disciplines and because it suggests an important source of Foucault's work.

Canguilhem focuses on Comte's adoption and adaptation of Broussais's thesis. As we read Canguilhem, we see that his text writes out for us the double movement that takes place in all revisionist modifications of the canon. Comte's interpretation of science took Broussais's thesis from the limited realm of physiology and, for

Comte's own purposes, so to speak, extended its applicability to other spheres and so re-authorized it. For reasons largely independent of Broussais's intention, then, Comte's rereading of physiology's founding discourse exemplifies how the material and institutional networks of authority and power establish what is rational and legitimate within the intellectual disciplines and across an entire spectrum of representations, opinions, rumors, and common sense. Comte's assumption of Broussais's thesis has a significant institutional intellectual function: it extends the space of rationality from the region of physiology to those newly state-related areas of politics and the positive social sciences. More precisely, Comte's revisionary move exemplifies how irrationally a concept is appropriated; no ideal procedures regulate Comte's revision; no humanist memory of a precedent guarantees the efficacy, rationality, or benevolence of such appropriation or its inscribing systems of representation. For reasons of social and political power, Comte's agency extends a concept into areas for which it has no scientifically justified immediate applicability and no certain progressive value. It is significant that Comte has extended this concept into discourses and institutions much less scientifically organized than either natural science or the law. At least one result of this move is that these other discourses then aspire to fix the notions of science to their practice and theory to acquire legitimacy and social position within the consensus that is the regime of truth, while at the same time assigning leading roles to the dominant intellectuals of their disciplines.

Canguilhem shows that this process succeeds because Comte derives his already enormous intellectual authority from his role as ideological representative of the new hegemony that is grounded in positive science. Comte's strategy is paradigmatic: appropriate a concept by dialectically emptying and overfilling it and so turn it into a functional trope. In this case, a metaphor becomes an ideological tool or weapon in the political battle to empower systems of representation and align them to the socially dominant forces of the economic and cultural order: what Foucault calls "the regime of truth." Canguilhem nicely summarizes the process:

> By stating in a general way that diseases do not change vital phenomena, Comte is justified in stating that the cure for politi-

cal crises consists in bringing societies back to their essential and permanent structure, and tolerating progress only within limits of variation of natural order defined by social statics. In positivist doctrine, Broussais's principle remains an idea subordinated to a system, and it is the physicians, psychologists, and men of letters, positivist by inspiration and tradition, who disseminated it as an independent conception.[29]

Canguilhem shows us how the positivists join the cadre of free-floating traditional intellectuals who, like clerics, rearrange systems of representation as if there were no historical limits to or consequences of their actions, no resisting "otherness" to whatever they revise: free-floating intellectuals are revisionists who are free to rip concepts from context and rearrange their tropes to whatever end they like; they are doing the bidding of the hegemony that the newly configured representations create and support; and, most important in this case, they legitimize and make constitutive *revision* as the fundamental practice of modern intellectual life. Such a discovery lets us see Toulmin's defense of the putative rationality of disciplines for what it is: a reflection of the self-conception of traditional intellectuals and an occluding of the role of such intellectuals in the production and dissemination of the regime of truth.

Canguilhem and Foucault offer one useful technique for clearing away this darkness and for controlling the modern intellectual practice of arrogant and self-interested (because self-creating) revision—and that is genealogy. This involves a peculiar stance toward the relationship of the present to the past and to historical study itself.

Canguilhem notes that his suspicions of the deployment of reason in modern science led him to look for its genetic origins. He tries to learn how the present configuration of political and cultural forces has positioned theory, science, and method in modern structures of knowledge. More suspicious and reflective than Toulmin, Canguilhem proposes a method for investigating the past's production of the present and the present's self-production out of its revision of the past (using Comte as an instance) which is perhaps most fully developed in Foucault's *Discipline and Punish:*

It may be surprising to see that an exposition of Comte's theory has turned into a pretext for a retrospective study. Why wasn't a

chronological order employed at the outset? Because a historical
narrative always reverses the true order of interest and inquiry. It
is in the present that problems provoke reflection. And if reflection leads to a regression, the regression is necessarily related
to it. Thus the historical origin is really less important than the
reflective origin. . . . What is certain in any case is that even
in the milieu of medical culture, the theories of general pathology originated by Bichat, Brown, and Broussais were influential
only to the extent that Comte found them advantageous. The
physicians of the second half of the nineteenth century were for
the most part ignorant of Broussais and Brown, but few were
unaware of Comte or Littré; just as today most physiologists
cannot ignore Bernard, but disregard Bichat to whom Bernard is
connected through Magendie. By going back to more remote
sources of Comte's ideas—through the pathology of Broussais,
Brown, and Bichat—we put ourselves in a better position to
understand their significance and limits.[30]

In his Nietzschean insistence that the present promotes reflection, Canguilhem displaces conventional genetic histories of science and establishes the importance of what he calls the "reflective
origin." The realities of the present provoke not a revision of the
past, not the sort of history of science Foucault rejects in "The
Discourse on Language"; but a critical genealogy that discovers how
in light of the issues pressing in the present and so reflected back into
the past, the past must be read to account for the present configuration of forces which, itself, emerged at that reflective origin. This is a
powerfully delegitimating method that is itself a form of resistance
(often taking the form of narrative) to the courses of things as they
have led, so to speak, to the present moment of reflection.

Toulmin cannot write such critical history. Despite his insistent
claim that practice forms disciplinary knowledge and its categories,
his specific assertions remain empty. They can have no content because the revisionist disciplines he defends constitute themselves by
Comte's method of dialectically overloading and emptying out concepts; the result is that they produce a vacuous rhetoric that cannot
reflect their origins, that is, their coming into being within the spaces
first defined by their own and affiliated discourses and institutions.

The critical genealogical model (which Foucault describes as the attempt to write the history of the present) always asks what is at stake in the individual events that constitute the disciplines and their discursive regularities, and how one can tell the story of their transformations and constitutive relationships to the regime of truth. Critical genealogy allows, among other things, for consideration of both the discursive structures in which or out of which an intellectual/political event emerges and the real material interests in which it may be inscribed. Also, it creates one of the conditions for theorizing how intellectual discourses and practices stage cultural and political conflicts. After Canguilhem it offers the terms *normal* and *pathological* as binaries through which the regulative ideals of cultural production can be reflected.

At this point one might adapt a generally Althusserian line to Toulmin's model of historical continuity. Such a reading would show that the common-law argument cannot rationalize fundamental historical contradictions of Toulmin's own moment; indeed, it would usefully see Toulmin's attempt as in itself a symptom of those contradictions.[31] Canguilhem's work, however, lets us see something more important and more general: that Toulmin can make no convincing claim that his evolutionary model of disciplines is demonstrative. On the contrary, it suggests how narrow and simple Toulmin's model is.

In the 1940s Canguilhem worked out a conception similar to Toulmin's which used populational models to describe how medical practice (as opposed to physiological science) creates norms and normatives. But Canguilhem's model is not only much more elegant and powerful, it is also more flexible: it genealogically figures each moment in a structure not as part of an assumed continuum of reason itself produced by a continuing commitment to rational disciplinary ideals held and acted upon by reasonable and disinterested men; rather it sees each event and its place within the site of a discipline (as well as the stability of a discipline itself) as much more tenuous, confused, and disharmonious than might appear on an unreflected surface.

The differences between Canguilhem's and Toulmin's adoptions of Darwin let us see, to put it in terms reminiscent of Adorno's critique of Mannheim, that Toulmin takes appearance for essence. Since Toulmin misreads Darwin as assuring evolutionary success, his revisionist model becomes a machine representing "normal" disciplinary practices as everywhere ensuring stability and harmony, rationality and disinterest. In literary criticism, Toulmin's model surely does not hold, despite Stanley Fish's propaganda for the regulative force of interpretive communities. (The significance of Fish's parallel interest in the law needs to be worked out elsewhere.) Criticism is surely an "unformed science," despite the great allure of Northrop Frye and his followers; but it is also the case that "inside" the field, "professional intellectual interests" are self-consciously implicated in relations of power among "generations" and "elites" of literary study. Revisionism is the only regulative ideal to be found at the top of the heap.[32] Furthermore, despite the recent "boomlet" in literary studies marked by the attempts of a number of elite universities to attract the best and brightest of a new generation,[33] Toulmin's model cannot account for the economic and cultural factors that threaten the very survival of advanced literary study in the United States.

But literary criticism is a perfect example of Canguilhem's version of the Darwinian scheme: a period of stability marked by the dominant New Criticism's supervention of other conflicting elements in criticism, followed by open conflict over disciplinary identity and attempts at revision necessary for the survival of the profession. Canguilhem schematizes the process around the figure of compensation:

> It would not express a specific stable equilibrium but rather the unstable equilibrium of nearly all equal norms and forms of life temporarily brought together. Instead of considering a specific type as being really stable because it presents stable characteristics devoid of any incompatibility, it should be considered as being apparently stable because it has temporarily succeeded in reconciling opposing demands by means of a set of compensations. A normal specific form would be the product of a normalization between functions and organs whose synthetic harmony is obtained in defined conditions and not given.[34]

Canguilhem's figure of compensation translates politically into Gramsci's notion of hegemony, that is, the dominant, which gives its identity to the stable moment, achieves its position by virtue of the set of concessions it offers to the conflicting groups it directs and leads. In other words, compensation is a political process in the creation of intellectual and disciplinary stability. It is not rational in the disinterested sense Toulmin hypothesizes. Figuring politics as practical reason is the traditional intelligentsia's ideological defense of its own privilege, a privilege provided by the dominant groups that benefit from its caste practices.

What Toulmin takes away from reason is the element of "critique" which Marx, for example, in *The German Ideology* insisted separated him from Feuerbach: a recognition that all discursive practice is part of class warfare and that mere skepticism, the mere demystification of religious visions, always forgets the primary task of critique—to join in the political battle (not, as Richard Rorty would have it, just "the conversation") of cultural, economic, and national conflicts.

As a genealogist interested in disclosing the history and structure of power from the point of view of the present, Foucault learns his basic lessons from Nietzsche and Canguilhem: he learns what we should call "the lesson of error." Accident or chance, Canguilhem argues, lies at the biological basis of life, in the genetic materials themselves. Errors in genetic coding always occur. For Foucault, and all genealogists, this implies that error and not reason is "at the root of what makes human thought and its history."[35] Not only does Canguilhem guide Foucault in studying genealogically how power/knowledge has grasped the body, but Canguilhem's positioning of biological error as an unavoidable feature of genetic information systems grounds (especially in *The Birth of the Clinic*) Foucault's own insistent claims for historical discontinuity and the role of power in the relationship between thought and history:

> The opposition of true and false, the values we attribute to both, the effects of power that different societies and different institutions link to this division—even all this is perhaps only the latest response to this possibility of error, which is intrinsic to life. If the history of science is discontinuous, that is, if it can be analyzed only as a series of "corrections," as a new distribution of true and false which never finally, once and for all, liberates the truth, it is because there, too, "error" constitutes not overlooking or delaying a truth but the dimension proper to the life of men and to the time of the species.[36]

We might say that Toulmin's expansion of reason is one of the latest forms of error, that always found among traditional intellectuals as they tell stories about and to themselves and their masters. Of course, error marks Toulmin's texts, and so like all humanistic texts they are inscribed within death, if I may extend Foucault's own reading of Canguilhem's figure of the origin of clinical medicine.[37] Toulmin's own thinking leads us nowhere near these questions, for as a traditional intellectual there is no reflective origin to be found in his work. He makes no effort to understand his own position within the regime of truth, that is to say, the space within which he practices is taken for granted, assumed to have natural status within the discourses of truth and judgment. The result, in part, is that his work goes on untroubled by any implications it might have within the apparatus of power/knowledge, especially as this affects those less empowered by this very apparatus. In effect, I take Toulmin to exemplify intellectual irresponsibility, a disregard for extension of the regime of truth across society and national borders, and a carelessness toward interrogating one's own intellectual function within such an apparatus.[38]

We can conclude that Toulmin is genealogically unselfconscious; his model errs in its theory of practice. Yet Toulmin is interesting because his is a form of error necessary to the truth apparatus of modern intellectual practice itself. We can see in Toulmin's work the extent of a particular problem that I have discussed elsewhere:[39] established liberal humanistic discourse, even when it claims to be historical and concerned with institutions, always effectively blocks entry into the workings of irrationality, desire, interest, and will within the professionalized disciplines. More important, it always substitutes its own normalcy and familiarity for the strange and difficult task of genealogically looking into the history and position of intellectuals and their work in the current regime of truth. Seen in this way, Toulmin appears as an exemplary instance of how institutionalized discourses in *our* regime of truth substitute abstract analytics for the complex genealogical narratives needed to recall our own history.[40] A more thorough critique of Toulmin would be necessary to fulfill the two primary aims that should motivate such criticism: to negate the very thingness, the ontic naturalness, the givenness, as it were, of Toulmin's kind of practice, but more important again, to exemplify in itself the kind of genealogical critique that takes seriously both the historical specificity of its subject and contemporary problematics: to write a history of the present which best accounts for the coming into being of the current regime while also recalling those few moments of alternative practice and discourse the present regime would rather have forgotten. Such a genealogical practice would recover for itself—and for others who take up that practice as a tool in their own struggles—the very critical impulse that amnesic liberal discourses misappropriate and deaden.[41]

Without such a genealogical critique, humanistic institutions will maintain the regime of truth even while engaged in reform. Humane motivation is not an adequate defense against mistakes that further the replication of the current regime. Without critical knowledge there can be no awareness of the pitfalls that confront the reforming or even revolutionary consciousness. If one hopes to avoid some of these pitfalls, one must recall a wide-reaching tradition of critical anxiety and responsibility that includes Benjamin and Adorno as well as Blackmur and Jameson,[42] that is, a tradition that insists upon difficulty, slowness, complex, often dialectical and highly ironic styles as an effective antidote to the uncritical professional prejudices of the current regime of truth: speed, slogans, transparency, and reproducibility. Although there are critical histories everywhere—indeed, even histories of these histories—they are variously positioned and nothing seems more definitely to mark their differences than their relative commitment to the tradition I have just mentioned. The farther such a history is from this tradition both in its style and its problematics of reading, the closer it is, so to speak, to that institution Toulmin so clearly represents.[43]

Notes

1. Stephen Toulmin, *Human Understanding: The Collective Use and Evolution of Concepts* (Princeton: Princeton University Press, 1971). Hereafter cited as *HU*.

2. See Michel Foucault, *Power/Knowledge: Selected Interviews and Other Writings, 1972–1977*, ed. Colin Gordon, trans. Colin Gordon et al. (New York: Pantheon, 1980), as well as his *Discipline and Punish: The Birth of the Prison*, trans. A. M. Sheridan Smith (New York: Pantheon, 1977).

3. I follow Richard Rorty in using the capital "P" to refer to the professional act of (and actors who do) thinking about certain problems like truth. See his "Pragmatism and Philosophy," in *Consequences of Pragmatism* (Minneapolis: University of Minnesota Press, 1982).

4. Max Horkheimer, *Critique of Instrumental Reason*, trans. Matthew J. O'Connell et al. (New York: Seabury Press, 1974), p. vii.

5. I cannot discuss here either Toulmin's indebtedness to or differences from pragmatism. For Toulmin, however, the pragmatic becomes the instrumental.

6. Max Horkheimer, "The End of Reason," in *The Essential Frankfurt School Reader*, ed. Andrew Arato and Eike Gebhardt (New York: Continuum, 1982), pp. 30–31.

7. A full discussion of Toulmin would have to include an investigation into the forces that, in part, account for Toulmin's decision to revise Darwin in this particular way.

8. See Michel Foucault, *L'Ordre du discours* (Paris: Gallimard, 1971), pp. 73–74.

9. Space does not allow a complete reading of Toulmin's text against Darwin's. Suffice it to say that Darwin's own hesitations disappear in Toulmin's systematizing.

10. Foucault, *L'Ordre du discours*, pp. 73–74; translated as "The Discourse on Language" by Rupert Swyer in *The Archaeology of Knowledge* (New York: Harper & Row, 1976), p. 235.

11. Antonio Gramsci, *Selections from the Prison Notebooks*, trans. and ed. Quintin Hoare and Geoffrey Nowell Smith (New York: International Publishers, 1971), pp. 323–333, 348, 419–425.

12. Rorty's "Pragmatism and Philosophy," pp. xiii–xlvii, suggests how near and how far Toulmin is to pragmatic conceptions of rationality.

13. See Toulmin, *Human Understanding*, pp. 329ff., and also Charles Altieri, *Act and Quality* (Amherst: University of Massachusetts Press, 1982), esp. pp. 318–331, for a similar attempt to revise Hegel.

14. See Paul A. Bové, *Intellectuals in Power: A Genealogy of Critical Humanism* (New York: Columbia University Press, 1986).

15. See Burton J. Bledstein, *The Culture of Professionalism: The Middle Class and the Development of Higher Education in America* (New York: W. W. Norton, 1976).

16. For a few thoughts on this see John Fekete, *The Critical Twilight* (London: Routledge and Kegan Paul, 1977).

17. One can only say this does not correspond to anyone's sense of the profession of English studies.

18. In a way that is particularly apropos for Toulmin's assumption of an interest-free legal model, see on this point Roberto Mangabeira Unger, *The*

Critical Legal Studies Movement (Cambridge, Mass.: Harvard University Press, 1986), pp. 28–30. It is here that Unger discusses the privileges of certain groups within North Atlantic democracies.

19. Horkheimer, "The End of Reason," p. 31.

20. See, for example, Theodor Adorno, "On the Fetish Character of Music and the Regression of Listening," in *The Essential Frankfurt School Reader*, pp. 270–299.

21. Horkheimer, "The End of Reason," pp. 31–32.

22. See Karl Mannheim, *Ideology and Utopia: An Introduction to the Sociology of Knowledge*, trans. Louis Wirth and Edward Shils (New York: Harcourt, Brace and World, 1936), esp. pp. 306–309.

23. Theodor Adorno, "Sociology of Knowledge and Its Consciousness," in *The Essential Frankfurt School Reader*, p. 459.

24. Paul Feyerabend, *Against Method* (London: NLB, 1975).

25. Alvin Gouldner, *The Future of Intellectuals and the Rise of the New Class* (New York: Continuum, 1979). See also, Bové, *Intellectuals in Power*.

26. Adorno, "Sociology of Knowledge," p. 455.

27. Georges Canguilhem, *On the Normal and the Pathological*, trans. Carolyn R. Fawcett (Dordrecht, Holland: D. Reidel Publishing, 1978), p. 70.

28. In this context, it is interesting that Fredric Jameson, writing on Sartre, should say something that sounds so Foucaldian. Given Jameson's dismissive position on Foucault, Sartre's common influence alone can account for the coincidence: "What if the power of the revolutionary idea came fully as much from the new temporal reorganization of experience that it permits, as from any practical consequences which might flow from it as effects from a cause?" *Marxism and Form* (Princeton: Princeton University Press, 1971), p. 258.

29. Canguilhem, *On the Normal and the Pathological*, p. 28.

30. Ibid., pp. 27–28.

31. See David Kairys, ed., *The Politics of Law: A Progressive Critique* (New York: Pantheon, 1982), esp. Edward Greer, "Antonio Gramsci and 'Legal Hegemony,'" pp. 304–309, and Duncan Kennedy, "Legal Education as Training for Hierarchy," pp. 40–61.

32. See Bové, *Intellectuals in Power*, and Daniel T. O'Hara, *The Romance of Interpretation: Visionary Criticism from Pater to de Man* (New York: Columbia University Press, 1985).

33. See *New York Times*, March 16, 1986, sec. 1, p. 1.

34. Canguilhem, *On the Normal and the Pathological*, p. 93.

35. Michel Foucault, Introduction to ibid., p. xix; see also Bové, *Intellectuals in Power*, esp. chap. 6.

36. Foucault, Introduction to *On the Normal and the Pathological*, by Canguilhem, p. xix.

37. See Bové, *Intellectuals in Power*, chap. 6.

38. I am aware of Toulmin's recent book, *The Return to Cosmology: Postmodern Science and the Theology of Nature* (Berkeley and Los Angeles: University of California Press, 1982), but do not believe that it any way invalidates my claim. On the contrary, one might say that even at its most postmodern moment when it evokes Heidegger and Keats (pp. 255–257), it continues to be nonreflexive. While worrying the relationship of the observer to the observed in true hermeneutic fashion, it never questions the position of the Philosopher or his discursive practice.

39. See, for example, Paul A. Bové, "Agriculture and Academe: America's Southern Question," *The Legacy of Antonio Gramsci*, special issue, *boundary* 2 14, no. 3 (Spring 1986), pp. 169–195.

40. See Bové, *Intellectuals in Power*; see also Jonathan Arac, *Critical Genealogies: Historical Situations for Postmodern Literary Studies* (New York: Columbia University Press, 1987).

41. It should be said that this critical impulse has positive as well as negative components, especially when positioned within the struggle for self-determination. See Bové, *Intellectuals in Power*, esp. chap. 6. I should also point out that I make the argument for a positive element in criticism despite Foucault's own powerful critique of emancipatory rhetorics.

42. For examples of this tradition see R. P. Blackmur, *Language as Gesture* (New York: Columbia University Press, 1981), esp. pp. 396–399 and 410–412; and Jameson, *Marxism and Form*, pp. xiii–xiv.

43. As so often in the past, I am indebted to Jonathan Arac for his extraordinary skills and patience as a reader and editor.

WHAT WAS FOUCAULT?

Daniel T. O'Hara

My title means to allude, of course, to Foucault's famous essay "What Is an Author?"[1] In addition, it intends a more distant echo, that murderously innocent question that in one form or another animates Nietzsche's career: "What Is Dionysian?"[2] Besides these specialized intertextual references, however, my title cannot help invoking a less intellectual mode of placement and definition, that of the typical, even the stereotypical. I am thinking of the way one asks what the political or sexual orientation was of someone now dead, whose literary corpus we identify, in subtler if no less discriminating ways, just as we tag the actual body by name and cause of death. Against this stark mass of more commonplace resonances, my title would project a first set of darkly twining figures, in a manner that will produce, I hope, a somewhat lighter music.

The Compensations of Parody; or, The Profession of Genius

Why should we read Foucault? I raise this question after a survey of recent uses to which he has been put in the humanities.[3] Three such usages outline an answer to this second question which leads us on, or rather, leads us back to Foucault himself and especially to the question, "What Is an Author?"[4]

Enabling constraints—these are what Foucault provides to the three critical projects under consideration. Lydia Blanchard deploys Foucault's critique of the repressive hypothesis from the first volume of *The History of Sexuality* to frame a recovery of D. H. Lawrence's *Lady Chatterley's Lover*.[5] She finds that Foucault, like several major

critics, "underestimates" (p. 18) Lawrence's work of liberation. For
Foucault sees in the novelist what he sees in Freud and his scientific
and theoretical followers. Like them, according to Foucault, Lawrence merely repeats the myth of sexual liberation from Victorian
repression, a myth that accompanies the climactic incitement to the
transformation of sex into sexuality which defines the modern period
as the end of Western culture. Foucault quotes Lawrence from *The
Plumed Serpent* and "A Propos *Lady Chatterley's Lover*" in cursory
illustration, the lines from the latter essay being particularly telling in
Foucault's eyes: "Now our business is to realize sex. Today the full
conscious realization of sex is even more important than the act
itself."[6] Blanchard in turn quotes Foucault's ironic gloss on these
lines:

> Perhaps one day people will wonder at [Lawrence's] concern.
> They will not be able to understand how a civilization so intent
> on developing enormous instruments of production and destruc-
> tion found the time and the infinite patience to inquire so
> anxiously concerning the actual state of sex; people will smile
> perhaps when they recall that here were men—meaning our-
> selves—who believed that therein resided a truth every bit as
> precious as the one they had already demanded from the earth,
> the stars, and the pure forms of their thought; people will be
> surprised at the eagerness with which we went about pretend-
> ing to rouse from its slumber a sexuality which everything—
> our discourses, our customs, our institutions, our regulations,
> our knowledge—was busy producing in the light of day and
> broadcasting to noisy accompaniment. And people will ask
> themselves why we were so bent on ending the rule of silence
> regarding what was the nosiest of our preoccupations. (pp. 157–
> 158)

Thus Foucault, in the first volume of *The History of Sexuality*, analyzes
and prophetically criticizes, according to the model of the confessional rite as viewed from some utopian future, this metamorphosis
of the body's interior into the field of psychosexual discourse, reading this transformation as the production of "bio-power" into or as
language. Foucault also claims that this discursive practice has actually defined Western culture for most of its history, especially since

the Enlightenment, and that the Victorian confinement of sex took place precisely when sexuality was beginning to be subjected to the most intense and disciplined of scientific articulations, which culminated, of course, in the invention of psychoanalysis.[7]

Blanchard's point against Foucault's lumping of Lawrence in this camp, however, is not to prove the philosopher and Lawrence's critics generally wrong and so the novelist and his ultimate novel particularly right. She does not use Foucault to demonstrate how Lawrence anticipates, transcends, and so precludes all the positions of his commentators, critical or not. Rather, she uses Foucault to enframe the transformation of sex into discourse. This process creates the modern conception of sexuality as the guilty secret of individual identity which has to be openly and endlessly discussed. Blanchard then finds this problematic transformation and its founding confessional imperative already operative, in a reflective and critical, even ironic, fashion in Lawrence's final and mistakenly abused novel (the Lawrentian motif of "sex-in-the-head").

For Blanchard, Lawrence is neither the dupe of discourse nor its demon, neither genius nor devil. Instead, like the figure of Foucault which she sees, Blanchard discovers a Lawrence who practices in his novel a kind of critical reflection, a human balance, which in his case takes the form of parody of inherited fictional and social conventions and self-parody of prophetic pretensions—that is, the sex scenes and love debates in *Lady Chatterley's Lover*, surprisingly enough, are as often as not intentionally absurd, Blanchard claims. Thus Lawrence here equally embraces and holds up to ridicule both horns of his (and, according to Foucault, *our*) imaginative dilemma of sexuality and discursiveness, of sex and talk, or what Lawrence derisively called in *Women in Love*, "sex-in-the-head."

> Foucault is right, of course, that Lawrence did want to realize sex; Lawrence, after all, maintained that the point of *Lady Chatterley's Lover* was "to think sex, fully, completely, honestly, and cleanly" (*Phoenix* II, 489). But Lawrence also argued that "in man's adventure of self-consciousness [he] must come to the limits of himself and become aware of something beyond him. A man must be self-conscious enough to know his own limits, and to be aware of that which surpasses him" (*Phoenix*, 185).

> *Lady Chatterley's Lover* is a study of the tension between these
> two ideas, between the need to rescue sexuality from secrecy, to
> bring it into discourse, and the simultaneous recognition that
> the re-creation of sexuality in language must always, at the same
> time, resist language. (pp. 32–33)

Blanchard, in short, uses Foucault to rehabilitate the reputation of
the novel within the canon of major works as established in Lawrence Studies since the 1950s. She does so, as we have seen, by
reading its weak points as parody and self-parody, consciously intended; and its strength as Lawrence's self-conscious human finitude.
Foucault thus serves to produce another reading in an essentially
New Critical or Leavisite mode. The arch-antihumanist among
poststructuralists here helps to recuperate Lawrence's humanity, in
support of the self-serving academic morality of critical humanism in
Blanchard's actual instance of reading as a woman.

My point, despite this sudden shift in tone, is not so much to
lament this familiar situation of professional assimilation of innovative work as to understand it. By her reading Blanchard would pull
not only Foucault's teeth but Lawrence's, too. But the form of this
reduction is more my concern than its morality. A double reduction
of Foucault and of Lawrence occurs, and this reduction corresponds
to or mirrors both the dilemma of the immediacy of sex being mediated by language and Blanchard's paradoxical, compensatory resolution of this dilemma in parody: both the parody of earlier novelistic
practices and that of Lawrence's own earlier and current practices.
The innovation, useful to Lawrence Studies, of discovering parody
and self-parody in *Lady Chatterley's Lover* exacts its price: the human-
ization of Foucault, what I am ironically calling the profession of
genius but could just as well be called the professionalization of genius. For all that appears different, provocative, or suggestively original; all that could mark both writers as creative, innovative, or as
what used to define the designation "genius" in its original sense as
the distinctive difference of an individual;[8] all this is done away with
or at least is severely modified, sacrificed to the professional constraints of doing business as usual within the code of Lawrence
Studies, which is still dominated by the critical ideology of the 1950s.
And yet, despite this conservative humanistic use of Foucault's ideas,

Blanchard, by helping to open Lawrence Studies enough to insert them here makes possible, perhaps, several points among the many that would be required to modernize and then postmodernize the subfield, to bring it in line or up-to-date with Romantic or Renaissance Studies, theoretically speaking.[9] Whether such a transformation would be more of a burden than a boon remains, of course, to be seen.

Like my first example from literary studies, the chapter on Foucault in Allan Megill's *Prophets of Extremity*, a contribution to intellectual history, professionalizes Foucault as well as its other three subjects. (The other figures are Foucault's assigned predecessors: Nietzsche and Heidegger, and his critical alternative, Derrida.) Although suspicious of Foucault's allegedly aesthetic or hermetic self-enclosure in discourse and of his pan-ironic crisis mentality (or his apocalyptic thinking with a vengeance), "Michel Foucault and the Activism of Discourse" finally produces a balanced portrait of a thinker caught in the dilemma of negating both a degraded present and the compensatory radical drive to envision any ideal alternative, nostalgic or prophetic, out of suspicion of this revisionary dialectic's complicity with the will-to-truth in Western culture from Socrates to Sartre. In the name of a self-parodic utopianism of oppositional discourse for its own sake, Foucault substitutes, according to Megill, the activity of critical reflection for the action of revolutionary political organization, in the desperate belief that his openly admitted historical fictions may provoke, absurdly enough, long-term structural changes in the networks of discursive power in the culture. Megill argues, of course, that unless these fictions in some sense contain truth for their professional readers—and their good professional readers already know they cannot do so, being imaginative lies in the service of what Foucault himself terms "a politics not yet in existence"—then Foucault's histories can only be taken as novel forms of literature, as texts full of—at best—creatively misleading rhetoric:

> If the "object" is created by an elusive power, rather than power the product of knowledge (as has been held since the seventeenth century), if everything is a lie designed to aid the continuing struggle against the extant order, then it simply does not matter who, objectively, is struggling against whom. Foucault

gives not an "analytic" but rather a "rhetoric" of power—or, perhaps better a vision of power as rhetoric. (p. 250)

And yet, Megill redeems Foucault precisely on an aesthetic or literary basis, that is, on the basis of the power of this vision of power, as being imaginatively productive of new ideas, perspectives, visions —"images that yet fresh images beget," as Yeats would say. Or, as Megill himself more temperately puts it: "Still there is much that we can learn from Foucault. By the very fact that his writings cut across accepted categories, generating a tension with analyses of a more conventional kind, they are not only intriguing but also sharply illuminating" (p. 256). Megill demonstrates this claim in his own brilliantly inventive and highly persuasive reading of *The Archaeology of Knowledge* (see "The Parody of Method," pp. 226–237), as a parodic and even self-parodic text that does for Descartes's *Discourse on Method* and its legacy of Cartesianism in French intellectual circles what Joyce's *Finnegans Wake* has done for literary modernism and its legacy of Mallarmé-ism: namely composed its ultimate satyr-play.

Like Blanchard, Megill humanizes Foucault, by which I mean that both critics cut Foucault down to size, assimilate him to the structure and procedures of their respective disciplines in ways that will stimulate more scholarly production but will leave the institutional apparatus not merely intact but actually untouched. Whatever may be distinctly, even originally challenging and so recognizably Foucaldian in Foucault, has been detached. Blanchard splits off Foucault's understandably human underestimation of Lawrence, produced by the requirement of taking a comprehensive, even "panoptical" overview in the first volume of *The History of Sexuality*. Megill isolates Foucault's essentially post-Kantian theory of the world-making-and-breaking powers of discourse, which Foucault had adopted not in blind hubris, of course, but out of a tragic dilemma—that of a post-Holocaust, post-1960s prophet of pandemic suspicion without a positive vision to announce, affirm, or sacrifice himself for. Blanchard and Megill thus reduce and then consign their subjects (their "Foucaults") to the sphere of literature, in the purely, even banally academic sense: in normalizing Foucault and Lawrence, in other words, they professionalize their genius of defining differences.

The double danger of such professionalization of genius, however, lies not only in the way it normalizes whatever does not fit preestablished procedures, but also, by its very reductiveness, in the way such professionalization retroactively projects the original sublimity upon the distinctive figure that is to be normalized by professional strategies of assimilation in the first place. That is, professionalization produces at least two Foucaults—one closet humanist and one romantic genius—and thereby represses and sublimates the critical differences his discourse would make. The subject of my final example, drawn from Paul Bové's *Intellectuals in Power*, is this ironic dialectic of revisionary professionalization, seen from within a space of judgment made possible by a certain reading of Foucault.

Although Bové's critique of the professionalization of genius in this double sense of repressive sublimation appears throughout his book, it can be found most abundantly isolated in the two longest and central chapters on Erich Auerbach. These are elaborately and brilliantly done, and it would be useless to attempt to redo them here. Besides, my analysis so far suggests what I want to underscore in this revisionary process: the way Foucault, as assimilated into the humanities, is split into a more human, secondary figure and an original, more sublime figure tacitly assumed and retroactively projected by the methods of assimilation themselves. This duality has already been exemplified in Megill's reading of Foucault as a pathetic aestheticist who, in *The Archaeology of Knowledge* at least, is yet a master of parody. Thus the balanced dialectic of critical humanism in action.

That certain reading of Foucault to which I referred a moment ago, Bové's enabling constraint, is also concentrated in its shortest chapter "Intellectuals at War: Michel Foucault and the Analytics of Power." Bové argues that Foucault refuses to envision, prophetically, alternatives to things as he claims they are in our present world of what I call "professionalism unbound." Foucault thus should be seen as evading rather than succumbing to the seductive cul-de-sac of aesthetic hermeticism and utopian discursiveness which Noam Chomsky (in an interview) and Edward W. Said (in a chapter from *The World, the Text, and the Critic*, "Travelling Theory") accuse him of. For although Foucault does claim that power is dispersed amidst networks of truth, he also claims that power provokes the production of positive visions as one of its superior ruses. But for Chomsky and Said—both like Megill in this one respect—Foucault's double negation of the existing repressive order (or regime of the will-to-truth) and of any and all possible intelligible alternatives to it necessarily leaves him affirming only a sublime power that, like God, is everywhere and nowhere at once; that is, with a stylishly ironic metaphysics (but no real analytics) of power. In short, for Chomsky and even more so for Said, Foucault's own words—from "Fantasia of the Library" (1967)—about the hero of Flaubert's *The Temptation of* author; for Foucault's later texts, especially, could be seen as Said tends to see them: in Foucault's own words, as "the composite result of a vision that develops in successive and gradually more distant levels and a temptation that attracts the visionary to the place he has seen and that suddenly envelops him in his own vision."[10] One could see things this way.

For Bové, however, Chomsky and Said especially have somehow failed to recognize or appreciate, to take into serious account, Foucault's career-long analysis of the revisionary dialectic of critical humanism, which since Kant and the Enlightenment generally has condemned the present in the name of an ideal selected from the past, in order to prophesy and oversee its apocalyptic realization in some actually utopian future. Unlike his critics, then, Foucault (for Bové at least) recognizes the pervasively intimate complicities of intellectuals and power, of academic professionals and the ideological apparatus of the modern nation-state. By arrogating to themselves the prophetic and executive power of envisioning alternatives to things as they are, Bové argues, they ensure their continuation as repressively ineffective overseers of the privileged knowledge of liberation; that is, precisely because of its status as the phantasmic property of leading intellectuals (accredited by the state), such liberation is no liberation at all:

> [L]eading intellectuals try to deny to the people the power of self-regulation and self-imagination, either individually or in groups, and try to prevent or at least to inhibit others from coming to political clarity. Leading intellectuals traditional or oppositional tend to assume responsibility for imagining alternatives and do so *within* a set of discourses and institutions burdened genealogically by multifaceted complicities with power

that make them dangerous to people. As agencies of these discourses that greatly affect the present lives of people one might say leading intellectuals are a tool of oppression and most so precisely when they arrogate the right and power to judge and imagine efficacious alternatives—a process that, we might suspect, sustains leading intellectuals at the expense of others. (p. 227)

Thus Foucault, in Bové's eyes, should be taken seriously when in "Nietzsche, Genealogy, History" (1971) he ironically proclaims, following Nietzsche's lead from *Daybreak*, that whereas "religions once demanded the sacrifice of bodies, knowledge now calls for experimentation on ourselves, calls us to the sacrifice of the subject of knowledge" in texts that enact a universal self-parody,[11] a cosmic auto-da-fé of the transcendental pretensions of Western culture. The conclusion to *Intellectuals in Power* strongly alludes to this vision of Foucault as demonic parodist of the Enlightenment mind-set via its own savagely parodic play upon the uncannily familiar imagery of birth as death and death as birth which attends the major texts in the tradition of critical humanism from Kant and Nietzsche to Foucault and his erstwhile American disciple, Said himself:

The temptations to build a better world, to discover the truth about human life, to rely on genius, sublimity, mastery, and prophetic wisdom: even though all these must be put aside, they will recur for a long time. The emergent cannot be forced. Forceps in the hand of male medical experts—can this image have benign force any longer? Such an appropriation of truth to political work, such a releasing of it from the shapeless, indeterminate background of the power structure of humanistic discourse might seem amoral or immoral. But the morality of humanism and its professionalization has worn out its welcome; it has announced its own betrayal of its own highest ideals, not only, as Auerbach would have it, by helping produce fascism, but by being structurally and institutionally allied with other "masters" whose "morality" is indefensible and, above all, by relying always and everywhere on death for its own survival. (p. 310)

Well, in Bové's book, we surely have a different use of Foucault from those found in my other two examples. In Blanchard's exercise in literary criticism, you will recall, Foucault appears as a device to transform the Lawrence of *Lady Chatterley* into a lover of parody and self-parody. In the section of Megill's volume devoted to him, Foucault himself appears as the desperate activist of a self-defeatingly parodic discourse of antiknowledge, of heuristically fictional histories of the will-to-truth in the service of "a politics not yet in existence" and known in advance never to be coming into existence, since as soon as any such politics should begin to come into existence it would have to be negated as complicitous with power in the worst sense of the word. Finally, however, in Bové's text we have seen Foucault, despite the critiques of Chomsky and Said, in an even more severely grand light—as the master critical parodist of all post-Enlightenment pretensions to mastery, to end all such figures of mastery. As such, Bové's Foucault would thus help to empty out and leave the spaces of representation in the culture open to the people's own acts of self-determination and self-imagination, so long as the institution of critical humanism, traditional and oppositional, in the form of leading professional intellectuals like Chomsky, Said, or William J. Bennett, does not usurp the role of envisioning for the people the proper alternatives—of the Left or the Right—to things as they are.

If we are to allegorize these three uses of Foucault with the help of what to my mind appears to be an appropriate literary text, we could say that Blanchard uses Foucault in such a way as to make him (and Lawrence as well) seem more like the narrator of Thomas Mann's *Doktor Faustus*, Serenus Zeitblom, Ph.D., that ordinary, normal, bourgeois humanist who is nevertheless indirectly and unwittingly complicit in the final destruction of an avant-garde genius and of a nation. Megill, to continue this play on point of view, then could be said to transform Foucault, especially the Foucault of *The Archaeology*, into Adrian Leverkühn, Mann's self-destructive Schoenberg-like composer, who, like Nietzsche, possesses a demonic gift for sublime parody. Finally, in Bové, Foucault emerges as the critical heir of modernist and postmodernist writers, I think, conceived along lines of someone like the implied author of *Doktor Faustus* or *Grav-*

ity's Rainbow, that elusive parodist of parodists, who in turn is best conceived on the original demonic model of Satan himself.

If we grant that these or similarly allegorized master-figures are guiding the uses of Foucault in the humanities, what can we say is being achieved through them? First of all, new readings of Lawrence, of modern critical theory, and of post-Enlightenment intellectual history. Second, a new placement of Foucault as a figure in his own right who can be used to get more interpretive work done, of whatever sort and however its effects are intended by these or other critics in and out of the humanities. That such an enabling or empowering use of Foucault also entails forms of constraint (on Foucault's work, on the critics concerned) goes without saying. The primary constraint is the ironic reinforcement of the ruling paradigm of scholarly production and distinction which has always been the hallmark of critical humanism in the modern university: *scholarship as an individual achievement or work.* Bové's book is particularly self-aware of this ironic aspect of its own or any use of Foucault in the academy today.

Even more significantly, I think, each of these uses of Foucault places him either near or actually in the sphere of literature—as, for example, a midwife to parody on Lawrence's part (Blanchard); as, for another, a parodist himself (Megill); and last, as the parodist par excellence of this very strategy of literary consignment and containment of the emergent and the different via the secularizations of the religious discourses, especially those of the prophetic texts (Bové). So in answer to my earlier question, "Why should we read Foucault?" we apparently can say that we should read him because he permits us to discover the effectiveness of parody for current critical discourse. In adducing such an answer we also address my title question "What Was Foucault?" by identifying him as, effectively, an intellectual parodist of the first order. That is, we should read Foucault as it appears we already do, for the parody's sake, because he was a parody himself in some sense or a self-parody of the prophetic or leading intellectual—the lead in the Enlightenment satyr-play now being played out everywhere in Western culture—whose textual performances can still promote our own scholarly productivity.

In the rest of this chapter, I would like to examine the issue of parody and of style generally, of what it may mean to say that a critical intellectual is an author in a literary sense, issues that are occasioned by these ironic literary institutionalizations of Foucault in the humanities, institutionalizations whose critical practices repeatedly invoke one author-figure in particular: Nietzsche.

The Practice of Criticism; or, The Culture of Parody

The *locus classicus* of this question regarding the author in Foucault is, of course, "What Is an Author?" One familiar reading of the essay, as suggested by Megill's remarks on it and related works of the time (1969), is to see it in the context of French intellectual life, that is, as a symbolic revolutionary destruction of the subject of knowledge projected by the discourses of the regime of the will-to-truth within the so-called liberal and democratic state. That is, one could read it as a discursive guerrilla action taken as a knowing form of therapeutic compensation for the collapse of actual revolution. In essence, then, one could read the essay as a belated, postmodern, perhaps parodic and even self-parodic repetition of the romantic reaction to the failure of the French Revolution (as classically represented by M. H. Abrams in *Natural Supernaturalism* [1971]).

Although such a reading is comforting precisely because of its familiarity and nice balance of realistic critique and reductive psychologizing, I propose another reading: "What Is an Author?" as a socialization of the natural history of authorship to be found in Nietzsche's *Ecce Homo*, particularly in sections 8 through 10 of the chapter entitled "Why I Am So Clever." I read Foucault's parodic style, therefore, not as a narcissistic economy of grandiose compensation. I see it instead as an instrument for a kind of musiclike metamorphosis, a singular transformation of Nietzschean themes into a different key and register, a revisionary recategorization of Nietzsche's "naturalistic" categories demarcating the conditions of possibility for authorship that has for its primary effect the potential assimilation, along already established institutional and professional lines, of Nietzsche's Dionysian stance.

Before proceeding any further, I want to define what I intend by my use of the term *parody* (or *self-parody*) in this context. Parody has traditionally taken two forms: that of the burlesquing subplot that ridiculously parallels the heroic main plot in Shakespeare and in Classical drama, and that of critical parody, the exaggerated imitation of a writer's characteristic style. Originally, "a song sung beside" a serious poem, parody achieves its broadest comic effects by applying high-flown language to trivial matters, or, more rarely and subtly, vice versa. Parody, in short, is an antithetical song placed adjacent to some conventional work of piety.

For my purposes, however, the intellectual self-parody I am isolating can be defined as the exaggerated imitation of a recognizably characteristic position or style that the parodist in question shares with others by virtues of a network of ideological and professional identifications and associations. Even more precisely and technically, intellectual parody, what I also want to call "radical parody," is a recognizably self-contradictory conceit of defensive hyperbole that arises from the exuberance of critical productivity, as if the parodist were almost beside himself with self-opposing forms. As we shall see, however, the intended target of such parody, some common aspect or other of the intellectual parodist's own mode of scholarly production, may only be the mask for another, more fundamental, repressed object.

I want to distinguish, in other words, this mode of radical parody, which I see as potentially operative both at any time in the post-Enlightenment cultural history of the modern nation-state and its professions and bureaucracies, and in any discourse or genre or artistic medium, from the historically specific and aesthetically limited conception of parody, in its relation to pastiche, found in Fredric Jameson's "Postmodernism, or The Cultural Logic of Late Capitalism." Jameson sees a shift from modernist parody like that of Mann's *Doktor Faustus*, with its moral imperative largely intact, to postmodern pastiche as in the wholesale "imitation of dead styles . . . stored up in the imaginary museum" of the past. "The producers of culture," Jameson claims, now practice "blank parody," a kind of neutral and neutralizing pastiche on the model of pop-art collage.[12] My own conception of radical parody would incorporate this recent development in a larger aesthetic and historical framework than that provided Jameson by the transition to late capitalism.

That parody, even self-parody, is operative in Foucault's "What Is an Author?" is signaled not only by his deployment of a quotation, "What matter who's speaking, someone said, what matter who's speaking," that comes from Beckett's *Stories and Texts for Nothing,* which occurs at the opening and then again, in truncated form, at the close of the essay's experimental argument as an ironic refrain or frame. It is also signaled at the very beginning of the initial statement that prefaces Foucault's text. When this statement claims that its speaker, presumably Foucault, is "conscious of the need for an explanation" simply for "proposing the slightly odd question" of the title as a serious subject for discussion and then goes on to assert that the general notion of "the author" itself remains an open question "to this day" both "with respect to its general function within discourse" and in what the speaker terms "my own writings"; or when we notice that the speaker then claims that "this question permits me to return to certain aspects of my own work which now appear ill-advised and misleading"; and we also notice, perhaps, that this speaker declares that this question even grants him the right, indeed the authority "to propose a necessary self-criticism and reevaluation" (p. 113) with respect to certain apparently misleading statements in *The Order of Things;*[13] and finally, when we reflect that in the space of the six short sentences of this small first paragraph of his brief prefatory statement there are five uses of the first-person singular pronoun or its reflexive pronominal and adjectival variants; then we may begin to feel, I think, that what is to follow in the text of "What Is an Author?" can be read in part at least as a revisionary parodic text of self-revision.

Even if we grant that the Foucault speaker is being wittily ironic here, even parodic and self-parodic, why should we also understand all his following remarks as similarly tainted or so stressed in part? And why should we see them, as I have suggested that we should, as a socialization of a naturalistic mode of conceiving authorship, especially since this speaker explicitly sets aside a sociohistorical analysis of the author in favor of an apparently highly restrictive rhetorical focus on "the singular relationship that holds between an author and a text," precisely by virtue of "the manner in which a text apparently points to this figure who is outside and precedes it" (p. 115). It is at this point that the speaker, to ironically emphasize his accredited seriousness, introduces the Beckettian citation and then digresses upon writing's self-referential nature these days and its antiheroic "kinship," in Kafka and Beckett certainly, with "death" (p. 118). And yet, I would argue, the banality of these digressive remarks as well as the ironic twist the speaker gives to them via the Beckett line suggest the continuation of the opening parodic move. For the self-referentiality of contemporary writing is conceived here not as constitutive of a heterocosmic interior totality, as a great sphere burning with a hard, gemlike flame; rather, it is said to constitute a new form of exteriority, a new Mallarméan stress on the impersonal, indeed anonymous materials of the linguistic medium itself, into whose surfaces the author is said to be disappearing, practically at this very moment: a sacrificial victim of the demolition by writing of the traditional epic assumption of the writer as hero whose work wins for him and his people the serene if purely symbolic immortality of posthumous fame as a classic text of culture (p. 117). I submit that the speaker's parodic practice at the opening of the essay, as throughout, therefore, specifically enacts the irony of the contemporary writer's "death" as theoretically thematized here by the Foucault figure in—with one notable exception—terms that were even for 1969 obviously clichéd.

A complete reading of this text along the lines suggested would continue by noting how the speaker not only suggests that "the function of an author is to characterize" in various ways "the existence, circulation, and operation of certain discourses within a society" (p. 124), particularly by a splitting and dispersion of the subject into different, even opposing discursive positions and functions, but also makes this suggestion in a way that recalls the conventional version of ironic point of view and the implied author to be found, as the editor helpfully notes, in Wayne Booth's *The Rhetoric of Fiction* (p. 129). That is, such a reading would further develop the innovative conventionality of this text revealed here and also in its tracing of the hermeneutic practices of today's critics who deal with today's revolutionary writing back to the medieval norms of Christian hermeneutics—specifically, to Saint Jerome's four criteria for textual authenticity (p. 127). A fully comprehensive reading of "What Is an Author?" could indeed demonstrate, ad nauseam, the evidently knowing way this text quite literally subverts or contradicts itself by invoking innovation and disclosing continuity—and vice versa.

This parodic self-contradiction and self-subversion is seen

nowhere more strikingly than in the speaker's simultaneous dismissal of and dependency on what he terms, derisively, the notion of the "transcendental anonymity" of *écriture*, by which he means the unwitting recapitulation and reinscription of "the historical and transcendental tradition of the nineteenth century" (p. 120) upon the theoretical plane of the then newest intellectual mode, deconstruction.[14] For the Foucault figure, after this outburst, proceeds to assume his own position of prominence among "those who are making a great effort to liberate themselves, once and for all, from this conceptual framework" of post-Kantian philosophy (p. 120). At the same time he also divides authors into those godlike few such as Homer, Aristotle, and the church fathers who occupy "a 'transdiscursive' position" as "old as our civilization itself" (p. 131) and "a singular type of author" which, though not classically sublime in the former sense, nonetheless remains remarkably distinctive, even uniquely original, as what "the nineteenth century in Europe produced" and left us, namely such "inescapable" "initiators of discursive practices" (p. 131) as Marx and Freud. Significantly, Nietzsche is omitted from this roster, indeed almost entirely from the essay as a whole, with the exception of one explicitly comic aside concerning the question of how one knows what to include in an author's corpus.[15] Once again, "What Is an Author?" parodies its own gestures of innovation as they are being made.

Let's take a closer look at this distinction between kinds of authorship for what it may betray about the workings of this text. A transdiscursive author, according to the Foucault speaker, "authors" "much more than a book . . .[authors] a theory, for instance, . . . a tradition or a discipline within which new books and authors can proliferate" (p. 131). Such authors, like the founder of a science, produce, in Thomas Kuhn's conception of scientific revolution, an organization or paradigm for doing certain things in a discourse or cutting across several discourses which subsequent workers in the field can follow, apply, refine upon, or normalize.[16] Both Saint Jerome and Newton could function as transdiscursive authors in this sense, as could Saint Augustine and Darwin. On the other hand, initiators of discursive practices in the nineteenth-century tradition, a tradition that for this text clearly still continues into our time, such figures as Marx and Freud, as the Foucault persona claims, produce new discursive constellations that, by their original omissions, logical aporias, and rhetorical fissures, cannot be totally assimilated into normalized discourse, even that inspired by these very original omissions. Consequently, I would argue, such initiators of discursive practices must provoke the further production of textual innovations and repositionings by this production of memorable images of sublime disjunctiveness. These further innovations can stand in opposition, even as they must always return to their founding ellipses in the works of the "initiators of discursive practices" from which these later texts have spring. Instead of ascribing the innovations of such writers as Marx and Freud, therefore, to their mysterious irreducible originality that functions as a daemonic or natural force of inspiration, the Foucaldian voice attributes them to the unique and founding "interstices of the text, its gaps and absences. . . . those empty spaces that have been marked by omission or concealed in a false and misleading plentitude." That is, this speaker attributes their innovations to "an essential lack" (p. 135). Such fundamental holes in these innovative texts, in other words, provoke an equally innovative, indeed transgressive progeny that are simultaneously marked by their own generic blanks, which in Foucault's case take the form of a radical, Dionysian self-parody. And in this instance of the distinction between transdiscursive writer and discursive initiator, Foucault's text openly selfdestructs. For it reinscribes the transcendental anonymity of *écriture* just banished for recalling the Kantian problematic; more generally, it revises, under the sign of negative inversion, of the original "essential lack," the romantic or daemonic conception of individual genius which, like the texts for nothing of Beckett or Kafka, "What Is an Author?" disperses—here, of course, into the four author-functions that the rest of the essay analyzes.

"Foucault" limits himself, he says, to the four characteristics of "the author-function" which seem "most obvious and important";

[T]he "author-function" is tied to the legal and institutional systems that circumscribe, determine, and articulate the realm of discourses; it does not operate in a uniform manner in all discourses, at all times, and in any given culture; it is not defined by the spontaneous attribution of a text to its creator, but through a series of precise and complex procedures; it does not refer, purely and simply, to an actual individual insofar as it simultaneously gives rise to a variety of egos and to a series of subjective positions that individuals of any class may come to occupy. (pp. 130–131).

In any text, this Foucault is saying, we can trace the lineaments of the legal and institutional codes that permit and constrain, that determine and articulate the production, circulation, and preservation—in the largest sense, the economy—of texts and their authors. In addition, by comparing texts produced in different times and cultures, we can trace the ways our attribution of authorship is *placed* in our present culture by these legal and institutional codes. (This is one thing it means to do "a history of the present.") Consequently, we can also learn how the attribution of authorship is an elaborate yet exact discursive practice of construction and positioning (and not one of interpretive discovery and re-creation). These procedures for constructing an author depend on the extant intellectual and cultural conditions far more than on the original intention of the individual writer. In fact, as this Foucault figure concludes, the text a writer produces in accordance with our discursive, institutional, legal, and intellectual or cultural conditions and conventions, disperses the individualized subject into a series of egos or author-functions and textual positions which a reader from any class can be educated to occupy, and which the writer, as reader, can occupy as well. One thinks in this regard of Kierkegaard's or Beckett's Chinese box–like nests of narration, of their innumerable author-figures and narrators, which infinitize the ironic play of point of view in their literary discourse.

In summary, these four characteristics of the "author-function" are: (1) the author's determination by particularized institutional codes; (2) the author's temporally and spatially specific placement vis-à-vis other times and societies; (3) the author's culturally irregular or heterogeneous construction and dissemination; and (4) the author's, indeed the subject's, serial dispersal as these author-functions into ego-positions and freely accessible personae for occupation by individual readers. These four characteristics of the author-function thus constitute the primary conditions of possibility, in a discursive and textual sense, for the emergence and institution of the author in

Western culture, especially since the inauguration of modernity with the rise and triumph of the bourgeoisie and their universal assumption of texts as the private property of a uniquely original individual.

In the articulation of the discursive conditions of possibility for authorship, therefore, "What Is an Author?" clearly lies, ironically enough, well within the field of a nineteenth-century transcendental tradition of critical philosophy founded by Kant. The distinction between two kinds of authors—transdiscursive and initiating—replicates, for instance, a transcendental move, namely, the division of an object's mode of existence into noumenal and phenomenal modes. This text, in other words, once again proves radically self-contradictory in a way that suggests self-parody, since it apparently intends to contribute to the current effort to break free from, once and for all, this very tradition, even as it demonstrates the impossibility of such a project being anything other than a purely rhetorical gesture.

Restrictions of space prohibit a demonstration of the positioning of this text within the field of the Kantian problematic. Suffice it to say, the various ways this text subverts itself—conceptually, structurally, and rhetorically—testify equally to the limits of instrumental reason (what Kant calls "the understanding") and to the imaginative power of the failure of rational representation ironically to resist the provocatively shattering effects of what Kant in *The Critique of Judgment* calls "the sublime." Although the identifiable causes differ in Kant and Foucault (nature and discourse, respectively), the textual production of the sublime effect, as such, is consanguineous. Foucault's own recently published essay "What Is Enlightenment?" reflects on this general intellectual situation of Kant's pervasiveness (see *The Foucault Reader*). Besides, there is another, more immediate predecessor text of discursive innovation within the field of the Kantian problematic, Nietzsche's *Ecce Homo*, which relates more directly to the question "What Is an Author?" An examination of one portion of *Ecce Homo* not only will demonstrate how the Foucaldian text transforms Nietzsche's naturalistic and late romantic characterizations of the conditions of possibility for authorship; but it also will explain, I think, why "What Is an Author?" repeats, parodically and self-parodically (that is, transgressively) in its institutional, discursive, professionalizing, and impersonalizing modes of socialization, the more generally romantic and demonic conception of individual genius it would ironically disperse. That is, in deconstructing, as it were, this cultural myth-theme of genius, "What Is an Author?" also reiterates, in a transformed register or key, a Dionysian problematic drawn from Nietzsche's text.

As Nietzsche's *Ecce Homo* generally does, so "Why I Am So Clever" reduces and disperses, in a climactic fashion, the subject of writing which its announced author has so far impersonated in his life career. Nietzsche's self, that is, is reduced and dispersed along the discursive networks of rules for the construction of the conditions of possibility for authorship which are wholly defined according to the biological and psychological imperatives of natural history as understood from the perspective created by the canon of Nietzsche's works their author is reviewing: in short, their natural history of the will-to-power.[17]

For Nietzsche, the "selection"—whether conscious or not—of "nutriment, of place and climate, of recreation" (p. 63) constitutes the author-organism's "whole casuistry of selfishness" (p. 66)—its defensive system of mimicry and self-mimicry, of chameleonlike effects that is claimed to have made possible the realization of this career's ruling principle or genius: self-overcoming through a form of writing which produces, almost as a side-effect, a revaluation of all values hitherto operative in the history of values and value judgments on the earth. These naturalistic or naturalizing categories of nutriment, place and climate, recreation, these conditions of possibility for "the whole casuistry of selfishness," which in turn enables and constrains authorship in Nietzsche, enact a Dionysian destruction of the religious and moral idealism, the mystique of the great spirit and beautiful soul associated with the romantic conception of genius. Moreover, Foucault's four "obvious and most important" "characteristics of the author-function" act as the revisionary reading of these Nietzschean categorizations that de-idealize their *über*-biologism, according to the largely professional economy of texts in present-day society, even as these Foucaldian revisions maintain the original critical configuration of Nietzsche's categories.

Being "tied to the legal and institutional systems" that "circumscribe, determine, and articulate the realm of discourse," for instance, rereads the first Nietzschean category of "nutriment," even as the "whole casuistry of selfishness" becomes in Foucault's hands the serial

dispersal of "a variety of egos" and "subjective positions that individuals of any class may come to occupy" (p. 131). The revisionary
relationship between the Nietzschean "place and climate" and "recreation," on the one hand; and the Foucaldian cultural heterogeneity
and construction of the author-function, on the other, appears too
obvious to belabor at this point. The revisionary relation between
these two texts can be summarized as follows: Where Nietzsche's text
allegorizes the author-function according to a natural history schema
or code, Foucault's text allegorizes the conditions of possibility for
authorship according to a textual and discursive, an institutional or
professionally social schema or code. The structures of these allegori-
zations of the author, as readings, remain, however, homologous,
almost musically so, as if each were the variation of the other's theme
and both were variations of a theme left unread and so unsounded.

This last point is best exemplified, I think, in a section of "Why
I Am So Clever" which reinscribes the dispersed ideology of genius
under the sign of creative repression, in much the same self-contradictory and self-parodic way that "What Is an Author?" reinscribes it
via the speculative conception of "initiators of discursive practices,"
which functions as a form of critical negation. After deconstructing
the author into this fiction's "naturally" defensive components of
nutriment, place and climate, and so on, the Nietzschean narrator
announces that he is ready at last to answer the question implicit in
the subtitle of *Ecce Homo: How One Becomes What One Is.*

According to this narrator, by means of such reductions and
dispersals found in this text, as well as by such "lies" as are found in
all sorts of idealisms, one can practice, knowingly or not, "the art of
selfishness," of "higher" self-protection and self-defense, until one's
"genius" or "organizing 'idea'," the intention of one's life as career,
has become powerful enough to leap forth "suddenly ripe," in its
"final perfection." For to be a great author, this Nietzschean narrator
claims,

> The entire surface of consciousness—consciousness *is* a sur-
> face—has to be kept clear of any of the great imperatives. Even
> the grand words, the grand attitudes must be guarded against!
> All of them represent a danger that the instinct will "understand
> itself" too early—. In the meantime the organizing "idea"

destined to rule grows and grows in the depths—it begins to command, it slowly leads *back* from sidepaths and wrong turnings, it prepares *individual* qualities and abilities which will one day prove themselves indispensable as means to achieving the whole—it constructs the *ancillary* capacities one after the other before it gives any hint of the domineering task, of the "goal," "objective," "meaning."—Regarded from this side my life is simply wonderful. For the task of a *revaluation of values* more capacities perhaps were required than have dwelt together in one individual, above all antithetical capacities which however are not allowed to disturb or destroy one another. Order of rank among capacities; distance; the art of dividing without making inimical; mixing up nothing, "reconciling" nothing; a tremendous multiplicity which is nonetheless the opposite of chaos—this has been the precondition, the protracted secret labour and artistic working of my instinct. (p. 65).

The romantic ideology of individual genius, of the daemon that is the great author's destiny, hereby returns from its previous diaspora in the Nietzschean text by means of the psychology of repression and unconscious creativity—a conception of the unconscious as a source of individual and individualizing ruling instincts, as capacities for domination of the entire psyche, as wills-to-power that function like artists, authors of one's fate.[18] Such is the Nietzschean understanding of the conditions of possibility for authorship.

As we can now see, "What Is an Author?" follows the Nietzschean precedent in more than the structure of its critical categories. For it also reiterates the founding self-contradiction of the earlier text, the essential lack of that text, in its own self-contradiction between the subject's discursive dispersal into various author-functions and positions for utterance and the author's partial recuperation of the status of genius as an inspirational source of discursive initiation due to an original omission to which later writers must always return. But whereas Nietzsche's text recuperates the ideology of genius under the sign of creative repression, Foucault's text does its recuperative work under the sign of the critical negation of a text or an entire corpus. That is, while Nietzsche envisions his organizing idea of the revaluation of all values as a natural development suddenly fully ripe and perfect in the prophet's mouth, as it were; Foucault improvises his transient speculative conception of initiators of discursive practices as an original omission, as a founding gap or provocative hole—as an essential lack often subsequently thematized in various ways and informing the corpus of later writers. This essential lack incites further scholarly innovations in the form of transgressive returns to the texts of these initiators of discursive practices. Abysses that yet fresh abysses beget.

Although one can easily read the desires of Nietzsche and Foucault into these different portrayals of authorship (full mouth versus inviting slit?), I am more interested here in summarizing what we can learn from reflecting on the general question of style which their interaction helps to define, especially in comparison to the recent critical appropriations of Foucault in the humanities already discussed.

What such a comparison teaches us, I think, is that some younger scholars of the modern and postmodern in the humanities appear to be replacing irony with parody as one of the first principles of their critical judgments,[19] and to be applying this literary principle of judgment to other than conventionally defined literary works, with the result that the style of intellectual work in the texts so treated is being read as contributing to, even at points contradicting, the explicit arguments or intentions of such works.[20] In the words of the title of Hayden White's recent book on the difficulties of doing history, more and more it is "the content of the form" that matters in the critical conversation.[21]

As my reading of the relations between Nietzschean and Foucaldian texts suggests, such an orientation toward the symptomatology of style both enables us to read the previously more esoteric, revisionary transformations of texts by other texts that have produced intellectual history, and at the same time, of course, constrains us to *humanize* that productive history via the assumption of an inevitable comic pathos that necessarily attends the fate of the critical intellectual at this time. In short, we tend to see the work of others and even our own work as chronically self-contradictory to the point of intentional self-parody. We see ourselves, in other words, as self-conscious avatars of that hero of the Nestor chapter of Joyce's *Ulysses*—that is, as figures of sublime parody—as, at best, *holy fools* of the various discourses that distort us: "On his wise shoulders through the checkerwork of leaves the sun flung spangles, dancing coins."[22] Such appears to be the culture of parody in our postmodern age.

But perhaps I had better let Foucault himself have the last word on this matter. So I will conclude with a quotation from his early book on Raymond Roussel that seems apropos: "In relation to this secret all of Roussel would be just so much rhetorical skill, revealing, to whoever knows how to read what [his texts] say, the simple, extraordinarily generous fact that they don't say it."[23] This ironic secret that Foucault refers to in relation to Roussel is naturally that of his style.

Notes

1. All citations of this essay are taken from the version of the text to be found in Donald F. Bouchard, ed., *Language, Counter-Memory, Practice: Selected Essays and Interviews by Michel Foucault*, trans. Donald F. Bouchard and Sherry Simon (Ithaca, N.Y.: Cornell University Press, 1977), pp. 113–138. Hereafter all page references to this work will be given in my text.

2. See Tracy B. Strong, *Friedrich Nietzsche and the Politics of Transfiguration* (Berkeley and Los Angeles: University of California Press, 1975).

3. My three examples are: Lydia Blanchard, "Lawrence, Foucault, and the Language of Sexuality," in *D. H. Lawrence's "Lady": A New Look at Lady Chatterley's Lover*, ed. Michael Squires and Dennis Jackson (Athens: University of Georgia Press, 1985), pp. 17–35; Allan Megill, *Prophets of Extremity: Nietzsche, Heidegger, Foucault, Derrida* (Berkeley and Los Angeles: University of California Press, 1985), pp. 181–256; and Paul A. Bové, *Intellectuals in Power: A Genealogy of Critical Humanism* (New York: Columbia University Press, 1986), pp. 209–237. All page citations from these works will be given in my text.

4. My decision to focus on "What Is an Author?" was based, in part, on the inclusion of this essay in the highly influential anthology edited by Josué Harari, *Textual Strategies* (Ithaca, N.Y.: Cornell University Press, 1979).

5. Significantly, Blanchard does not refer to any other major work by Foucault.

6. As quoted in Michel Foucault, *The History of Sexuality*, trans. Robert Hurley (New York: Pantheon, 1978), 1:157.

7. See Daniel T. O'Hara, "The Power of Nothing in *Women in*

Love," in *Rhetoric, Interpretation, Literature,* ed. S. Mailloux (Lewisburg: Associated University Presses, 1983).

8. See the entry for "Inspiration" in *Princeton Encyclopedia of Poetry and Poetics,* ed. Alex Preminger, enl. ed. (Princeton: Princeton University Press, 1974), pp. 396–398. See also, Linda Hutcheon, *A Theory of Parody* (New York and London: Methuen, 1985).

9. For the best reading of the theoretical modernization of Romantic Studies, see Jonathan Arac, *Critical Genealogies: Historical Situations for Postmodern Literary Studies* (New York: Columbia University Press, 1987).

10. Bouchard, *Language,* p. 99.

11. As quoted in ibid., p. 163.

12. See the entry for "Parody" in Preminger, *Princeton Encyclopedia,* pp. 600–602. See also, Fredric Jameson, "Postmodernism, or The Cultural Logic of Late Capitalism," *New Left Review,* no. 146 (1984), pp. 64–65.

13. Bouchard's remarks in the footnotes to "What Is an Author?" and Megill's history of the critical relations between Foucault and Jean Wahl, who presided at the session where "What Is an Author?" was first delivered, both provide a biographical motivation for Foucault's parodic self-critical display in this initial statement.

14. Foucault's claims that certain recent critical developments grant writing "a primordial status" ("What Is an Author?" p. 120) are taken by Bouchard to refer to phenomenology. I think they refer as well to that philosophy of language associated with Barthes and Derrida which has come generally to be known by the term *deconstruction.*

15. The terms in which Foucault discusses this problem may have inspired, along with his critical remarks on those who grant "a primordial status" to writing, Derrida's self-parodic play in *Spurs: Nietzsche's Styles* on the fragment in Nietzsche's own handwriting, "'I have forgotten my umbrella.'"

16. See Thomas S. Kuhn, *The Structure of Scientific Revolutions,* 2d ed., enl. (Chicago: University of Chicago Press, 1970).

17. All references to this work will be to the following edition: Friedrich Nietzsche, *Ecce Homo: How One Becomes What One Is,* trans. R. J. Hollingdale (New York: Penguin, 1979). Hereafter all citations will be given in my text.

18. For different discussions of Nietzsche's aestheticism, see Daniel T. O'Hara, *The Romance of Interpretation: Visionary Criticism from Pater to de Man* (New York: Columbia University Press, 1985), and Alexander Nehamas, *Nietzsche: Life As Literature* (Cambridge, Mass.: Harvard University Press, 1985).

19. For the most comprehensive and insightful overview of the

modern/postmodern debate, see Jonathan Arac, ed., *Postmodernism and Politics* (Minneapolis: University of Minnesota Press, 1986).

20. On this subject, see my *Lionel Trilling: The Work of Liberation* (Madison: University of Wisconsin Press, 1988).

21. See Hayden White, *The Content of The Form: Narrative Discourse and Historical Representation* (Baltimore: Johns Hopkins University Press, 1987).

22. James Joyce, *Ulysses* (New York: Random House, 1961), p. 36.

23. Michel Foucault, *Death and the Labyrinth: The World of Raymond Roussel* (Garden City: Doubleday, 1968), p. 10.

THE RENAISSANCE
Foucault's Lost Chance?

Marie-Rose Logan

Do not seek Truth—Rather seek to develop those forces which make and unmake truths. Seek to ponder the same matter at greater length, more rigorously,—so as to catch yourself in the very act—so as to keep yourself in suspense—so as to precipitate out what is getting clogged. Make coordinations for yourself. Try out your ideas as functions and means.

—Paul Valéry, *Cahiers*

Michel Foucault's entire endeavor can be read in the light of the intellectual challenge set forth by Paul Valéry. Through his questioning of historical, social, and cultural values, Foucault impresses on his readers that the study of discursive practices does not yield truth but it can reinforce or undermine prevailing assumptions about the notion of truth. The truths Foucault made and unmade usually revolve around the exploration of a single issue—representation, insanity, incarceration, or sexuality—and involve the resources of several disciplines ranging from philosophy, history, linguistics, and anthropology to biology and psychiatry. In pondering any one issue at more length and with more rigor, Foucault searches through the past centuries of Western civilization. In *The Use of Pleasure* and *The Care of the Self*, he even ventures in the Greco-Roman past. A blend of epistemological inquisitiveness and linguistic ingenuity radiates from those pages of *The Order of Things* in which layers of the past are unraveled before the reader's eyes. There and in *The Archaeology of Knowledge*, the coordinations that are established between the realm of discourse (*verba*) and that of historical, social, and cultural realities (*res*) rest on the intellect's attempt to point out the ineluctable discrepancies that exist among ourselves, the world, and our representations of the world.

In both works, Foucault displays a sharp awareness of the boundaries that language imposes on the coming and going between pure thought and raw facts. The mathematical overtones present in Valéry's admonition to "try out your ideas as functions and means" aptly convey the challenge of the epistemological thrust at play in those works where conventional labels (such as Renaissance, Classical Age, Enlightenment) are used side by side with a new terminology (such as archaeology, heterotopias, discursive formations). Language is viewed as a mode of representation "that names, patterns, combines, and connects and disconnects things as it makes them visible in the transparency of words."[1] As such, it stands out as one of the essential functions associated with any effort to grasp and render the process of knowing (*mathesis*). Yet it also engenders an object of knowledge (*mathema*) which forever only resembles the so-called real object, while also resembling previous linguistic representations of that object. According to Foucault: "It is not that words are imperfect or that, when confronted by the visible, they prove insuperably inadequate. . . . it is in vain that we attempt to show, by the use of images, metaphors, or similes, what we are saying."[2] Such a strategy of watchfulness leads him "to catch" himself "in the very act" of interrogating the underpinnings of his own discourse:

> Perhaps I am a historian of ideas after all. But an ashamed, or, if you prefer, a presumptuous historian of ideas. One who set out to renew his discipline from top to bottom; who wanted, no doubt, to achieve a rigour that so many other, similar descriptions have recently acquired; but who unable to modify in any real way that old form of analysis, to make it cross the threshold of scientificity (or finding that such a metamorphosis is always impossible, or that he did not have the strength to effect that transformation himself), declares that he had been doing, and wanted to do, something quite different.[3]

In an effort to "renew his discipline from top to bottom," Foucault viewed the totality of history as a set of discontinuities. While resorting to the periodizations usually advocated by historians of ideas, he also introduced the possibility of thinking out the phenomena that characterize a given period as isolated entities. In exploring alternatives to traditional values of intellectual history, Foucault also opened the way for a methodology of conceptual cognition which departed from the primacy of the ontological argument that in one way or another has so far guided the formulation of criteria in the human sciences, be they history, philosophy (at least, the continental variety), or literary criticism and theory. The practitioners of those disciplines view their craft as a process directed toward the reaffirmation of meaning as it emerges from a set of given premises: the unity of the Western tradition with its corollaries of evolution and continuity in the realm of history of ideas, the powerful ontological logos in continental philosophy, and the primacy or even the transcendental function of the text in literary criticism and theory.

In recent years, postmodernist and poststructuralist trends have radically questioned the foundational aspects of the disciplines. According to Jean-François Lyotard, "A postmodern artist or writer is in the position of a philosopher: the text he writes, the work he produces are not in principle governed by preestablished rules, and they cannot be judged according to a determining judgment, by applying familiar categories to the text or to the work."[4] In many ways, Foucault's openended, dialectical understanding of the historical and philosophical processes challenged and still challenges the postmodernist program.[5] Does Foucault address a similar challenge to scholars who are entrenched in the study of a given period? What about the Renaissance? Throughout his writings, Foucault expresses a preference for the Classical Age, for the secular and empirical thrust that was the hallmark of the Enlightenment, and for the nineteenth century during which new disciplines like linguistics, anthropology, and psychoanalysis took shape. He could, like Nietzsche, envision the Renaissance as a "high point of the millennium" and acknowledge that "what happened since then is the great reaction of every kind of mob impulses against the 'individualism' of that period."[6]

In the wake of the publication and translation of *Madness and Civilization* and of *The Order of Things*, a number of reviews appeared in France and in America. In one way or another, Foucault's stance on the Renaissance was bound to be controversial on both sides of the ocean. By and large, French scholars displayed a greater willingness to accept Foucault on his own terms, while American historians expressed reserve if not outrage at Foucault's handling of Renaissance material.

As early as 1962, Robert Mandrou and Fernand Braudel cele-brated *Madness and Civilization* as an important contribution to the history of *mentalités*.[7] A decade later, Foucault earned a well-deserved place in the blossoming new school of history.[8] Yet his contributions to the study of sixteenth-century epistemes remained largely ignored with the exception of two articles by Jean-Claude Margolin.[9] By training a philosopher and historian of ideas, Margolin is perhaps best known for his work on Erasmus and for translating and editing Erasmus's pedagogical treatise, *De Pueris Instituendis* (1529). Most appealing to this French scholar were the thematic resources made available in Foucault's treatment of madness and resemblance. Mar-golin's response to Foucault was paradoxical but not untypical of an open-minded but nonetheless traditional historian of ideas. While expressing some reservations vis-à-vis Foucault's antihumanism and structuralism, he could at once elaborate on Foucault's findings on the correspondence between words and things and situate them within the sociocultural web of the period. For instance, in a com-parative analysis between *De Pueris Instituendis* and the seventeenth-century pedagogue Comenius, Margolin observed that although the equivalency between words and things prevailed in the Renaissance,

> for a pedagogue like Erasmus, preoccupied above all with prac-tical effectiveness and rather removed from abstract specula-tions—by natural reluctance as well as by will—the major problems in the education of the young, and primarily of the very young, are: the simultaneous experience of words and things, in other words of language—or the language *par excel-lence*, Latin; and acquiring the knowledge contained in the books of the ancients (since they had dealt with every subject) as it is dispersed over the surface of the globe, in surrounding nature immediately perceived, which is itself nothing but a large open book—the book of the world—which the tutor must teach children to read and decipher.[10]

Precisely because he was interested in theories of education, Margolin was also interested in theories of interpretation. From there stemmed his concern for Foucault's failure to articulate a reading of the texts by Aldrovandi, Crollius, Porta, Belon, Paracelsus, or Campanella which were so eloquently evoked in "The Prose of the World." It is certainly true that hermeneutics has not found a place in Foucault's work; it is also not too surprising given the fact that, as I have indicated earlier, Foucault's intellectual inquiry skirts any form of ontological argument. The very gesture of reading involves a correlation between ontology and hermeneutics insofar as it implies the postulation of a transcendental function of understanding. Such a postulation, no matter how mediated, rests on the assumption that it is possible to formulate the truth of a text through the use of tools devised for that purpose. Foucault's position may explain why there are few references to his work in the writings of some poststructuralist literary critics.

By and large, the rereading of Renaissance texts fostered by those critics centers on issues of textuality, poetics, and semiotics. I am thinking here, in particular, of Terence Cave's *The Cornucopian Text* and François Rigolot's *Le Texte de la Renaissance.*[11] Neither Cave nor Rigolot adopts a specific contemporary model of analysis, but each of them presents a mapping of sixteenth-century French literature which mirrors contemporary critical concerns without reducing "the sixteenth-century texts to the status of local illustration of a modern theory."[12] Foucault's endeavor revolved around, and unfolded in, discourse but, as he himself stressed, his investigations lay outside the models derived from linguistics and thereby outside the rhetoricity of literary or historical discourse.[13] Cave and Rigolot investigate the central role played by notions of writing, reading, and rhetoric in sixteenth-century literary texts. Therefore, Foucault's approach is of little use to them.

I should like to point out, however, that some Anglo-American theorists, whose orientation is more socioanthropological than textual, have incorporated Foucaldian insights in a most seminal fashion into their work. Under the banner of new historicism and cultural materialism, these critics carry on a reevaluation of patterns of thought as they emerged during the sixteenth century in England. Despite methodological and ideological divergences, critics like Stephen Greenblatt and Jonathan Dollimore tend to concern themselves with issues pertaining to the representation of power in language as well as with questions involving class and gender struggle, issues that permeate Foucault's writings.[14] In so doing, they have succeeded in providing English Renaissance studies with a new momentum. In many ways, their work reflects the way in which Foucault and other social scientists have led to the rethinking of a nineteenth-century periodic and cultural phenomenon called the Renaissance. In a reciprocal manner, Foucault's endeavor and theirs join to open the way for a reexamination of disciplinary boundaries within which history and classical scholarship hold a central place.

Greenblatt's new historical perspective is exemplary in provoking such reexamination. For instance, in *Renaissance Self-Fashioning,* Greenblatt shows that the study of human response to reality takes on its full meaning within a historical framework. Foucault engages in a similar task when he probes the Greco-Roman past. In focusing on the Renaissance, Greenblatt successfully confronts opposing and interacting tendencies that have prevailed in the disciplines since the age of Burckhardt. While considering Burckhardt's *Civilization of the Renaissance in Italy* as "one of the best introductions to Renaissance self-fashioning," Greenblatt also analyzes the pressures that societal rules exerted on individual freedom.[15] The latter insights owe something to Foucault's *Discipline and Punish.*[16] By the same token, in the introduction to *The Use of Pleasure,* Foucault refers to the pertinence of Greenblatt's account of Burckhardt's "techniques of the self." In the same introduction, Foucault states that he is "neither a Hellenist nor a Latinist" but that he has acquired sufficient familiarity with the Greek and Roman texts "to examine both the difference that keeps us at a remove from a way of thinking in which we recognize the origin of our own, and the proximity that remains in spite of that distance which we never cease to explore."[17] Furthermore, in an essay entitled "What Is Enlightenment?" Foucault observes that the nineteenth century had a tendency to oppose the Renaissance and the Enlightenment "at least as much as to confuse them."[18] The convergence of these remarks points to Foucault's awareness of the dominant role played by disciplines that combine the search for textual truth with the practice of historical scholarship. Foucault does not explicitly explore the implications of that role nor does he probe the ideological and methodological affinities that classical scholarship and Renaissance historiography have entertained since the nineteenth century.[19] The breadth of his rigorous speculations about the role of the individual in society has, however, contributed to shape current attempts in literary-critical scholarship to "estrange" the Renaissance from its nineteenth-century models.[20]

"Controversial but stimulating," writes social historian Guido Ruggiero when referring to Foucault's *Discipline and Punish* in his recent study on sex crime and sexuality in Renaissance Venice.[21] In a somewhat cynical manner, the author notes nonetheless that "with apologies to Michel Foucault, sexuality was not a discovery of the modern world."[22] To be sure, in choosing to write a history of sexuality, Foucault, as in the case of all his projects, seized upon the controversiality of a current issue in order to problematize it through its historization. In all likelihood, at the time he was composing his book, Ruggiero had only the first volume of *The History of Sexuality*, subtitled *An Introduction*, at his elbow. But Foucault did display at least some familiarity with Renaissance attitudes toward sex when in this first volume he contrasted them with seventeenth-century mores: "No seventeenth-century pedagogue would have publicly advised his disciple, as did Erasmus in his *Dialogues*, on the choice of a good prostitute."[23] Ruggiero's remark may have been incidental, but it can serve to illustrate the reticent fascination with which Foucault has been received among many Renaissance historians in America.

When reading the essays devoted respectively by George Huppert to *The Order of Things* and by H. C. Midelfort to *Madness and Civilization*, one is tempted to quip with Allan Megill: "Foucault was an animal of a sort that Anglo-American historians had never seen before."[24] They perceive Foucault as a fashionable Left Bank thinker whose criteria for historical research were at best questionable; they are quick to point out errors in his information. For instance, Huppert—quite rightly— states that several quotations including those from Belon and Montaigne are "garbled up."[25] Conversely, Midelfort summons evidence to prove that in the late Middle Ages and Renaissance, "many of the mad were in fact confined to small cells or jails or even domestic cages, and not just gate towers as Foucault suggests."[26] Since he is writing nearly twenty years after the publication of *Madness and Civilization*, Midelfort has to contend with a wealth of cross-disciplinary responses to Foucault's book. This he does by taking a harsh stance: "Indeed, in his quest for the essence of an age, its *episteme,* Foucault seems simply to indulge a whim for arbitrary and witty assertion so often that one wonders why so much attention and praise continue to fall his way."[27] In his 1973 condemnation of Foucault, Huppert had already anticipated Midelfort's criticism: "He claims, within the chosen stratum, to understand not this or that idea, movement, or school: he claims *total understanding.*"[28]

How are these polemical responses to be interpreted? One can, of course, reply that the Anglo-American perspective from which both historians are writing is characterized by a kind of pragmatism that leaves little room for abstractions. But one can also choose to take into consideration that they assume the posture—and this is especially true for Huppert—of guarantors of scientific history, a branch of intellectual history whose roots plunge right into Renaissance humanism. By adopting this second choice, one can hope to gain a better understanding of the meaning involved in the use of the terms *rigor* and *scientificity* on both sides of the fence and thereby to put into perspective the divergences involved. In order to do so, and to help clarify the reasons for the dismissal of Foucault's approach to the Renaissance, I shall now turn to Huppert's *The Idea of Perfect History: Historical Erudition and Historical Philosophy in Renaissance France.* In the wake of Momigliano, Huppert views historical research as a perfectible craft that has attained a greater degree of veracity in contemporary times. Textual truth lies at the core of his methodology. Furthermore, he argues that current developments in historiography owe a mighty debt to the learned work of French sixteenth-century scholars like Etienne Pasquier and La Popelinière. In his opinion, rigor and scientificity emerged when these scholars, following in the footsteps of their Italian predecessors, incorporated the collecting and editing of primary sources into their writings.[29] Like historians of classical scholarship, historians of learning, and practitioners of textual criticism, Huppert considers texts as objects (*res*). The historians' task is thus faithfully to reconstruct the texts they examine and to account for their contents through language (*verba*). It is certainly legitimate to combine the search for textual truth with the practice of historical scholarship, provided that such an attitude does not lead to academic dogmatism for the sake of upholding truth.

The remarks made so far underscore that Foucault and Huppert approach the past from opposite poles. The use and proper handling of sources coupled with erudition which are central in Huppert's endeavor leave little room for the questioning of the premises upon which his method rests. Foucault's methodological claims call for an ongoing questioning of one's premises. The contrasting outlooks of these scholars exceed the boundaries of their own discourse as it shapes current debates in French sociological and historical circles. For instance, in *Les Grecs ont-ils cru à leurs mythes?* Paul Veyne envisages both methodologies as constitutive of our heritage.[30] In showing how an ambivalent attitude toward the past prevailed throughout different periods, Veyne quotes Huppert: "For it seems clear that historical research was practiced for centuries without seriously affecting the writing of histories. The two activities were kept separate, even on occasion in the mind of a single man."[31] Huppert makes a choice and opts for scientific history. Veyne, on the contrary, stresses the impossibility of choosing since according to him imagination shapes all forms of scientific and fictional discourses. To illustrate this point, Veyne evokes the figure of Einstein:

One must give the imagination its fair share if one thinks that there is nothing down to earth in Einstein, to take a legendary example; he built a theoretical skyscraper which one has not yet been able to test; should it be tested, the theory would still not be proved: it would only be not invalidated.[32]

The same argument could be made about Foucault's treatment of the Renaissance insofar as it cannot be proved to be completely right or completely wrong. Depending on the methodology used, one can at best prove that he was partially right or partially wrong. So should the question "The Renaissance: Foucault's Lost Chance?" which frames this chapter remain unanswered? Of course not; but it can only be answered by taking into consideration the intellectual challenge that Foucault set for himself. The role he ascribes in "The Prose of the World" to the episteme of the sixteenth century informs us as much about his distrust of language as it does about the sixteenth century. There, he opposes the correlation between words and things as it did indeed prevail in the sixteenth century to their disjunction in the seventeenth century—the century of Descartes—when, in his own terms, "this massive and intriguing existence of language . . . is eliminated."[33] Wrought in a diachronic chain, the thesis is controversial for its dogmatism. For instance, Vico still held to the impossibility of separating the institutions and ideas of a society (*res*) and the myths and symbols (*verba*) of that society.[34] The thesis can also shed light on some aspects of Renaissance discourse as well as on Foucault's own perspective on language.[35]

Even in their shortcomings, Foucault's provocative remarks on the proliferation of commentaries invites a closer look at a genre that has always been taken for granted. For instance, Foucault writes: "Perhaps for the first time, in Western culture, we find revealed the absolutely open dimension of a language no longer able to halt itself, because, never being enclosed in a definite statement, it can express its truth only in some future discourse and is wholly intent on what it will have said."[36] A reading of some specific commentaries, which Foucault does not mention, such as those of Guillaume Budé (1467–1540), reveals that the French humanist departed from his Italian predecessors and from his French colleagues in his handling of the genres of commentary and oratory. Budé, who never engaged in biblical scholarship to the extent that some of his contemporaries did (Erasmus, Lefèvre d'Etaples, Dolet), inscribed within works labeled as commentaries his desire to come to terms with self-portrayal through language, on the one hand, and with the necessity to provide generations to come with an "objective" body of knowledge, on the other hand. Thus in the "unbroken plain of words and things," there was room for individual practices of the same genre.[37]

In addressing the Renaissance conception of language, Foucault implicitly voiced his own critique of the representational function of language. As I have already indicated, Foucault's analyses unfold within and through discourse but are never carried out through the means of rhetoric or linguistics. Magritte's painting, *Les Deux Mystères*, perhaps best illustrates Foucault's epistemologico-historical approach to historical periods. Two pipes are represented: one is framed and rests on an easel, while the second one appears somewhat enlarged on the upper left hand corner of the painting. The framed painting carries the caption "Ceci n'est pas une pipe." Let us assume that the painting stands for Foucault's outlook on a historical period, in this case, the Renaissance. He visualizes two renderings: the pipe drawn in a conventional setting stands in for prevalent interpretations of the Renaissance and the other one represents the same object. On the first one, he writes "Ceci n'est pas la Renaissance." The two images persist. They will not go away for there will be no fusion between the two objects.[38] Therein lies the challenge that Foucault addresses to humanistic knowledge and to himself in trying out his "ideas as functions and means."

Notes

1. *The Order of Things* (New York: Random House, 1970), p. 311.

2. Ibid., p. 9.

3. Michel Foucault, *The Archaeology of Knowledge*, trans. A. M. Sheridan Smith (New York: Pantheon, 1972), p. 136.

4. Jean-François Lyotard, *The Postmodern Condition: A Report on Knowledge*, trans. Geoff Bennington and Brian Massumi (Minneapolis: University of Minnesota Press, 1984), p. 81.

5. See, for instance, Gilles Deleuze, *Foucault* (Paris: Minuit, 1986), and John Rajchman, *Michel Foucault: The Freedom of Philosophy* (New York: Columbia University Press, 1985), pp. 9–41.

6. Letter to Franz Overbeck written in October 1882 in Friedrich Nietzsche, *Werke*, ed. Karl Schlechta (Munich: Carl Hanser Verlag, 1966), 3:1193. Translation mine.

7. See, for instance, Robert Mandrou, "Trois clés pour comprendre la folie á l'époque classique," *Annales* 17 (1962), pp. 771–773. For more details on Foucault's reception here and abroad, see also Allan Megill, "The Reception of Foucault by Historians," *Journal of the History of Ideas* 48, no. 1 (1987), pp. 117–142.

8. On Foucault and the "new" school of history, see, for instance, Marie-Rose Logan, "Rethinking History," in *Rethinking History: Time, Myth, and Writing*, ed. Marie-Rose Logan, special edition, *Yale French Studies* 59 (1980), pp. 3–6, and Dominick LaCapra, "Rethinking History and Reading Texts," in *Modern Intellectual History: Reappraisal and New Perspectives*, ed. Dominick LaCapra and Steven L. Kaplan (Ithaca, N.Y.: Cornell University Press, 1982), pp. 47–85.

9. Jean-Claude Margolin, "Tribut d'un antihumaniste aux études d'Humanisme et Renaissance: Notes sur l'oeuvre de Michel Foucault," *Bibliothèque d'Humanisme et Renaissance* 29, no. 3 (1967), pp. 701–711, and his "The Methods of 'Words and Things' in Erasmus *De Pueris Instituendis* (1529) and Comenius's *Orbis Sensualium Pictus* (1658)" in *Essays on the Works of Erasmus*, ed. Richard L. DeMolen (New Haven: Yale University Press, 1978), pp. 221–238.

10. Margolin, "Methods of 'Words and Things,'" pp. 225–226.

11. Terence Cave, The Cornucopian Text: Problems of Writing in the French Renaissance (Oxford: Oxford University Press, 1979), and François Rigolot, Le Texte de la Renaissance: Des Rhétoriqueurs à Montaigne (Geneva: Droz, 1982).

12. Cave, The Cornucopian Text, pp. xvi-xvii.

13. Michel Foucault, "Vérité et pouvoir: Entretien avec M. Fontana," L'Arc, no. 70 (1977), p. 19.

14. For an overview of the distinction between new historicists and cultural materialists, see, for instance, Jonathan Dollimore and Alan Sinfield, eds., Political Shakespeare: New Essays in Cultural Materialism (Ithaca, N.Y.: Cornell University Press, 1985), pp. 2–15.

15. Stephen Greenblatt, Renaissance Self-Fashioning: From More to Shakespeare (Chicago: University of Chicago Press, 1980), pp. 161–162.

16. Ibid., p. 80.

17. See Michel Foucault, The Use of Pleasure, vol. 2 of The History of Sexuality, trans. Robert Hurley (New York: Pantheon, 1985), p. 11.

18. Michel Foucault, "What Is Enlightenment?" in The Foucault Reader, ed. Paul Rabinow (New York: Pantheon, 1984), p. 45.

19. See, for instance, Jean Bollack, "Ulysse chez les philologues," Actes de la recherche en sciences sociales 5–6 (1975), pp. 9–34.

20. The expression is appropriately used in Marjorie Garber, ed., Cannibals, Witches, and Divorce: Estranging the Renaissance (Baltimore: The Johns Hopkins University Press, 1987).

21. Guido Ruggiero, The Boundaries of Eros: Sex Crime and Sexuality in Renaissance Venice (New York: Oxford University Press, 1985), p. 169.

22. Ibid., p. 4.

23. Michel Foucault, The History of Sexuality, trans. Robert Hurley (New York: Pantheon, 1978), 1:27.

24. Megill, "The Reception of Foucault by Historians," p. 133.

25. George Huppert, "Divinatio and Eruditio: Thoughts on Foucault," History and Theory 13 (1974), pp. 201–204.

26. H. C. Erik Midelfort, "Madness and Civilization in Early Modern Europe: A Reappraisal of Michel Foucault," in After the Reformation, ed. Barbara C. Malament (Philadelphia: University of Pennsylvania Press, 1980), p. 253.

27. Ibid., p. 259.

28. Huppert, "Divinatio and Eruditio," p. 193.

29. George Huppert, The Idea of Perfect History: Historical Erudition and Historical Philosophy in Renaissance France (Urbana: University of Illinois Press, 1970), pp. 5–11.

30. Paul Veyne, *Les Grecs ont-ils cru à leurs mythes? Essai sur l'imagination constituante* (Paris: Seuil, 1983), pp. 15–19.

31. Huppert, *The Idea of Perfect History*, p. 5, quoted in Veyne, *Les Grecs ont-ils cru à leurs mythes?* p. 14.

32. Veyne, *Les Grecs ont-ils cru à leurs mythes?*, p. 126.

33. Foucault, *The Order of Things*, p. 79.

34. See, for instance, Michael Mooney, *Vico in the Tradition of Rhetoric* (Princeton: Princeton University Press, 1985), pp. 185–186.

35. Jean Céard, "Les transformations du genre du commentaire," in *L'Automne de la Renaissance (1580–1630)*, ed. Jean Lafond and André Stegmann (Paris: Vrin, 1981), pp. 101–103.

36. Foucault, *The Order of Things*, pp. 41–42.

37. Ibid., p. 40.

38. For a discussion of Magritte's *Les Deux Mystères* by Michel Foucault, see his *This Is Not a Pipe*, trans. and ed. James Harkness (Berkeley and Los Angeles: University of California Press, 1982), pp. 15–31.

FOUCAULT, GENEALOGY, HISTORY
The Pursuit of Otherness

H. D. Harootunian

Opposed to an other, the "I" is its own self, and at the same time it overreaches this other which, for the "I," is equally only the "I" itself. . . . But, in point of fact, self-consciousness is the reflection out of the being of the world of sense and perception, and is essentially the return from otherness.

—Hegel

Our period is not defined by the triumph of technology for technology's sake, as it is not defined by art for art's sake, as it is not defined by nihilism. It is action for a world to come, transcendence of its period—transcendence of self which calls for epiphany of the Other.

—Emmanuel Levinas

Since we have witnessed the virtual explosion of a culture industry committed to interpreting Foucault and transmitting his texts to ever greater numbers of readers, it would be hard to imagine a meaning or explanation that has not yet been uncovered in this apparent craze to confer authorial authority on the man who proclaimed its death. Studies on Foucault have proliferated at varying paces and on a number of related, but still autonomous, levels, illuminating his critique of subjectivity, his ruminations on oppression and domination, his privileging of discourse over the empirical domain, and his inversion of historical narrativity in what he first called archaeology but later described as genealogy. All of these considerations have turned on Foucault's reapprehension of how disciplines, the human or social sciences, have been formed, how they have attempted to divert the act of representation from calling attention to itself, and how they have been authorized by knowledge that is constituted on a prior will-to-power. Foucault probably would not have consented to this program, since it seems to have been his intention to contest the claims of coherence, continuity, unity, and totality, advising us in *The Archaeology of Knowledge* to "renounce all those themes whose function is to endure the infinite continuity of discourse and its secret presence to itself in the interplay of a constantly recurring absence."[1] But the authority of his own authorship authorizes us to see in his texts precisely those conventions of disciplinary practice he sought to put under erasure.

It is not my intention to discount or dismiss this large and very informative literature on Foucault, even though one can easily justify destroying Foucault's own texts after reading, rather than writing a book about them, and not feel any remorse for having committed an act of cultural transgression. That would be the kind of activity he would have endorsed before he became big business. The literature has, in any event, underscored the principal concerns his texts have tried to articulate, despite his own subversive efforts to induce playful disseminations and avoid becoming mired in fixed positions, which interpretation aims to accomplish when it tries to stabilize meaning and understanding. As a result, it no longer appears possible merely to read Foucault without the mediation or intervention of this interpretive literature, which has presented him as the founder of a discourse. Reading Foucault means forgetting one of the enabling principles of disciplined historiography, which is the necessity of separating social theory from practice. His texts prompt us to rethink, and even to see for the first time, relationships that have escaped notice, owing either to the familiarizing conventions of the historian's discourse or to a refusal to dissociate representation from the Real, culture from reference.

As for my own concern, I shall try to situate Foucault between Hegel's confident supersession of the Other and Levinas's hopeful reunion with it, after history has been transcended. As a condition for subsequently showing how this reading of Foucault authorizes recognizing him, at least in one incarnation, as the historian of alterity, we must acknowledge that he problematized the relationship between ourselves and the Other and, in fact, recentered the question of otherness altogether, asserting what Bakhtin elsewhere called "exotopy," the affirmation of the Other's exteriority which requires acknowledging its subjectivity.[2] With this in view, I will try to suggest how this discourse on otherness opens up the possibility for reapprehending the intellectual experience of the Other, in this case, Japanese before World War II, as something more than an atavistic or traditionalistic reaction to the condition of late development, as a prescient critique of the Western *ratio*, in and on its own terms.

In Foucault's texts, as in Bakhtin's, we find offered a way of experiencing and externalizing alterity, and come to recognize that those who have been absented from the practice of historical narrative have empowered the story that has been told. Yet, the move to resituate the Other, and to propose that discourse permits the articulation of a field consisting of a variety of subject positions, questions narrative's claim to representation and closure. Any consideration of the status of the Other, as both Foucault and Bakhtin demonstrated in their own ways, invariably calls into question the construction of narrative itself as the privileged story line of subjectivity and the unfolding of consciousness in time. It also reveals how a supposedly neutral form, the signifier, is made to serve an ideological purpose by sliding it under the signified, the content. One of the regular complaints Japanese writers registered before World War II, concerning the domination of Western epistemological categories and disciplines of knowledge, was that historical narrative reconstructed only a story about European subjectivity, which, by its very nature, excluded the entry of others like themselves, unless and until they assimilated forms of knowing which claimed universal application. Since the referent for this history was the Real, it was easily assumed that those who had been excluded from the narrative possessed no substantial reality. If the Japanese intellectual interlude constituted a return of the repressed of European culture, it also represented a full-scale attack upon the conceits of identity itself and prefigured the later poststructuralist critique of Foucault, Barthes, and Derrida, in order to contest one of the most cherished pieties of the Western philosophic endowment. Yet, without this later intervention and the deconstruction of the enabling metaphysical claims underlying the conviction that self-identity constituted the source of knowing, the earlier Japanese experience would have remained merely a moment or stage in the process leading to the supersession of the Others.

Critics of Foucault have regularly complained that Foucault's critical project has been decidedly ahistorical or antihistorical. No less a luminary than Jean-Paul Sartre dismissed Foucault's *The Order of Things* in an early review as an "eclectic synthesis in which Robbe-Grillet, structuralism, Lacan and *Tel Quel* are each invoked in turn so as to demonstrate the impossibility of historical thought. Behind history, of course, the target is Marxism. This is an attempt to constitute a new ideology, the last bulwark which the bourgeoisie can still erect against Marx."[3] Since the time Sartre delivered his judgment against Foucault, the historians' first line of defense has been to discount the status of Foucault's texts as history, a sentiment that Foucault has, in the past, shared, since he consistently has done his best to prevent being recuperated for the historians' discourse. What Marxists and non-Marxists have objected to is the critique of history implied in Foucault's observation that history itself is a Western myth that needs to be laid to rest. In fact, it was precisely this recognition that prompted Foucault to confess that he saw no real difference between being a Marxist and being a historian. Far from denying the writing of history, Foucault saw in a certain discursive practice a refusal of history, stemming from the recognition of otherness-as-merely-Other as a condition for its necessary exclusion. Here, he tried to envisage a "sober conception" of history after the twilight of the Hegelian idol.[4] What distinguished his so-called histories from the conventional practice was his decision to see history as both a form of knowledge and power at the same time, like any other discourse. By apprehending the historian's practice in this way, he was able to show how an activity that appealed to knowing the truth about the past was merely a mask for a will to domination. The desire to know the past was driven, not by the disinterested quest for knowledge and truth, but by the urge to domesticate and control it in order to validate the present. In this regard, Foucault also demonstrated how the past itself, as a locus of genuine difference, was incorporated into a narrative attesting to the regime of identity and sameness. The evidence for this will-to-power is everywhere manifest in the way narratives invariably exclude certain objects for discourse while privileging others, and how they smooth out heterogeneous elements in order to secure the appearance of homogeneity. Although Foucault undoubtedly aimed to show how the form of narrative serves the interest of power and domination by appealing to a neutral, natural story line, he sought from the beginning to write a history (first called archaeology, later changed to genealogy) that would not only account for the traces of the Other suppressed by conventional historiography but would also allow the Other to speak across the barrier established by the regime of reason.[5]

In his *Madness and Civilization* (a seriously truncated version of *Histoire de la folie à l'âge classique*), a work that can profitably be paired with Bakhtin's classic study of Rabelais in any interrogation of otherness, Foucault rejected the decision to write simply a history of psychiatry in order to permit the mad to speak their own history. "As for a common language," he wrote, "there is no such thing any longer; the constitution of madness as a mental illness, at the end of the eighteenth century, affords the evidence of a broken dialogue, posits the separation as already effected, and thrusts into oblivion all those stammered, imperfect words without fixed syntax, in which the exchange between madness and reason was made."[6] Psychiatrists talk to and about the mad, much like ethnographers, until recently, talked to and about the Other, but the mad are never permitted to speak or even to reply. "The language of psychiatry, which is a monologue of reason about madness, has been established on the basis of such a silence. I have not tried to write the history of that language, but rather the archaeology of that silence."[7]

History, Foucault observed, recounts the past, and an absence itself left only in traces inscribed imperfectly in the present; but the past of history was the present of an even more remote past, what he called the archaic, the rubble of an older, other city left in the midst of a later arrival, an other temple, perhaps pagan, occupying the site of a more recently constructed church.[8] It is this absent presence that constitutes the appearance of history. Later, in *The Archaeology of Knowledge*, Foucault redesignated archaic absence as historical a priori, in order to identify the conditions of possibility attending the appearance of history and what could be said about it.[9]

What Foucault sought to write was a history of madness itself, speaking about itself on the basis of its own experience, unmediated by another's language, and on its own authority, in order to avoid writing a history described from the language of reason. In fact, he proposed to write a history of madness not yet "crushed beneath [the language of] psychiatry, dominated, beaten to the ground, interned, that is to say, a madness made into an object and exiled as the other of a language and a historical meaning which have been confused with logos itself."[10] Yet, this was precisely the kind of history Husserl intended to do, in order to reach an origin of geometry before its constitution into conventional theorems and axioms, before it was captured in a language on geometry, "before being captured by knowledge."[11] Moreover, while Foucault restricted the historical a priori to the enabling of certain statements, the conception nevertheless promised, as apparently it did for Husserl, a way to retrieve an absent origin, a past of the past, the archaic, by launching the historical itinerary backward from the present. Where Foucault differed from Husserl was in his refusal to first question the concept of history, which is precisely the starting point of the latter's interrogation.[12] Ultimately, Foucault changed his mind about the retroductive operation and abandoned archaeology for genealogy. Even so, he was willing to carry the idea of origin as one of the possible meanings of genealogy as envisaged by Nietzsche.

If the search for the absent archaic authorized a different mode of historical inquiry, it also disclosed the limits of what the West had recognized as its history. At the heart of this history, and perhaps any history, identity presides to ensure that a single culture has enabled a specific group of individuals "to articulate the subject position of a collective 'we'."[13] According to *The Archaeology of Knowledge*, continuous history promises that "one day the subject, in the form of historical consciousness, will once again be able to appropriate, to bring back under his sway, all those things that are kept at a distance by difference, and find in them what might be called his abode."[14] But identity can be secured only at the price of deferring difference indefinitely, or to a last instance that never comes, through a series of exclusions. Here, it is important to note the kinship between Foucault's understanding of identity and the formulations of Levinas, which envisaged "history as a blinding to the Other" and as the ceaseless and laborious procession of the same. Commenting on this displacement of historicity, Derrida wondered, significantly I believe, whether history, under these circumstances, can any longer be history. But he also recognized the impossibility of avoiding the establishment of exclusionary discourses so necessary to the historiographical program. "If all cultures are finite or limited, this is not to be explained in negative terms by the fact that no one culture could succeed in universalizing itself. It is because in an initial decision, the first 'division,' each culture rejects a certain number of alternatives."[15] In *Madness and Civilization*, Foucault elicits some of the consequences of this initial decision, the production of a number of divisions or oppositions which conferred upon the Western *ratio* its identity: the opposition between East and West, dream and reality, tragic and dialectical, ourselves and Other, traditionalism and modernity, and all the other pairings. Underlying all these divisions was the even more basic opposition established between reason and madness, or unreason. Foucault acknowledged that this divide constituted for Western culture one of the dimensions of its originality; indeed, it differentiated the West from all other cultures, even as he came to realize that it also authorized the "disciplinization" of forms of knowledge as a condition for dominating, and even silencing, the Other. Yet, the model for the discursivity of knowledge and power was not the history of madness, per se, but the form of history itself, which, directed by a knowing subject that fixes the axis of identity and difference, banishes the signs of heterogeneity wherever they are found. Exclusion must, therefore, signal voicelessness, suppression, and even deliberate repression. History now involves what Foucault described as a "confrontation beneath the language of reason." What this confrontation required was an interrogation free from the familiar constraints that follow reason in its horizontal trajectory, but that, nevertheless, seek to "retrace in time the constant verticality which confronts European culture with what it is not," thereby establishing its own "*dérangements*."[16]

Foucault acknowledged that the endpoint of the destination was quite unknown to him. What seemed certain, and even necessary, was to elude the reductions of progressive time and its vast propensity for the homogenization of differences, in order to enter a realm, a place, which is neither the history of knowledge nor history itself as conveyed in closed narratives that tell the tale of reason and its place in the world. Once the fateful decision is left behind, once, in fact, the "sign has been inverted," the human sciences are relieved of all responsibility of accounting for the "rational sequences of causes," because this strategy belongs to the world of the division, not to its other. Indeed, Foucault is free to enter a domain "where what is in question is the limit rather than the identity of culture." But limits involve encountering what is genuinely different, other than what is self-same. It is for this reason that Foucault declared early on that the history of madness equaled a history of the possibility of history.[17] Otherness, the historical a priori of Western culture, whether it appears in the guise of unreason or of the alien, strange, and incomprehensible, launches history upon its course to speak of what it is not. In Foucault's understanding, historical practice in the West was realized in the production of works and the steady transmission of words endowed with reasonable meaning.

Madness, accordingly, produces no books or texts. Like the Other, it either has no written language, or its spoken sounds sound like gibberish, an observation made first and lastingly in the West by Herodotus. Above all else, otherness deserves only inattention. The mad, or any constituency denied entry into the subject position of discourse, are committed to communicating in a world lacking referentiality and meaning. Just as internment removes the mad (that is, the different), from the world of norms, so exclusion of the Other from discourse confines them to silence. Language, in the Foucaldian project, does not represent a thought but expresses a subject. Hence, the possibility of history, as imagined by Hegel, rests upon the decision to reject all utterances, all gestures that have no positive significance, as unreason. History, then, is really work, praxis, that ensures the surety of identity, when, according to Levinas, "negativity is enclosed within the circle of the same" and when work does not encounter alterity, "providing itself with resistance."[18] Otherness, in this connection, becomes everything that finds no role to play in a linear and progressive history, and can never make a contribution to its end. But, Foucault believed it can have its own narrative— an observation that Japanese reached years before French poststructuralists launched their assault on the knowing subject and its History.

Foucault announced in the French edition of *Madness and Civilization* that even though the great work of world history is accompanied by an absence of work, it is always there: before history, in a primitive decision; and after it has ended, victorious with the last word history pronounces. If the end of history proclaims the triumph of meaning, as Hegelians believed, it marked the "apogee of non-meaning" as well, since nothing remains to be done or said. Hegelians prided themselves in believing that dialectical identity included everything written within its conception of totality, even no-thing itself. Yet, this inclusiveness amounted to sameness in the end, and the very alterity the dialectic was supposed to include remained unaccommodated, ready to reappear after history was supposed to be over. Derrida, commenting on Levinas, posed the possibility of a history beginning with this relationship with the Other, which is placed beyond history, that is, beyond reason and work.[19] With this in view, the historical narrative that conveys the *ratio* of Western culture represents a caesura, a long interlude between the possibility of history at the beginning and at the end, since we know, according to Foucault, that the Other is present even as the great drama of reason unfolds.

When Foucault discovered that the madman appeared once reason and history had established their dynasty, he found the form of otherness. Reason and its "history," he observed, establish what is other from itself, different, a distinction that could not be made before the decision to install reason in its privileged place and to favor history, that is, work. The division of reason and its other constitutes the latter as unreason, opposing reason, and it thereby becomes an object submitted to knowledge. Whether it was the mad, the diseased, or even the criminal, it was no different from the Other when it became specified as non-European, non-Western, always in its negativity, as something to be incorporated and superseded by the dialectic of identity. In this respect, the disciplines of psychiatry and Orientalism or, indeed, any effort to constitute otherness in discourse, to be disciplined by the knowledge generated by a centered and fixed subject, share a common ancestry or tenancy in the world of power. Yet, Foucault has already discounted the capacity of conventional historiography to teach us anything about the conditions of discursivity, because psychiatry, no less than any other form of "disciplinizing" the Other, knows nothing of the enabling division between ourselves and otherness, and is therefore prevented from moving beyond this great divide. Disciplines, he believed, can do no more than reiterate their founding principles and prejudices, and reaffirm their blindness. By abandoning a history of psychiatry as a suitable method for understanding unreason, Foucault was effectively bypassing narrative and its presumed capacity to recount the history of the world. Nothing was more remote from the world of the Other than a reasonable recording of an ever more enlightened and human history, and the inevitable triumph of science over disorder, thereby testifying as to how the different becomes assimilated to the same. What Foucault seemed to accomplish in his refusal of a history of psychiatry was a rejection of progressive history, which tells the story of the rise and spread of rational knowledge and the final extinction of "unreason" everywhere. But, we know that once the Other appeared in African or Asian dress, there began new so-called scientific inquiries that aimed at understanding and dominating these new objects. In this projection of reason underlying the formation of new disciplines, a rational knowledge was always juxtaposed to ignorance, humanity to inhumanity; new territorial claims were instituted to fix the boundaries separating truth from falsehood, reason from unreason. As a result, a cultural ethos was confused with an imperial *ratio* as the privileged position of morality was increasingly identified with rational knowledge and the subject who was in a position to know it.[20] The consequences of this move consisted in alienating humans from truth and, ultimately, committing all those who failed to meet certain social standards to forms of confinement and segregation. Their failure made them subject to fundamental moral condemnation and dismissal from the narrative of modernization. "Anyone interned is placed within the field of this ethical valorization," Foucault wrote, "and long before being an object of knowledge or pity, he is treated as a *moral subject.*"[21]

Although Foucault early called this method, pledged to reconstituting otherness/madness, an archaeology, he seems to have abandoned it for what later is described as a genealogy. Initially, archaeology resembled its later incarnation principally in its opposition to any form of a retrospective history presumed capable of narrating the history of progress. When he embarked upon his analysis of madness, it is important to note, he assumed the pose of a methodical ignorance of what unreason consisted of, even though Derrida later demonstrated, correctly I believe, the impossibility of speaking for the mad outside of language. The "misfortune of the mad," Foucault observed,

> the interminable misfortune of their silence, is that their best spokesmen are those who betray them best, which is to say that when one attempts to convey their silence itself, one has already passed over to the side of the enemy, the side of order, even if one fights against order from within it, putting its origins in question.[22]

Nevertheless, Foucault proceeded to show how the production of that identity with oneself known as reason involves the expulsion from the common space (and the coupling of confinement with designated spaces) of all those who refuse to submit to such an identity, all that is negatively denoted as difference, incoherence, and irrationality. All dialectical history fails because madness must be envisaged as the negative of reason, despite the final negation of the negation, its absence (deficiency) and its refusal (the irruption of the irrational). An expanded reason, supplied by dialectical logic or even structuralism based on binary oppositions, might have easily accommodated this negativity, but Foucault, inverting the Hegelian inventory, argued that reason can never return to its origin in a division between itself and its Other.[23] In an intimation of Levinas, he also discounted a necessary symmetry between the self and other, the I who knows and speaks, and its lack.

Reflecting on this methodological operation later (1971), Foucault formally appropriated genealogy to best describe the combination of a critique and the traces of otherness which his texts were devoted to elucidating. In the essay "Nietzsche, Genealogy, History," he explained that genealogy rejects "history whose function is to compose the finally reduced diversity of time into a totality fully closed upon itself," one that ceaselessly encourages subjective recognitions and attributes a form of reconciliation to all the displacements of the past, in order to "imply an end of time, a completed development."[24] By accepting Nietzsche's original equation between genealogy and origin, or, better yet, descent (*Herkunft*) and emergence (*Entstehung*), Foucault believed he had found a strategy that would permit a dissociation from the certainty of absolutes and an engagement with something called "effective history," that is, a history free from constants and self-recognition.[25] "Effective history," he urged, "deprives the self of the reassuring stability of life and nature," and will not submit to the "voiceless obstinacy toward a millenial ending."[26] Hence, it seeks what is close at hand to reach what is distant, it avoids depths for a search of the surfaces of events, details, shifts, and subtle contours. If genealogists see history as contingency, they also recognize that it has no subject, neither individual nor collective, moving its course. But, it requires the additional acknowledgment that subjectivity is itself constituted by discursive practices that must claim fixity, stability, and permanence in order to suppress the very historicity that has enabled its condition of possibility but that it can never know. With this observation, Foucault discerned that subjectivity was merely constituted by discourses, which themselves obeyed no laws of motion. The method of genealogy seeks to provide a pedigree for the subject, which might thereby unveil the mechanisms that have served all systematic attempts to understand and define man. Genealogy opens up the perspective on discourses in general and promises to reveal their claims as diversions for power and domination. Following a Lacanian formulation concerning the unconscious and the language of the Other, Foucault's genealogical strategy sought to analyze man's discourse as something that mediates identity and difference, the "Other and the Self it manages to reconstruct."[27] Yet, it is important to add that genealogy functions as a device to defamiliarize what is familiar, or taken for granted as natural or commonsensical, to jar stock responses into grasping ones, making the past look strange and different again, reasserting its heterogeneity, not numbly recognizing what was always there, present by an absence. That is to say, because Foucault's genealogy is the mode designated to grasp the Other, it seeks to avoid merely seizing the meanings or the images generated by discourse, and proceeds directly to making explicit all that is conspicuous by its absence, the past areas of silences outlined when discourses proclaim to represent essences, absolutes, constants, and eternal truths, the "not-saids." Consequently, it is the Other, the being of nonbeing, that becomes the objective of Foucault's own discourse.

eternal truths, the "not-saids." Consequently, it is the Other, the being of nonbeing, that becomes the objective of Foucault's own discourse.

Effective history defamiliarizes the familiar in order to show how the past not only differs from the present, but also refuses to offer the present its sanction and resists assimilation to its own requirements. In addition, effective history is a practice that must begin and end with the present, with what Marxists once called the "current situation." "I would like to write a history of the prison," Foucault acknowledged in *Discipline and Punish*, "with all the political investments of the body it gathers together in its closed architecture. Why? Simply because I am interested in the past? No, if one means by that a history of the past in terms of the present. Yes, if one means writing the history of the present."[28] But it would be wrong to accuse him of an incurable presentism, which proleptically projects contemporary interests back in time, revealing the meanings of the past in terms recognizably familiar to the present in order to show a shared identity, a continuity, between the two moments. The impulse to write a history of the present stems from the genealogical impulse to apprehend otherness by beginning with the contemporary ritual of power or the political technology of the body, to locate the point in the past when it constituted a difference, a discontinuity. Exploring the past provides not its history, but a genealogy of contemporary phenomena by isolating their components and showing the route by which they arrive in the present. Such an operation, however, takes place in a space, not in a temporal continuum. "The spatializing description of discursive realities," Foucault explained in *Power/Knowledge*, "gives on to the analysis of the related effects of power."[29] To reject space is to misunderstand how to throw into relief "processes, historical ones, needless to say, of power." It is almost as if spatiality, once condemned to the domain of the dead, the immobile, and the undialectical, the suppressed other of a rich, fecund, and dialectical time, is now reinstated as the place of the Other, as Japanese observed years ago, whereas the self only presides as the subject over the temporal process, which must presume a stability it can never realize.

Finally, the genealogical arsenal provides the instruments for disrupting and disorienting inventories received in the present. "Let us give the term genealogy," Foucault answered in *Power/Knowledge*, "to the union of erudite knowledge and local memories which allow us to establish an historical knowledge of struggles, and to make use of this knowledge tactically today."[30] In fact, he continued, "it entertains the claims to attention of local, discontinuous, disqualified, illegitimate knowledges against the claims of a unitary body of theory which would filter, hierarchize and order them in the name of some true knowledge and some arbitrary idea of what constitutes a science and its objects." Genealogies are, in this respect, "antisciences," insurrectionary knowledges, "opposed to the effects of centralizing powers which are linked to the institution and functioning of an organized scientific discourse within a society such as ours."[31] Hence, Foucault saw the method as an intervention into contemporary conditions of politics and domination, by virtue of its capacity to represent problems and phenomena in an entirely new and unfamiliar way. As strategic intervention, genealogy disclosed the operation by which disciplines dispense knowledge of larger enabling discourses founded on the will-to-power and calculated the results from the effort to remove them from their conditions of possibility and from knowing the circumstances of their own production. Underlying this conception of intervention was the conviction that structures of knowledge, especially those classified as the human or social sciences, were the effects of discourses devoted to enforcing recognitions and identities sanctioned by the fixed position of a subject as possessor and producer of knowledge. The task of Foucault's own intervention was to dissolve all claims to subjective fixity in order to make way for a fundamental shift in perspective toward an unconscious subject, from the same to the different—the Other. But, an other who stood in an asymmetrical relationship to the self. After the shift, the truth of the subject would be displaced from an inner subjective certitude to the realm of the symbolic and, therefore, would be situated in a discourse that is always historically contingent. In Foucault's genealogy, the function of the statement (*énoncé*) ultimately "deprives the subject of its integrative and causal privileges," as it now comes from a symbolic pool prior to empirical experience, and "presents discourses as a field of regularity for various positions of subjectivity."[32] As a result, the subject loses both the status of the "pure, founding authority of rationality" and the role of an "empirical function of synthesis."[33] Genealogy offers a conception of the subject now functioning as a space that can be articulated by anyone involved in a particular enunciative configuration. With this in view, genealogy is not locked or fixed in a closed chain of identities, but articulates the space for the other to reclaim its subjectivity, its difference, by seizing the enunciative function. By submitting to this operation, the suppressed Other of historical discourse becomes merely the other.

If Foucault's reconstitution of genealogy promises to supply the space in which the other's subjectivity will appear by revealing the suppressed alterities that have made possible the dominant historical narrative in the West, it is possible to imagine it authorizing the production of the other's history and narrative. Foucault's texts, together with those of contemporaries such as Roland Barthes and Pierre Bourdieu, have opened up a perspective that seeks to encounter the other, to "welcome the Other" as Levinas would have expressed it, and interrogates its own conditions of possibility. In making this move, he—Foucault—has cautioned us against relying on any articulatory practice that would try to reaffirm the primacy of identity and recognition, and bend us into complying with the iron laws of what he called the "Science of the Same." By the same measure, his own example, his own explorations into alterity, whether that of madness, imprisonment, deviancy, or the past itself, marks a starting-point from which to seek out for traces of otherness, and thereby alerts us to contest established signs of a knowledge of sameness as the necessary condition for excavating another discourse, submerged and forgotten. Foucault's program succeeds in imparting a sensitivity to the problematic of otherness itself. Before his intervention, it had remained hidden, the "black sun of language" as Michel de Certeau described it. Foucault therefore obliges us to recognize in the familiar the buried outline of the different. The importance of the Foucaldian project is not in providing merely a methodology, which he, in any case, invariably eschewed. Rather, it provides a critique of forms of subjectivity, which instantiates the problematic that poses the question of otherness. Foucault's own critical intervention delineated a task for us: to reread the experience of the Other as the suppressed second term in a discourse that had confidently instated a subject of rational knowledge and its centrality in the historical process.

Although Foucault's texts have managed to deconstruct the claims of cultural unity and, by extension, Western superiority, the disclosure of this problematic encourages us to see a Japanese discourse on subjectivity, culture, and difference as something more than an instance of how otherness was assimilated by the categories of rationality as a necessary stage in the final modernization of Japanese society. Instead, we can now read this particular episode as an attempt by Japanese to resist their recuperation by and incorporation into a Western *ratio* masquerading as a universal ethos. Moreover, a genealogical unpacking of contemporary (1980s) Japanese declarations of cultural uniqueness as the cause of their global economic success, claiming to derive their authority from earlier, prewar discussions on identity, will reveal not simply two different movements, but the "ideologization" of an earlier critical effort to find a place for difference, in a discourse whose enabling principle necessitated its exclusion, into a noisy declaration of cultural exceptionalism. What was once envisaged as an example of Japanese modernizing by entering a Western-dominated discourse can now be seen as an instance of a critique that questioned the very entitlements of subjectivity and rational knowledge. Yet, beyond the identity of this problematic, Foucault's conception of knowledge, *savoir*, which institutes discursive practice as the producer of utterances and the place from which the subject speaks, authorizes the search for precisely those entitlements that, in every culture, empower some to speak and others to remain silent. By locating the subject of otherness in the field of knowledge (*savoir*), Foucault opened the way to question the claims of every operation that seeks to center a subject who is in the position to know and to recognize the vast consequences of this arrangement for power and domination.

It was, in fact, this particular observation that Japanese, before World War II, sought to articulate within the frame of a philosophical and historical discourse that had effectively denied a place to alterity, even as it granted entry to others who were willing to master the rules of the game in and on its own terms. In the 1920s and 1930s, a generation of Japanese writers, intellectuals, academics, and even bureaucrats contributed to the formation of a cultural discussion that must now be read as an attempt to forestall the process of assimilation to new forms of knowledge and developmental theories of history. After the war, interpreters quickly "misrecognized" this intellectual interlude as an instance of reified traditionalism, dangerous atavism, fascism, and jingoism. Depending on the persuasion, prewar philosophers and thinkers who had grappled with questions of subjectivity, history, and value were represented as either talented imitators or anguished modernizers, yearning to rescue and even retain the certainty of traditional values in the transforming process leading to a modern and rational society. Such efforts often risked reification, which invariably occurred in the hands of appropriators, who saw in dead or dying forms the hope of national revival in the desperate war that was soon to come. But inscribed in these discussions was the more fundamental recognition of the decision, explained by Foucault, that had divided reason and unreason, and subsequently confused *ratio* for ethos by privileging rational knowledge as a moral norm. Japanese were probably the first, but by no means the last, to systematically challenge the claims of an instrumental knowledge and the story of its progressive dissemination throughout the world. Yet, this confrontation produced a cultural discourse that had, perhaps paradoxically, assimilated the very forms of knowledge, cognitive strategies, and historical consciousness which it wished to call into question. Ironically, the Japanese critique proceeded from within the self-same categories of thought—theories of representation and action it aimed to discount—to dissemble into even more adequately cosmopolitan and universalistic forms of understanding. What thinkers frequently risked was recuperating a simple symmetry, implied in Western discourse in the distinction between self and other, by juxtaposing what was essentially West to what was irreducibly East. Only a few were able to escape the urge to fill the lack, the second term, with what amounted to a reverse image of the West, by trying to think through the alterities Western discourse had so successfully suppressed.

When Japanese, therefore, sought to dethrone the claims of what Derrida had called the "culture of reference" and to propose the massive project of decentering an imperial subject who was in a position to know, they were, of course, referring to the world of contemporaries and teachers, such as Husserl, Heidegger, Scheler, and others, in and on terms negotiable across cultural and racial frontiers. But, when Husserl announced in one of his last texts that only the West had known philosophy, any attempt to enter the precincts of philosophy entailed submitting to the requirements of the West. For Japanese, this meant that they would have to accept the very oppositions authorized by self and other; even though they produced a set of fixed dualities that were supposed to account for alterity and difference, they suppressed them in the interest of sameness and the logic of likeness—the homogeneity of order. Corresponding oppositions signifying cosmopolitanism and cultural essentialism, universalism and particularism, philosophy and history, the West and Japan, became complicitous in the suppression, inasmuch as the second term was made to stand in a symmetrical and necessary relationship to the first. Although some Japanese remained bound to these constraints, others recognized the implications of a philosophical view that could easily be employed to sanction certain kinds of domination and to eliminate the possibility of realizing genuine difference. The very terms that Japanese used to see themselves were provided by the signifying powers of the self.

An earlier (1920s) program to install a cosmopolitan vision was actually founded on this philosophic presumption of sameness, not of difference, even though it was often represented as providing a place for local differences in the great chorus of humanity. In this way, the other was easily incorporated into the self, and was seen either as a replication of the self, a mirror image, an alter ego, or worse, as a lack that still needed completion. Often, this understanding led thinkers and writers on a search for the spiritual resources in the world's civilization; more frequently, it prompted Japanese to concentrate on their own cultural traditions in order to demonstrate the itinerary of the spirit. What started, then, as a quest for universal value in the West was invariably supplemented by the pursuit of the particular as a manifestation of spirit, which ultimately led to a "return to the native place," *Nihon kaiki*. Driven by this quest for universal value (produced by spirit and expressed in art), for the true, the good, the beautiful (*shin, zen, bi*), a generation of thinkers and writers turned to Japan's own cultural endowment in the effort to show equivalence between the West and Japan, to demonstrate that

Japan was merely a local manifestation of the universal spirit. Yet, this move to cosmopolitanism betrayed the fundamental and underlying oppositions that the idea of a universal culture was supposed to conceal. Throughout the twenties and thirties, scholars eagerly produced a number of cultural histories and texts testifying to Japan's unique contribution to a global culture and praising its accomplishments as equivalents to Western achievements. All of these works and others positioned values and ideals such as beauty, goodness, and truth as central to Japan's creative capacity and reflective of its claims to universality, instances of how local culture manifested the inner workings of self and spirit. Watsuji Tetsurō's *Studies of the History of the Japanese Spirit* (1926),[34] for example, was an explicit attempt to grasp the "existence or life of the Japanese throughout the ages in order to show how the self realized itself as it passes through a number of cultural artifacts."

But if the tortuous and often tragic efforts of Japanese to imagine a cultural identity for themselves are envisaged in these terms, it is clear that all of those later claims attesting to uniqueness amounted to nothing more than hollow litanies, announcing not difference and otherness but the primacy of the self of Western philosophy. Hence, the central problematic of Japanese thought in the crucial decade before the Pacific War was to resolve the aporetic nature of this fearful symmetry and all of the oppositions it authorized. One obvious example was Watsuji Tetsurō's rather desperate attempt to tease out of Heideggerian categories of time and the grounding of history in being an alterity that emphasized space and collective social relationships. Watsuji provided the idea of a spiritual community, derived from his reading of Nietzsche, and the conviction that cultural struggle (which he saw first in terms of classes) demanded a contest between Asian spirituality and Western materialism. Convinced that Asia, and Japan, saw the world differently than the West, owing to Buddhism and the role played by nature, he concluded that the rational self had remained outside of nature rather than within its embrace. To articulate this view, he believed it was necessary to consider the operation of human society within nature and to explore customs, habits, and mores in their pure—natural—setting. In the world, he wrote, there had always been two basic but different ways of thinking: logical reasoning and intuition.

While the former belonged to the traditional West and the latter to the East, Watsuji risked supplying the self with its complementary other when he proposed in "Climate and Character" (*Fudo*, 1935) that, if timefulness explained the particular form of Western subjectivity, spacefulness of the East constituted its philosophical equivalent. To explain the reasons for this difference, he appealed to climate and environment, which in the West explained the development of individualism but in monsoon Asia mandated social relationships based upon cooperation and community. Owing to the moderate climate of the Mediterranean, nature was seen as benign and subservient, predictable, geometrical, and calculable. "Where nature shows no violence, she is manifested in logical and rational forms. . . . Thus, Europe's natural science was clearly the product of [its] meadow climate."[35] By contrast, monsoon Asia projected the spectacle of a nature both violent and unpredictable, a place teeming with plants and life, where people resign themselves to its caprices and do not resist it. As a result, human life is completely engulfed by nature and compelled to submit to its harsh dictates.

If Watsuji ran the risk of reproducing sameness, even as he tried to establish a place for heterogeneity, he nonetheless called into question the presumptions of Western universality and imagined a different conception of subjectivity—a decentering—which was capable of claiming comparable validity for acceptance. As an attempt to establish the conditions of possibility for the production of differing forms of subjectivity, Watsuji's conception of climate functioned similarly to Foucault's *savoir* and Bourdieu's *habitus*, not to mention later Japanese versions, such as the "communal sensibility" (*kyōdō kansei*) of Yoshimoto Takaaki[36] and all of those variations of a unique intersubjectivity which fall under the classification of the "household" (*ie*) society. Other contemporaries from the prewar period resorted to different referents in an effort to explain the instance of otherness in Japan. Hence, the novelist Tanizaki Junichirō sought to delineate this place of otherness as the "world of shadows" of Japan's remote past;[37] the philosopher Kuki Shūzō tried to catalyze the "concrete particular" in an irreducible cultural style (*iki*) derived from the eighteenth-century urban experience of merchants and townspeople, which now constituted an untranscendable cultural horizon;[38] and, the ethnologist Origuchi Shinobu sought a time before time, in which the authentic voice of the folk was expressed in speech, not writing, and which was still self-present in traces of custom and religion.[39] All of these efforts sought to imagine an elsewhere from which knowledge about the social order and the real order of the world might be gathered. Yet, this real order was vastly different from the social order which prevailed in the modern Japan of the prewar period. And all testified to the conviction, shared by numerous contemporaries, that it was still possible to reconstitute different forms of subjectivity from elsewhere. Accomplishing this reconstitution would succeed in dismissing the universalistic claims of the Western *ratio* and decenter its knowing subject from its stable moorings by promising the encounter with manifold otherness.

In order to realize this program of an alterity liberated from the symmetrical oppositions informing Western philosophical discourse, thinkers like Nishida Kitarō and Miki Kiyoshi, especially, concentrated their considerable energies on resisting the very fixity of the relationship between self and other which contemporaries were trying to supplement.[40] They tried to think through it to a place beyond the logic of identity, where there was only *other* and *other*, identity and difference. With Nishida, the most original thinker modern Japan has produced, virtually dominating the intellectual landscape of the twenties and thirties, the attempt was made to break through the logic of symmetry to make available to human consciousness varieties of experience: a pure experience as he described it in a *Study of the Good* (1911), and what had hitherto been formless and voiceless, which Western thought had consistently excluded as incomprehensibly Other. Nishida proposed that the true self could never be grasped as consciousness, willing, or acting, which invariably fell short of its nature and constrained its place in the world. Instead, the self must always have available the possibility of negating the world by negating it-self and thereby recognizing the presence of an absolute other. In this regard, the presumed unity of continuity is really a radical discontinuity, just as the self, in its propensity to negate, is different from moment to moment. Only an other makes the "I" that becomes simply other. "True self-identity," Nishida wrote in 1933, "means neither the unity of the subject nor the unity of the predicate. True self-identity is neither . . . noematic nor simply noetic. It has its proper meaning only when the subject is the predicate and the *noema* is the *noesis.*"

Nishida moved to envisage a *topos* (*basho*, place) to contest the idea of a self-determining individual, since he already believed that such determination depended upon the interaction of others. This *topos* was effectively outside of the logic of noncontradiction; it was, in fact, the site of the unity of absolute contradictories and, therefore, free from a dialectic that continuously reaffirmed the primacy of self-same identity and the exclusion of genuine difference, able to resemble later deconstructions of reason and the sovereignty of the self-conscious subject. Although many have tried to freight Nishida's thinking with Zen quietism and the mystifications of Oriental religions, trivializing its genuinely critical force, he denied that it was his intention either to revive Buddhism as a supplement to philosophy or to preach it. Rather, he claimed that his own reflections aimed to find a philosophically stable basis of life which might successfully move beyond the constraints of Western conceptions of ego and self, material interests and willful, possessive individualism, and the continuity of time and progressive historical change. In the final analysis, he saw the category of a universal negative—*mu*—as the location of place, that is, difference, unconstrained by history, individual ego, and Western absolutes such as God.

Yet, others in Japan would try to specify the sense of *topos*, and its adequation to a definable place or space outside of history and its social relationships based on individualism, free from the sameness that the fixed conception of the self demanded in its itinerary through time. Throughout the thirties, a number of thinkers and writers like the Japanese Romantic, Yasuda Yojūrō,[41] tried to foreground a recognizable place that conformed to this site of self-determination, such as the "landscape" (*fukei*) or the "scene" (*bamen*) of the linguist Tokieda Motoki,[42] "one's native place" (*kyodō*) of the folklorist Yanagita,[43] presided over by the departed ancestors, or the "land beyond the seas" (*tokoyo*), where all desire to go, which Origuchi Shinobu detected inscribed in the folk memory and still present in traces, or in the "spirit of language" (*kotodama*). Regardless of the terrain, these sites of self-determination all amounted to the privileging of the place of cultural production and praxis as an alterity, which the necessity of progressive history threatened to banish.

Ultimately, meaning, Japanese believed, was unavoidably de-
layed, because the drive for value depended upon the ceaseless quest
in time and history to act and create. If, moreover, temporality was
the condition for action, as Japanese believed the Western discourse mandated, then movement and historical change were its
inevitable consequences. Individuals, in their unending search for the
real, have been propelled on a dizzying journey in time to change
the world around them by imposing their will at the price of forfeit-
ing any chance for securing permanent meaning in human life.
The paradox of this view of knowledge and the history that nar-
rated the quest, as many Japanese noted, is that the very process
of change produced by human willfulness is always destined to fail,
because individuals are condemned to disappear in the flow of time.
The quest seeks everywhere to install identity and recognition in a
doomed effort to extinguish difference or perhaps even death itself.
At the heart of this unending process is the propellant that, in this
case, happens to be the desire of the Other. To revise this rather
unfortunate legacy, Japanese writers, intellectuals, and philosophers
began to explore the traces of what they believed to be the absent
signified of this restless process, which was the integration of self into
place, cosmos, nature, or community, and the privileging of fixed
social relationships as a corrective to the corrosions of temporal
change. Declaring an exemption from historical change invited writers and thinkers to begin imagining a permanent locus of value in a
timeless place, which represented the site of heterogeneity. By the
same token, they believed that the production of value occurred only
in a place, perhaps a "no-place" (whether metaphysical or metaphor-
ical) that had successfully resisted the confinements of progressive,
historical time. A crucial requisite of this resolution was the drive to
dissolve all oppositions by dismantling the subject as the founding
notion of consciousness. In the void created at the center of this
critical discourse—the "no-place" of textuality—it appeared possible
to recover a prior but repressed place, which had been the original
site of form and meaning and which constituted the real determinant
of history rather than merely being determined by it. Under these
circumstances, Japanese writers and thinkers were emboldened not
only to question the spurious claims of a narrative devoted to likeness
but also to envisage the possibility of constructing a different kind of
story line, founded on difference and cultural nonidentity.

From the assault on the philosophy of the subject, and the production of new, decentered subjectivities based on collectivities, place, scene, and landscape grew a critique that sought to resituate difference against the imperial claims of identity. Yet, in the postwar era these new subjectivities were wrenched from the context of criticism, which had given them expression, to signify a sense of Japanese uniqueness, a national subjectivity in order to guarantee homogeneity and sameness in a world teeming with dangerous differences, in a world that demanded global interaction on a scale never before imagined. The consequences of consensus, which I reread as the Japanese attempt to install sameness within domestic society, the "we Japanese" of countless pronouncements proclaiming Japanese homogeneity for the mobilization of domination and control, are beyond the scope of this chapter but are apparent to anyone who has seen how the Foucaldian project managed to demonstrate the intimate relationship between knowledge and power.

When Hegel proposed that self-consciousness invariably has an Other that it recognizes and supersedes, he wanted to show that its trace is vanishing and insubstantial. Self-consciousness, he proposed, feels the unity of this seeming other with itself in the form of a desire to abolish the otherness of the Other. The result would be a genuine supersession of the Other as the locus of difference and alienation. This "difference *is not*," he wrote, "and *it* [self-consciousness] is only the motionless tautology of: 'I am I.'"[44] Examination of Foucault's own encounter with the question of otherness and the example of Japanese thinkers trying to find a way out of a Western metaphysics of depth (and death) oblige us to confront the problem of desire ceaselessly seeking to eliminate otherness for the surety of identity, in preparation for rethinking the stages of reconciliation with a genuine other, not Other. Foucault's discourse has shown us how Western metaphysics has, since the Age of Reason, sought especially mightily to suppress any strategy for reunion by representing otherness as nonidentical to likeness. Foucault demonstrated that a culture so committed to historical consciousness was itself driven by a demon to banish history altogether, for the promise of a Hegelian certitude in absolute identity. Yet, he, along with others elsewhere, has been able to persuade us to search for the Other in its place of difference and radical heterogeneity, by recognizing, first, that we are masters of neither desire nor language (as consciousness transparent to itself).

We are only bodies capable of avoiding fixed identities because of an inexhaustible capacity to represent ourselves differently and to find new placements in shifting economic, social, and ideological practices. In this way, Foucault showed how we might all begin to construct discourses aimed at subverting established identities and settled dominations as a condition for serving both ourselves and others.

Notes

1. Michel Foucault, *The Archaeology of Knowledge*, trans. A. M. Sheridan Smith (New York: Pantheon, 1972), p. 25.

2. Tzvetan Todorov, *Mikhail Bakhtin: The Dialogic Principle*, trans. Wlad Godzich (Minneapolis: University of Minnesota Press, 1984), pp. 99–103, 109.

3. Quoted in Vincent Descombes, *Modern French Philosophy*, trans. L. Scott-Fox and J. M. Harding (Cambridge: Cambridge University Press, 1980), p. 110.

4. Ibid.

5. This is the problem Jacques Derrida engages in "Cogito and the History of Madness," in *Writing and Difference*, trans. Alan Bass (Chicago: University of Chicago Press, 1978), pp. 31–63.

6. Michel Foucault, *Madness and Civilization*, trans. Richard Howard (New York: Vintage, 1973), p. x.

7. Ibid., p. xi.

8. The imagery has been suggested by Descombes, *Modern French Philosophy*, p. 111.

9. Foucault, *Archaeology*, pp. 126–131; see also, Jacques Derrida, *Edmund Husserl's Origin of Geometry: An Introduction*, trans. J. P. Leavey (Stony Brook: Nicholas Hays, 1978), pp. 158, 175. In fact, much of Derrida's introductory commentary on this text is concerned with history, historicity, and historical a priorism.

10. Derrida, *Writing and Difference*, p. 34.

11. Derrida, *Edmund Husserl*, p. 158; and his *Writing and Difference*, p. 34.

12. Derrida, *Writing and Difference*, pp. 36, 38.

13. Descombes, *Modern French Philosophy*, p. 111.

14. Foucault, *Archaeology*, p. 12.

15. Derrida, *Writing and Difference*, p. 94.

16. Foucault, *Madness*, p. xi.

17. Descombes, *Modern French Philosophy*, p. 111.

18. Derrida, *Writing and Difference*, p. 94.

19. Ibid.

20. Karlis Racevskis, *Michel Foucault and the Subversion of Intellect* (Ithaca, NY: Cornell University Press, 1983), p. 43.

21. Quoted in ibid., p. 44.

22. Derrida, *Writing and Difference*, p. 36.

23. Descombes, *Modern French Philosophy*, p. 115.

24. Michel Foucault, *Language, Counter-Memory, and Practice: Selected Essays and Interviews* ed. Donald F. Bouchard, trans. Donald F. Bouchard and Sherry Simon. (Ithaca, NY: Cornell University Press, 1977), p. 152.

25. Ibid., p. 153.

26. Ibid., p. 154.

27. Racevskis, *Subversion*, p. 41.

28. Michel Foucault, *Discipline and Punish: The Birth of the Prison*, trans. A. M. Sheridan Smith (New York: Pantheon, 1977), p. 31.

29. Michel Foucault, *Power/Knowledge: Selected Interviews and Other Writings, 1972–1977*, ed. Colin Gordon, trans. Colin Gordon et al. (New York: Pantheon, 1980), p. 71.

30. Ibid., p. 83.

31. Ibid., p. 84.

32. Racevskis, *Subversion*, p. 73.

33. Foucault, *Archaeology*, p. 54; also Racevskis, *Subversion*, p. 73.

34. Watsuji Tetsurō (1889–1960) was an influential philosopher before World War II, who taught ethics at Tokyo Imperial University. Watsuji was an early enthusiast of Nietzsche, whose views on middle-class culture he incorporated into his own critique of contemporary Japanese life in the 1920s. He studied in Germany with Heidegger and inverted his conception of temporality and historical groundedness into a category of relationality determined by space and place, not history. Watsuji was one of the first of a long line of Japanese thinkers who contested the primacy of history for the privileging of unmediated aesthetic form, which revealed the itinerary of the national spirit in its unfolding. In English, see Robert Bellah, "Japan's Cultural Identity," *Journal of Asian Studies* 4 (August 1965). In Japanese there is a very fine intellectual biography of Watsuji by Yuasa Yasuo, *Watsuji Tetsurō* (Tokyo: Mineruba shobō, 1981).

35. Watsuji Tetsurō, *A Climate*, trans. Geoffrey Bownas (Tokyo: Hokuseido Press, 1961), p. 74.

36. Yoshimoto Takaaki is a prolific contemporary critic and poet whose intellectual positions have ranged from ultranationalism through Marxism to cultural exceptionalism based upon the conception of "communal feeling" (*kyōdō kansei*). Yoshimoto's most current activity involves modeling men's fashions and extolling the virtues of consumerism.

37. The writings of Tanizaki Junichirō (1886–1965), novelist and short-story writer, explore the effect of Westernization on Japanese sensibility and traditional modes of life. In the early 1930s Tanizaki wrote an elegiac meditation on the meaning of modern civilization for Japanese aesthetics, which has been translated as *In Praise of Shadows* by Thomas Harper and Edward Seidensticker. During the war, he rewrote the *Tale of Genji* for modern readers. His best known novel *Sasameyuki* was translated as the *Makioka Sisters* by Edward Seidensticker.

38. A Japanese philosopher, Kuki Shūzō (1888–1941) was briefly associated with Sartre in the late 1920s and may have introduced German phenomenology to him. Kuki studied with both Husserl and Heidegger; his major work *Iki no kōzō—The Structure of Style* (1930)—employed Heideggerian hermeneutics to examine style in Japan as a cultural horizon. An interesting book by Stephen Light, *Shūzō Kuki and Jean-Paul Sartre* (Carbondale: Southern Illinois University Press, 1987), includes translations of some of Kuki's shorter essays.

39. Origuchi Shinobu (1887–1953) was a scholar of folk religion and ancient Japanese texts, poet and ethnologist, whose writings tried to identify an authentic folk voice in antiquity before it was suppressed by the adoption of Chinese cultural standards and script.

40. Nishida Kitarō (1870–1945), twentieth-century Japan's premier philosopher, established the terms of philosophical discourse with his explorations into the phenomenological tradition. It is difficult to measure Nishida's impact on the Japanese intellectual world, since he was such a commanding figure for so long a time, and since so many of Japan's outstanding philosophers were his students. But there is no question about his originality, or about his conviction that he was participating in a philosophical discourse that observed no cultural or national boundaries. It is one of the tragedies of Nishida's career that although he was able fully to master texts in German, French, English, and Greek, his own writings in Japanese never received the readership they required from non-Japanese. A number of his texts have been translated into English, but none of them are very reliable. A brilliant doctoral dissertation by William Haver, "The Body of This Death: Alterity in Nishida-Philosophy and Post-Marxism" (University of Chicago, 1987), offers insight into Nishida's career.

Miki Kiyoshi (1897–1945), Nishida's most gifted student, was, briefly during the late twenties, an enthusiast of Marxism. In a number of articles, Miki tried to establish the terms of action in the present, employing phenomenological categories without appealing to more formal conceptions of class struggle. Miki ultimately abandoned Marxism for existential phenomenology in the 1930s, became involved in the (in)famous brain trust of

Konoe Fumimaro *(Shōwa kenkyukai)* in the late 1930s, with all of its associations with the war in China; and was later imprisoned where he died.

41. Yasuda Yojūrō (1910–1985) was a leading figure in a group called the Japan Romantics *(Nihon romanha)* which was organized around a magazine of the same name in the mid-1930s. Many of the group's members were former Marxists who saw in Marxism merely another surrender to modernism and realism. The group called for an "ironic" return to Japan *(Nihon kaiki)*, stressed its kinship with the generation of German romantics, who were also young, and contested the claims of machine civilization, arguing for a restoration of nature. Yasuda was clearly the leading ideologue of the group, whose own critical writings bordered on racism and jingoism during the war.

42. Tokieda Motoki (1900–1967), a leading Japanese linguist, had already written a penetrating critique of Saussure before the war. Yet Motoki accepted Saussure's more basic privileging of speech in order to construct an autonomous theory of the Japanese language based on a conception of the inaugural scene.

43. Yanagita Kunio (1875–1962) was a leading Japanese ethnologist and founder of folkloric studies in Japan *(minsokugaku)*. Yanagita spent most of his life collecting information relating to village customs, religious practices, language, and so on, ever fearful that a communal way of life would disappear before the demands of modernization. In the end, he imagined Japan as the *place* of a timeless community held together by common practices and worship to the ancestors.

44. G.W.F. Hegel, *Phenomenology of Spirit*, trans. A. V. Miller (Oxford: Oxford University Press, 1977), p. 105.

DISCIPLINING WOMEN
Michel Foucault and the
Power of Feminist Discourse

Isaac D. Balbus

In this chapter I stage a confrontation between the genealogy of
Michel Foucault and the feminist psychoanalytic theory of Dorothy
Dinnerstein, Nancy Chodorow, Jane Flax and myself. I am obliged
to resort to this artifice because—as far as I am aware—none of the
parties to this confrontation has ever before addressed the position of
the other: the feminist psychoanalytic theorists have yet to make the
discourse of Foucault the object of their critique of masculine discourse as a simultaneous reaction to and denial of the power of the
mother, and neither Foucault nor his followers have extended their
deconstruction of the disingenuous discourse of the true to the discourse of the theorists of mothering. This confrontation is by no
means arbitrary, however, because we shall see that the discourse of
the mother looks like a paradigm case of what Foucault would call a
"disciplinary true discourse," while from a feminist psychoanalytic
standpoint the Foucaldian deconstruction of true discourse betrays
assumptions that can only be characterized as a classically male flight
from maternal foundations. If feminism necessarily embraces these
foundations, then a Foucaldian feminism is a contradiction in terms.

I shall argue that this opposition between feminism and Foucault can be resolved in favor of feminism and—in part—against
Foucault. This argument will entail a demonstration that there are
aporias or internal inconsistencies in the Foucaldian position that can
only be overcome through a reformulation of this position that would
require us (a) to distinguish between libertarian and authoritarian

An earlier version of this essay appeared in *Praxis International* 5, no. 4
(1985): 466–483. Reprinted by permission of Basil Blackwell.

true discourses and (b) to assign the feminist mothering discourse to the former rather than the latter category. Thus Foucault's discourse points—against itself—to the power of the very feminist discourse it would undermine.

Foucault versus Feminism

Let me begin with a summary comparison of some of the constituent elements of feminist and Foucaldian discourse.

Foucault on History

The object of Foucault's genealogies are the variety of "true discourses" through which the will-to-power has been simultaneously expressed and denied in Western societies.[1] Expressed: true discourses function as "regimes of truth" that "induce regular effects of power" by virtue of the self-sacrifices they demand in the name of "Truth" and the "status [they grant to] those who are charged" with enunciating it. (P/K, p. 131). Denied: true discourse makes it difficult if not impossible to recognize the power it produces because it insists on the opposition between power and truth: "True discourse, liberated by the nature of its form from . . . power, is incapable of recognizing the will to truth which pervades it; and the will to truth, having imposed itself upon us for so long, is such that the truth it seeks to reveal cannot fail to mask it."[2] The task of the genealogist is not to produce yet another, but rather to unmask all forms of, true discourse by determining their conditions of existence and their political effects.

Since the eighteenth century the prevailing true discourse of the West has been what Foucault calls "anthropology" or the discourse of "continuous history." Practitioners of continuous history—traditional historians—seek to disclose the truth of the present by uncovering its origins in the past; they are committed to a concept of historical continuity, the necessary presupposition of which is the assumption that history is the unfolding of the essential attributes of man. Man, in short, can become the object of history precisely insofar as he is its subject. This commitment to historical continuity, in turn, both sanctifies the present with the tradition of the past and privileges it as the unique vantage point from which the past can be definitively known. Thus, "the traditional devices for constructing a comprehensive view of history and for retracing the past as a patient and continuous development must be systematically dismantled."[3]

Hence Foucault's attempt to dismantle or deconstruct the assumption of man-as-the-simultaneous-subject-and-object-of-history on which continuous history rests. He argues that the effective material presuppositions for the existence of "man as object" and "man as subject" are the disciplinary technologies (that render the body at once docile and productive) and the "technologies of the self" (which oblige the subject to speak the truth about itself) that have flourished since the eighteenth century in Western societies. Thus power—exercised over both the body and the soul—is the condition of existence for that form of knowledge which the discourse of continuous history makes possible. This form of knowledge, in turn, functions to reinforce and renovate the objectifying and subjectifying technologies through which this power is produced.

This deconstructive history of the present demonstrates the *discontinuity* between the present and the past and thus withdraws both the familiarity and the privilege conferred on the present by the relationship that the discourse of continuous history establishes between it and the past. The demonstration of discontinuity becomes the task of genealogy: to practice it is to "discover that truth or being do not lie at the root of what we know and what we are, but the exteriority of accidents . . . the forms operating in history are not controlled by destiny or regulative mechanisms, but respond to haphazard conflicts" (*LCMP*, pp. 146, 154). History, in short, has no meaning (*STT*, p. 91).

Feminism on History

Feminist psychoanalytic theorists—along with other feminists—understand the history of all hitherto existing societies as a history of the subordination of women by and to men. Women have always been experienced by men as the "dangerous sex" and men have always sought to avert this danger by excluding women from positions of authority outside the family.[4] Thus ostensibly different, even

antithetical cultural and/or political arrangements are merely variations on the common overriding theme of misogyny and patriarchy.
Beneath the apparent discontinuity of transitory historical forms lies
the massive continuity of male domination. It is precisely this continuity that allows us to speak of "history" rather than "histories."[5]

Western philosophical discourse oscillates between a justification and a denial of this history. Either men have been explicitly
defined as superior to women (in order to rationalize their exclusion
from extrafamilial authority) or both men and women have been
subsumed under a category of "human being" which purports to be
gender-neutral but in fact always entails an equation of the human
with what (up to the present) happen to be disproportionately masculine characteristics. Gender difference is either transformed into
hierarchical opposition or homogenized out of existence. In neither
case is that difference understood to be consistent with nonhier-
archical, egalitarian relationships between women and men. Thus it
is possible to speak of a history—a patriarchal history—of Western
thought notwithstanding the otherwise profound differences among
its various representatives.[6]

The heretofore culturally universal phenomenon of patriarchy is
rooted in and reproduced by the equally universal fact of virtually
exclusive female responsibility for early child care. In all cultures it is
a woman—either the biological mother or mother-substitute—who
is both the source of the satisfaction and the frustration of the imperious needs of the infant; she is at once the being with whom the child
is initially indistinguishably identified and the one who enforces the
(never more than partial) dissolution of this identification. Thus it is
the mother who becomes the recipient of the unconscious hostility
that accumulates in children of both sexes as the result of this in-
escapably painful separation. The mother who is loved is also necessarily the mother who is hated.

The culturally universal fear and loathing of the female results
from the subsequent transfer of this hatred of the mother to all those
who come to represent her, that is, to women in general. And the
exclusion of women from positions of authority outside the family
reflects the terror of ever again experiencing the humiliating submission to the authority of the mother within it. (In *Marxism and
Domination* I have shown that the starkness of this exclusion varies

directly with the painfulness of this submission.) It is in this sense that mother-dominated childrearing must be understood as the source of patriarchy. History has a meaning, and that meaning is the flight from and the repudiation of the mother.

It follows that women and men must become more or less equally the agents of the gratification and frustration of infants and young children if the inevitable hostility resulting from this combination is no longer to be directed exclusively at women. And only when men, by virtue of their complicity in this fateful combination, are no longer available as blameless, overidealized refuges from maternal power will it be possible for people to come to terms with, and outgrow, the resentment that will remain but that will no longer be directed at one sex alone. Thus coparenting is an indispensable condition for the overcoming of patriarchy and the emotional immaturity of which it is an expression.

Foucault on Totality

The same will-to-power that accompanies the discourse of global historical meaning informs the discourse of society as a totality that is present in each of its parts. The theoretical pretension to grasp the social whole betrays a commitment to a "transparent society" in which "there no longer exist . . . any zones of darkness . . . or disorder" (P/K, p. 152): an epistemological attachment to the category of totality necessarily implies a political attachment to totalitarianism (P/K, p. 80).

Because this epistemological holism grants to a theoretical avant-garde the unique privilege of representing the whole to all those who are presently, if not permanently, unable to see it, it also enshrines the indispensable presence of this avant-garde in the transition to, if not the operation of, this form of society (P/K, p. 83). For both reasons, Foucault condemns the "tyranny of globalizing discourses" (P/K, p. 83), warns us that "the 'whole of society' is precisely that which should not be considered except as something to be destroyed," and insists that political thinkers who would resist totalitarianism must "reject [totalizing] theory and all forms of general discourse" (LCMP, pp. 233, 231).

This repudiation of totalizing theory extends to the effort of theorists to envision an alternative to the society whose all-embracing logic they purport critically to comprehend. Utopian thought merely substitutes yet another totality for the one it is sworn to eliminate, and thus it reproduces all the authoritarian political tendencies to whose eradication it is ostensibly committed. Hence the stark Foucaldian conclusion: "to imagine another system is to extend our participation in the present system" (*LCMP*, p. 230).

Intellectual resistance to this system demands not general discourse but rather an analysis of the plurality of specific technologies of power which traverse it. This commitment to specificity over generality is the sociological parallel to the genealogical commitment to discontinuity over continuity. In Foucault's work it manifests itself in careful attention to the "specificity of mechanisms of power . . . which each have their own history, their own trajectory, their own techniques" (*P/K*, pp. 145, 99). Thus one book on the power of the medical "gaze" (*Birth of the Clinic*), another on the power of "surveillance" (*Discipline and Punish*), and yet another on the power of the "discourse on sexuality" (volume 1 of *The History of Sexuality*). Thus the intelligibility of Foucault's otherwise perverse insistence that "je suis Pluraliste."[7]

A pluralism of powers necessarily gives rise to a pluralism of resistances. Foucault insists on the multiplicity of the sources of resistance and refuses to privilege one as any more revolutionary or universal than any other. He does not exclude—indeed, he is committed to—the possibility that these resistances might eventually combine to create a new (nondisciplinary) form of power[8] and thus a "new politics of Truth,"[9] but his principled theoretical reticence precludes him from naming this new form of power/knowledge. The much more modest but far less dangerous task of the intellectual —the specific rather than the universal intellectual—is simply to struggle against the power that operates in his or her own local disciplinary domain.

Feminism on Totality

The overcoming of patriarchy would entail a complete cultural transformation. Patriarchy is not an isolated part of, but rather a pervasive presence within, any given human society.

The mother is not merely the first woman we encounter but also the first representative of the world we encounter. The hitherto culturally universal symbolization of the earth as a woman captures this connection between our relationship with the mother and our relationship with nature. Nature, in short, becomes Mother Nature because it is the mother who nurtures. Under certain conditions of this nurturance—to which I refer in some detail in *Marxism and Domination*—the hostility that accompanies its termination is translated into a hostility toward the nature that the mother represents. The symbolization of nature as an absolute, dangerous other that must be tamed lest it destroy us is rooted in the unconscious, childhood symbolization of the mother as an other who must be punished for having betrayed our love. If the domination of nature is the domination of the mother, it follows that a less hostile, more cooperative relationship with (nonhuman) nature requires a less painful, emotionally explosive relationship with the mother. As we have seen, this is precisely what coparenting would make possible.

The mother is also the "first, overwhelming adversary" of the will of the child, the first representative of authority that he or she confronts.[10] Thus the relationship with the mother within the family sets the emotional stage for our subsequent relationship with the variety of authorities we will encounter outside the family. The fear and loathing of women that the intolerable exercise of maternal power engenders becomes the unconscious basis for the acquiescence in, or even the affirmation of, first the authority of the father and then the authority of men as a whole. Under conditions of mother-monopolized childrearing, "male authority is bound to look like a reasonable refuge from female authority."[11] The struggle against political domination therefore demands that this form of childrearing be replaced with childrearing that is shared equally by women and men.

So it is that coparenting is essential not only for the overcoming of male domination but also for the supersession of political and technological domination. It is in this sense that the struggle against patriarchy must be understood as a struggle for an entirely new civilization, a civilization without domination.

Foucault on Subjectivity

We have already seen that Foucault argues that the individual whom anthropological discourse conceives as the subject of history is but the product of apparatuses of power/knowledge, of technologies of the self and the discourses that both sustain and are sustained by these technologies. Since the subject "is not the vis-à-vis of power [but rather] one of its prime effects" (P/K, p. 98), the constitution of the subjectivity of the individual is simultaneously the constitution of his or her *subjection*.[12]

The theme of the "founding subject" enables us to "elide the reality" (AK, p. 227) of this power effect; it would have us believe that the very power/knowledge complexes that produce individual subjects have been produced by them, and thereby makes it impossible even to formulate the problem of the subject as an object to be explained (STT, p. 101). Thus the genealogist must "dispense with the constituent subject . . . get rid of the subject itself" (P/K, p. 117) in favor of an analysis of the various technologies of the self and associated discourses by means of which the subject has been historically constituted.

Foucault locates psychoanalysis as a, or perhaps even *the*, master discourse/technology of the self in contemporary society (P/K, p. 219). It unites the confessional mechanisms that have long characterized Western civilization—procedures that incite individuals to reveal their hidden, inner truths—with a more recent, post–nineteenth-century deployment of sexuality, in order to ensure that the truth of the individual subject will be his or her sexuality. Since the subject-to-be is initially unaware of, indeed resistant to, this truth, becoming a subject requires subjection to the power of a "Great Interpreter" (BSH, p. 180) who is assumed to have privileged access to the truth. And, since this interpretive process culminates in the subject's affirmation of an unambiguously sexual identity, this process "categorizes the individual, marks him by his own individuality, attaches him to his own identity [and] imposes a law of truth on him which he must recognize and which others have to recognize in him." The result is a thoroughly subjugated subject in the twofold sense of being "subject to someone else by control and dependence, and tied to his own identity by a conscience or self-knowledge" (*BSH*, p. 212).

In this remarkable passage Foucault dispenses not only with individual sexual identity but with individual identity *tout court*. An attachment to an identity that one recognizes and is recognized by others is not the inevitable outcome of any form of social interaction but rather the result of the form of interactions peculiar to the technologies of the self which proliferate in the contemporary disciplinary society. The celebration of an individual identity that is somehow unrealized or distorted in that society does not contest but merely confirms its power. The genealogist refuses this ruse and recognizes instead that "nothing in man—not even his body—is sufficiently stable to serve as the basis for self-recognition or for understanding other men" (*LCMP*, p. 153). It follows that the struggle against the disciplinary society must be waged against, rather than on behalf of, sexual, or any other form of, identity. Thus Foucault's cryptic conclusion to the first volume of *The History of Sexuality*: "the rallying point for the counterattack against the deployment of sexuality ought not to be sex-desire but bodies and pleasures."[13]

Feminism on Subjectivity

The development of the identity of children of both sexes depends on a period of primary identification—of symbiotic union—with the mother that results from her nurturant responses to their imperious infantile needs *and* on a subsequent separation from her, the perception of which can only be enforced through the mother's frustration of these very same needs. But here the symmetry ends. Since both the girl and the mother are female, the intense identification that the girl establishes with the mother is consistent with, and becomes the basis for, her feminine identity. This means that "for girls and women, issues of femininity or female identity do not depend on the achievement of separation from the mother."[14] Thus, despite this separation, the mother continues to be symbolized as an other with whom the girl is connected and on whom the development of her self depends.

Hence women typically develop a relational orientation within which others are understood not as a threat to, but as essential for, the realization of their identity. In Nancy Chodorow's words, they come to experience themselves as "continuous with and related to the external object world" and "emerge with a strong . . . basis for experiencing another's needs . . . as one's own."[15] This means that women are unconsciously predisposed to fulfill the needs of the other—to *empower* rather than excerise power *over* the other—and thus that they are emotionally prepared for the nurturing in general and the mothering in particular for which they have heretofore been disproportionately responsible.

It is otherwise for the boy. Whereas primary identification with the mother is the source of the female child's recognition that she, too, is a woman, this feminine identification is an obstacle that must be overcome if the male child is to become a man. Thus the development of his masculinity demands that the male child suppress the feminine within him through the repudiation of any attachment to or identification with the mother. In order to become a man he must learn to symbolize his first and most significant other as an absolutely separate, alien object with which no connection or communion can be established.

This unconscious symbolization of the mother as an object sets the stage for a generalized objectifying stance toward the entire world of others which the boy will subsequently encounter. Since "masculinity is defined through separation," the very relationships that women perceive as essential for the realization of their gender identity will characteristically be experienced as a threat to the identity of men.[16] Men will attempt to ward off this danger by avoiding intimate relationships or by transforming them into relationships in which the self establishes invulnerability by achieving distance from, and control over, the other. Thus men are emotionally prepared for the manifold ways—violent and nonviolent—in which they will seek to excerise power over the variety of others they will confront.[17]

Western philosophical discourse operates entirely within the limits of this masculine horizon. The emotional orientation of men is transformed into the master assumption that the appetites or passions are self-seeking at best and antisocial at worst. What divides Western philosophers is merely the answer they give to the question of whether it is possible and/or desirable for humans to rise above these passions. Idealists from Plato through Kant to Habermas have argued that the faculty of reason enables human beings to discover or elaborate universal principles of social obligation which can override the appetites and thus make social justice possible—that, in short, reason should rule over passion. Materialists from Thrasymachus through Hobbes to Nietzsche counter that the ostensibly rational articulation of universal principles of social obligation is itself part of the passionate struggle to excerise power over others and that justice is merely the name given to the outcome of this struggle—that, in other words, reason is forever a slave to passion. This masculine oscillation between a self-seeking materialism and a dispassionate or disembodied rationalism has recently been transformed by Lawrence Kohlberg into an evolutionary theory in which the passage from materialism to rationalism is conceptualized as an invariant sequence of moral development. But as Carol Gilligan has pointed out, what is missing in Kohlberg (and in the entire Western philosophical tradition that his theory attempts to synthesize) is precisely the assumption that the passions are or can be social, and that social interaction might be informed neither by self-seeking passion nor by abstract, rational obligation but by the nurturing or caring that has hitherto been the distinctive orientation of women.

The realization of this possibility requires the elimination of the asymmetries in the pre-Oedipal experiences of male and female children. Once the father joins the mother as an early caretaker of the male child, this child will now experience a primary identification with a parent of his gender; the formation of his masculine identity will, therefore, no longer demand the suppression of his primary identification and the assumption of an exclusively oppositional stance toward his first love object. Under these conditions, boys can be expected to grow up far more relationally oriented than they are under mother-dominated child-rearing. Thus it is reasonable to suppose that they will no longer be driven to exercise power over others and will instead be emotionally inclined to empower others as they are empowered by them. Coparenting is the key that can unlock the possibility of a society in which the nurturance and caring that have thus far been largely restricted to the arena of the family come to inform the entire field of human interaction.

By now the opposition between Foucaldian and feminist psychoanalytic discourse should be clear. Each treats the other as part of
the problem for which it understands itself to be a remedy. The
Foucaldian perspective indicts feminist psychoanalytic theory for relying on all three of the constituent, interrelated elements of a
contemporary true discourse: continuous history, the concept of totality, and the theme of the founding subject. The idea of a universal
patriarchy that is rooted in an equally universal mother-dominated
childrearing simultaneously masks the strangeness of the contemporary disciplinary society and privileges one form of the struggle against
it, namely the struggle for coparenting, over all other types of resistance. The nightmare of a patriarchal society—a whole that is present in the way in which we work, decide, philosophize, and even
feel—as well as the vision of a postpatriarchal society in which these
parts of life would all be thoroughly reorganized betray the inevitably
totalitarian pretensions of a reason that believes itself to be capable of
objectifying the conditions of its own existence. And the reliance on
psychoanalysis to reveal the hidden origins of an allegedly pre-ex-
isting, gendered subjectivity at once contributes to the constitution
of this subjectivity and veils this constitutive process. Thus, from a
Foucaldian perspective, Dinnerstein, Chodorow, and Flax are disciplining women; that is, they are committed to a form of true discourse that is both cause and consequence of the disciplinary society
that Foucault contests.

From a feminist psychoanalytic perspective, Foucault's deconstruction of disciplinary discourse/practice betrays all the signs of its
masculine origin. His ban on continuous history would make it impossible for women even to speak of the historically universal misogyny from which they have suffered and against which they have
struggled, and would appear to reflect the blindness of a man who so
takes for granted the persistence of patriarchy that he is unable even
to see it. His gender-neutral assumption of a will-to-power (over others) that informs true discourses and the technologies with which
they are allied transforms what has in fact been a disproportionately
male orientation into a generically human orientation, and obliterates in the process the distinctively female power of nurturance in
the context of which masculine power is formed and against which it

reacts. His critique of totalizing reason condemns as totalitarian the very awareness of the pervasiveness of male domination which women have so painfully achieved, and entails an equation of identity with loss of freedom that is but a conscious translation of the unconscious opposition that men experience between autonomy and identification with the (m)other. Finally, the dismantling of all psychoanalysis as a technology of the self dissuades us from taking seriously the particular form of psychoanalysis which alone can enable us even partially to undo this—and other—patriarchal oppositions. In short, Foucaldian genealogy disciplines women by depriving them of the conceptual weapons with which they can understand and begin to overcome their universal subordination.

Foucaldian True Discourse

The disciplining of women or women who discipline? How is it possible to adjudicate these competing claims? Do not be misled by the reference to adjudication. I write not as a neutral observer but as a partisan of feminist psychoanalytic theory, as someone who is committed to its truth and the practice with which it is connected. My goal, therefore, is to persuade Foucaldians to take feminist psychoanalytic theory seriously. But this is precisely what Foucaldians will not do, as they believe that the only way to contest the inevitably authoritarian effects of all true discourses is militantly to refuse their seductive appeal to truth. Since it is the belief in the invariably authoritarian effects of all true discourses which prevents Foucaldians from taking feminist psychoanalytic theory seriously, my first task is to disabuse them of this belief. That I approach this task not only as a partisan of feminist psychoanalytic theory but also as someone who shares the Foucaldian abhorrence of authoritarian effects (and whose effort to annul the equation between true discourse and authoritarianism is, therefore, principled and not merely strategic) establishes, I believe, the common ground on which the dialogue necessary for this task can take place.

This task begins with a demonstration that Foucaldians are implicitly committed to the very true discourse that they explicitly reject. Although Foucault's manifest discourse repudiates continuous history, totality, and founding subject, it is not difficult to detect in his writings a latent discourse in which each of these interrelated themes assumes a prominent place.

Consider first his critique of continuous history. According to Foucault, the concept of historical continuity is merely the effect of an anthropological discourse that defines man as the subject and object of history, a discourse that is by no means historically continuous but rather coeval with the relatively recent emergence of disciplinary technologies and technologies of the self. It is precisely the discontinuous—that is, the specific nature of the disciplinary power/knowledge complex—that the concept of continuous history conceals and the genealogist must reveal. But this appeal to discontinuity is undermined by the assumptions that the disciplinary age is by no means the only one in which power and knowledge have been inextricably intertwined, and that this unholy alliance is, rather, almost as old as Western civilization itself (*AK*, p. 218). Western history, Foucault tells us, is nothing but the succession of different power/knowledge complexes, different regimes of truth (*STT*, p. 90). So we are back to a notion of historical continuity, even if the continuous object of Foucault's history is not "man" but the will to power/knowledge through which "he" is created and transformed. As Hubert Dreyfus and Paul Rabinow have observed, to make the incestuous relationship between knowledge and power the object of dicourse is to seek to convey a truth about this power relationship by means of which it can be subverted (*BSH*, p. 132). Thus Foucault remains within the very opposition between power and truth which he opposes. He remains, in other words, within the discourse of the true.

The totalizing reason against which Foucault inveighs is likewise present in his work. Despite his explicit repudiation of "all forms of general discourse" and his insistence on the "specificity of mechanisms of power," he speaks of disciplinary power as an "integrated system," of the "spread [of disciplinary mechanisms] throughout the whole social body," of an "indefinitely generalizable mechanism of 'panopticism,'" the "omnipresence of the mechanism of discipline [and] the judges of normality," and the "formation of what might be called in general the disciplinary society."[18] Here we are a long way from the pluralist Foucault. As Frank Lentricchia has pointed out, a concept of the disciplinary society "is nothing if not the product of a totalizing theory of society."[19] Indeed, we should scarcely expect otherwise. To hold, as Foucault does, disciplinary technologies responsible for the very constitution of the modern-individual-as-object-and-subject is necessarily to attribute to them a totalizing power that only a totalizing theory can name. And, if these technologies lacked this totalizing power—if they were less globally and dangerously determinative—what would be the point of Foucault's prodigious effort to dismantle the true discourses that sustain them? The point is that the mere identification of the object against which the genealogist struggles requires the very concept of totality which the genealogist would unambiguously condemn.[20]

So too, finally, does the conceptualization of the struggle against this disciplinary object demand that genealogists violate their prohibition against the founding subject. We have seen that Foucault argues that the subject is but an effect of disciplinary power/knowledge and that theorists who would subvert this form of power/knowledge must therefore get rid of the subject. But the one subject who cannot be gotten rid of is the theorist him/herself. The very intention to identify knowledge/power complexes as objects for deconstruction presupposes a subjectivity that is not an effect of these complexes but, rather, an animating source of the deconstructive discourse. And the problem is not merely that Foucault cannot account for his own resistance without revoking the ban on the constituent subject. It is also that he cannot account for *any* nonreactive resistance—any resistance that anticipates the new form of power/knowledge to which he is committed—without making reference to a subjectivity that is more and other than an effect of discipline. Thus Lemert and Gillan are correct to observe that "there is more subjectivity in Foucault than a casual reading would suggest" (*STT*, p. 106), as Foucault himself appears to acknowledge when he tells us in an interview that "it is through revolt that subjectivity . . . introduces itself into history and gives it the breath of life."[21] The difficulty is that this subversive subjectivity cannot be explained within the framework of a discourse for which subjectivity and subjugation are correlative terms. By speaking of a subjectivity that breathes life into history—that is, in short, its animating source—Foucault embraces the very theme of the constituent subject with which, he informs us, we must dispense.

I have demonstrated that there is a Foucault who is committed to a form of true discourse in opposition to the Foucault who insists on the pernicious consequences of all forms of true discourse. There are two possible ways to resolve this opposition. We can accept the position of the latter Foucault, in which case we will be obliged to refuse to take seriously everything that the former has to say about a transhistorical domination, the disciplinary society, and the possibility of its subversion. Or, we can take seriously these global claims to truth, in which case we will have to reject the thesis that all such claims have necessarily authoritarian effects. I assume that radical, politically conscious Foucaldians prefer to be able to speak of the continuity and pervasiveness of domination as well as the possibilty of its transcendence, and that they will therefore reject the Foucault who maintains that this can not be done without contributing to its contemporary reproduction. I assume, in other words, that the thesis of the inevitably authoritarian effects of all true discourses will have to be abandoned in favor of the authoritarian effects of some true discourses and the libertarian effects of others.

How might this distinction be drawn by Foucaldians who come to recognize its necessity? I believe that Foucault has already implicitly established the criteria for this distinction and that we need only to make them explicit by contrasting the specific form of true discourse to which one Foucault is, in fact, committed with the specific form of true discourse that indeed entails the authoritarian political consequences that the other Foucault incorrectly attributes to all forms of true discourse.

Recall, to begin with, the genealogical remedy for continuous history: "the traditional devices for . . . retracing the past as a patient and continuous *development* must be systematically dismantled" (emphasis added). This suggests that historical continuity understood as an evolutionary development is the real danger that the genealogist must combat. The conceptualization of historical continuity as a rational progression does indeed privilege the present as the necessary culmination of that progression, and the thinker who would undermine rather than privilege the present must therefore also strive to undermine this conceptualization. But historical continuity need not be conceptualized as development or progress and, as we have seen, is not so conceptualized by the Foucault for whom history has been nothing but the succession of different apparatuses of power/knowledge, "transitory manifestations of relationships of domination-subordination."[22] That Foucault is able to develop a powerful critique of the contemporary, disciplinary form of these relationships of domination-subordination despite—or perhaps because of—this notion of historical continuity demonstrates that this notion does nothing to privilege the present. By linking the present to the past it may make the present more familiar, but it is a familiarity that breeds contempt.

Reconsider next Foucault's critique of what he calls "totalizing reason." The equation he establishes between the epistemology of totality and the politics of totalitarianism is based on the argument that the impulse to know the whole—to see its presence within the manifold parts—implies a commitment to a society in which individuals are allowed no hiding places from the surveillance of those who presume to represent it. But the plausibility of this argument rests entirely on an asserted but undemonstrated identity between seeing and surveillance. Surveillance, as Foucault understands it, recognizes individuals only as more or less interchangeable parts of the power machine; it robs them of any individuality that is not functional for the reproduction of society as a whole. It is, in short, a way of seeing the other that homogenizes the differences between it and any other, and thereby obliterates its autonomy. But this is not the only way of seeing the other. The other can be recognized as an other with whom we share connections—with whom we are identified—yet from whom we are nevertheless different. Thus the impulse to see the whole can be an impulse to recognize—and celebrate—the persistence of heterogeneity and autonomy within the context of community and identification.

In his leap from totality to totalitarian Foucault ignores this crucial distinction between a homogeneous and a heterogeneous totality. Yet his own (totalizing) critique of the disciplinary society implies a commitment to the latter: if he were not an epistemological holist, it would be impossible for him to conceptualize that society, but if his holism were of the homogenizing variety, he would have no grounds on which to condemn its impulse to obliterate heterogeneity. (Unless one were to argue that Foucault is an empirical holist and a normative pluralist, an argument that entails an ultimately indefensible separation of description and evaluation.) That he argues for a multiplicity of sources of resistance to the disciplinary society should not mislead us, for he recognizes the necessity for alliances among those whose resistance flows from these different sources, and the possibility of an alliance (that is not purely tactical and therefore short-lived) presupposes the possibility of recognizing what these otherwise heterogeneous agents have in common (*LCMP*, pp. 216–17). Thus Foucault demonstrates, despite himself, that a thinker who is committed to an epistemology of "heterogeneous totality" will resist, rather than succumb to, the totalitarian temptation.

We have seen that the Foucault who tries to get rid of the subject is at odds with the Foucault who embraces subjectivity as a vital source of history. He is silent about the nature of this subjectivity, but I think we are entitled to infer from his reference to "bodies and pleasures" as the "rallying point for the counterattack against the deployment of sexuality" that the subjectivity which manifests itself in transformative resistance has a *bodily* basis. To account for this type of resistance, Foucault appears obliged to take recourse to a concept of an embodied subjectivity that is a source rather than an effect of power, a "lived body that is more than the result of the disciplinary technologies that have been brought to bear on it" (*BSH*, p. 167). But a concept of embodied subjectivity or a "lived body" entails that the body *is* "sufficiently stable to serve as the basis for self-recognition or for understanding other [people]," that is, it necessarily implies precisely that notion of bodily integrity or identity that Foucault refuses. [23]

In his equation of individual identity—sexual or otherwise—with individual subjugation Foucault has confused the identity of the embodied with the identity of the disembodied subject. The latter, but not the former, is the proper object for a Foucaldian deconstruction. It is the individual who can only relate to his or her body as an object from which he or she is separate and over which control must be exercised—the individual with a simultaneously docile and productive body—whose subjectivity has been shaped by disciplinary technologies and technologies of the self, and it is the traditional epistemological subject of either empiricism or idealism—the subject that is distinct from its object of knowledge—which both reproduces and is reproduced by these technologies. Thus any true discourse that relies on a disembodied founding subject does indeed both mask and justify the authoritarian process by means of which such a subject has (at least in part) been formed. But a true discourse that posits an embodied founding subject is a prerequisite for any material appeal against this very process.

Conclusion: Feminist Psychoanalytic Theory as a Liberatory True Discourse

I believe that I have established that our Foucaldian interlocutor would be obliged to agree that a true discourse whose constituent elements were (a) a concept of continuous but *nondevelopmental* history; (b) a concept of *heterogeneous* totality; and (c) a concept of *embodied* subjectivity would satisfy the criteria for a nonauthoritarian, potentially liberatory true discourse. My final task is to demonstrate that feminist psychoanalytic theory is a true discourse that satisfies these three criteria and thus that the Foucaldian should take it seriously.

Feminist psychoanalytic theory clearly satisfies the first criterion. The historical continuity that it takes as its object is not development but domination; not the triumphant march of reason as such but rather the hegemony of a particular form of reason which is shot through and through with the poisonous passion of patriarchy. Thus the feminist theorist does not privilege, but demands a fundamental break with, the present, one that involves the construction of a new form of reason and a new form of power. In this it is at one with the Foucaldian project.

Feminist psychoanalytic theory is also committed to the concept of a heterogeneous totality. It is based on the assumption that the development of the self depends on an identification with the other and thus that community and autonomy are not only consistent but, in fact, mutually constitutive. It demonstrates that when the first significant other is a woman, the male experiences the very identification that is essential for a genuinely autonomous self as a threat to the self, and that the inevitable result is both a damaged self and a damaged community. And it is animated by the impulse to undo this damage by helping to create the conditions—namely coparenting —under which the identification with our initial significant others would be experienced not as an obstacle to but, rather, as what it really is, an essential source of an authentic sense of self. The feminist mothering discourse makes explicit the implicit Foucaldian commitment to a heterogeneous totality and specifies the conditions under which this commitment can be fulfilled. It is, therefore, as militantly (and perhaps more realistically) antitotalitarian as the thought of Foucault.

Finally, the self to which the mothering discourse is committed is an eminently embodied self. It is through an intimate, continuous, and nurturant contact with the body of the mother that our earliest, most fundamental needs are satisfied. The identification with the mother which results from the satisfaction of these needs is, therefore, an identification with the mother's body. Since the formation of the self initially depends on this identification with the mother's body, it follows that the self can only be an embodied self. It also follows that our sense of bodily self will depend on our (unconscious) relationship to the body of the mother within us. If boys under mother-monopolized childrearing are obliged to suppress the mother within them in order to become men, this can only mean that they will be obliged to suppress their bodies as well. Only when the male child internalizes the body of a nurturer of his own gender —only under coparenting—will the mortifying repudiation of the body no longer be associated with masculinity.

Thus feminist psychoanalytic theory gives an account of the formation of embodied subjectivity which purports to explain the conditions under which it will be denied in order to contribute to the conditions under which it will be embraced. If we insist on calling the therapy that flows from this theory a technology of the self, then we will have to admit that there are technologies of the self which can enhance, rather than destroy, the embodied subjectivity of which Foucaldians are the covert partisans.

To conclude: I believe I have shown that feminist psychoanalytic theory satisfies all three Foucaldian criteria for a nonauthoritarian, potentially liberatory true discourse, and thus that there are no good Foucaldian reasons for refusing to take seriously its claims to truth. But there are, of course, other, perhaps more fundamental reasons than Foucaldian ones for not wanting to listen to this eminently subversive, deeply disturbing discourse.

Notes

1. Michel Foucault, *Power/Knowledge: Selected Interviews and Other Writings, 1972–1977* (New York: Pantheon, 1980), p. 131. Hereafter cited as *P/K*. See also Charles C. Lemert and Garth Gillan, *Michel Foucault: Social Theory and Transgression* (New York: Columbia University Press, 1980), p. 90. Hereafter cited as *STT*.

2. Michel Foucault, *The Archaeology of Knowledge and the Discourse on Language* (New York: Harper and Row, 1972), p. 219. Hereafter cited as *AK*.

3. Michel Foucault, *Language, Counter-Memory, and Practice: Selected Essays and Interviews*, ed. Donald F. Bouchard (Ithaca, NY: Cornell University Press, 1977), p. 153. Hereafter cited as *LCMP*.

4. H. R. Hays, *The Dangerous Sex* (New York: G. P. Putnam's Sons, 1984).

5. Dorothy Dinnerstein, *The Mermaid and the Minotaur: Sexual Arrangements and Human Malaise* (New York: Harper and Row, 1976); and Isaac Balbus, *Marxism and Domination: A Neo-Hegelian, Feminist Psychoanalytic Theory of Sexual, Political, and Technological Liberation* (Princeton: Princeton University Press, 1982).

6. Jane Flax, "Political Philosophy and the Patriarchal Unconscious: A Psychoanalytic Perspective on Epistemology and Metaphysics," in *Discovering Reality*, ed. Sandra Harding and Merrill B. Hintikka (Boston: D. Reidel, 1983), pp. 245–281. See also Balbus, *Marxism*.

7. Michel Foucault, "History, Discourse, and Discontinuity," *Salmagundi*, no. 20 (Summer–Fall 1972), pp. 225–248.

8. *P/K*, p. 133. See also, Herbert Dreyfus and Paul Rabinow, *Michel Foucault: Beyond Structuralism and Hermeneutics* (Chicago: University of Chicago Press, 1983), p. 223. Hereafter cited as *BSH*.

9. Cited in Jacqueline Zinner, review of Michel Foucault, *La Volonté de Savoir*, in *Telos*, no. 36 (Summer 1978), p. 224.

10. Dinnerstein, *Mermaid*, p. 166.

11. Ibid., p. 175.

12. *P/K*, p. 97; Michel Foucault, *Discipline and Punish: The Birth of the Prison* (New York: Pantheon, 1977), pp. 27–28, 192–194. Hereafter cited as *DP*.

13. Michel Foucault, *History of Sexuality* (New York: Pantheon, 1978), 1:157.

14. Carol Gilligan, *In a Different Voice* (Cambridge, Mass.: Harvard University Press, 1982), p. 8.

15. Nancy Chodorow, *The Reproduction of Mothering: Psychoanalysis*

and the Sociology of Gender (Berkeley and Los Angeles: University of California Press, 1978).

16. Gilligan, *Different Voice*, p. 8.

17. For an effort to relate the different ways in which men have exercised power over others to the different modes of mothering they have experienced, see *Balbus, Marxism*, pp. 327–333, and Balbus, "Habermas and Feminism: (Male) Communication and the Evolution of (Patriarchal) Society," *New Political Science*, no. 13 (Winter 1984), pp. 27–47.

18. Foucault, *Discipline and Punish*, pp. 176, 209, 216, 304, 209.

19. Frank Lentricchia, "Reading Foucault (Punishment, Labor, Resistance)," *Raritan* 1, no. 4 (Spring 1982), pp. 5–32.

20. As Mark Poster has recently reminded us, Sartre demonstrated that "all perception requires totalizations, that an observer is always privileged in drawing together disparate acts in an historical field revealing a totalization, even though individual actors may not be cognizant of it" (*Foucault, Marxism and History* [Oxford: Polity Press, 1984]), p. 21. See also Jean-Paul Sartre, *Search for a Method* (New York: Knopf, 1963), pp. 85–166. Gestalt psychologists also provide support for the proposition that what they call "totalizing reason" is inherent in perception.

21. Michel Foucault, "On Revolution," *Philosophy and Social Criticism* 8, no. 1 (Spring 1981), p. 8.

22. Barry Smart, *Foucault, Marxism, and Critique* (London: Routledge and Kegan Paul, 1983), p. 76.

23. Whether bodily identity also implies *sexual* identity depends on and Kegan Paul, 1983), p. 76.

24. Whether bodily identity also implies *sexual* identity depends on what is meant by sexual identity. Since the object-relations version of psychoanalytic theory on which the mothering feminists rely repudiates the orthodox Freudian conceptualization of the sexual drives or the libido as a- or antisocial in favor of the conceptualization of "the libido as directed toward the other . . . as 'object-seeking'" (Jessica Benjamin, "The End of Internalization: Adorno's Social Psychology," *Telos*, no. 32 [Summer 1977], p. 47), the mothering theorists share Foucault's critique of the notion of a primordial, presocial sexuality that the power of sociality can only repress. (For Foucault's critique of this repressive hypothesis, see volume 1, Chap. 1 of *The History of Sexuality*.) Since they also reject—at least implicitly—the orthodox Freudian assumption that heterosexuality is the normal outcome of the process through which an embodied identity is formed, they would also be obliged to agree with Foucault's critique of psychoanalytic and other technologies of the self that constitute individual identity as a specifically heterosexual identity.

Since, on the other hand, our bodies are gendered bodies—since under any conceivable circumstances (short of a genetically engineered transformation) human beings will have to make cultural sense of their physiological maleness and femaleness—the commitment of the mothering theorists to embodied identity perforce entails a commitment to a specifically gendered identity. Thus, even if it were the case that under coparenting bisexuality became the normal form of sexual preference, the assumptions of the mothering theorists lead us to expect that bisexual people would continue to define themselves as men or women and that this definition would continue to constitute an important dimension of their identity or sense of self. It is in this limited sense that a notion of embodied identity necessarily implies a notion of sexual identity, and thus that Foucault's implicit commitment to the former puts him at odds with his explicit repudiation of the latter.

FEMINISM
AND THE POWER OF
FOUCALDIAN DISCOURSE

Jana Sawicki

Is Foucaldian feminism a contradiction in terms? I would not have thought so. After all, Foucault and feminists both focus on sexuality as a key arena of political struggle. Both expand the domain of the political to include forms of social domination associated with the personal sphere. And both launch critiques against forms of biological determinism, and humanism. Finally, both are skeptical of the human sciences insofar as they have participated in modern forms of domination. Indeed, rather than link the growth of knowledge with progress, both describe how the growth of specific forms of knowledge—for example, in medicine, psychiatry, sociology, psychology—has been linked to the emergence of subtle mechanisms of social control, and the elision of other forms of knowledge and experience.[1]

Yet, as focused as Foucault was on domains of power/knowledge in which many of the bodies disciplined and the subjects produced and rendered docile were female, he never spoke of male domination per se; he usually spoke of power as if it subjugated everyone equally. As feminist critic Sandra Bartky, who is sympathetic to Foucault, rightly points out: "To overlook the forms of subjection that engender the feminine body is to perpetuate the silence and powerlessness of those upon whom these disciplines have been imposed."[2]

This charge of androcentrism notwithstanding, Bartky, myself, and many other feminists have found Foucault's discourses and methods useful tools for feminist criticism.[3] Moreover, in the first volume of his *History of Sexuality* Foucault isolated the "hysterization" of women's bodies and the socialization of procreative behavior as two key domains in which disciplinary technologies should be analyzed.

Perhaps as an advocate of what he called the "specific intellectual" he would have thought it best to leave specifically feminist research to those engaged in feminist struggle. In any case, he would have been the first to admit that one could do a genealogy of the genealogist. As an engaged critic the genealogist does not transcend power relations. Indeed, the very idea of power-neutral theory is one that Foucault's own genealogies continually questioned.

Thus, I find it paradoxical that, in his chapter in this volume, "Disciplining Women: Michel Foucault and the Power of Feminist Discourse," Isaac Balbus stages a confrontation between Foucault and feminist mothering theorists in which he ultimately interprets Foucaldian genealogy as an example of the very type of emancipatory theory which it has consistently questioned. Assuming that, to a Foucaldian, mothering theory would look like a "paradigm case" of a "disciplinary true discourse," Balbus concludes that a Foucaldian feminism is a contradiction in terms (see p. 138 in this volume). In order to resolve this so-called contradiction, Balbus reformulates the Foucaldian position and presents us with two Foucaults, one who rejects mothering theory and another who is forced to concede that mothering theory is a liberatory discourse.

Balbus's argument for the latter idea rests on his uncovering of a latent discourse within Foucault's writings in which Foucault implicitly appeals to categories that he manifestly rejects, namely, continuous history, the social totality, and a founding subject. According to Balbus, these categories are indispensable to feminist theory. Even more important, Balbus believes that for genealogy to be effective as social criticism, it must be grounded in an appeal to truth which is itself detached from the disciplinary power that it describes. If his discourse is not to be judged arbitrary and ineffective, argues Balbus, Foucault must exempt it from those forms of power/knowledge which it discloses. And once the Foucaldian admits the distinction between emancipatory and authoritarian true discourse, he or she has no principled reason to reject the emancipatory claims of a psychoanalytic feminist theory.

My initial reaction to Balbus's essay is to ask: Do these two discourses really need to be reconciled? Would a Foucaldian reject mothering theory *tout court*? Are appeals to totality (whether historical or social), or to a continuous subject of history, indispensable to feminist theory? Must feminist theorists embrace the notion that all forms of patriarchy have maternal foundations? Clearly, the answer to the last question is "no." Many feminists have rejected psychoanalytic theory for non-Foucaldian reasons. More important, feminism is not monolithic but represents many different theoretical strategies.

Suppose, however, that we do identify feminism with its psychoanalytic versions. Would a Foucaldian then be committed to rejecting feminism? Again, I think not. Neither, apparently, does Balbus, but for different reasons. In his view, we must interpret Foucault either as an antifeminist who, in his words, "disciplines women" by robbing them of the conceptual tools required in order to theorize and overcome male domination, or as an advocate of a humanistic feminism that, as I shall argue, employs a juridico-discursive model of power and appeals to a quasi-biological, universal practice, namely, mothering as explanatorily basic.

In what follows I shall argue that Balbus presents us with a false alternative. We can slip between the horns of this dilemma by offering an interpretation of Foucault's genealogy which is neither inherently antifeminist nor a masked version of the type of discourse it challenges. In the course of supplanting Balbus's paradoxical reading of Foucault, I shall also suggest the outlines of an alternative Foucaldian response to mothering theory which preserves the radical and innovative features of genealogy.

Genealogy: Grand Theory or Antitheory?

The principal targets of Foucault's genealogies of power/knowledge are the grand theories of society, history, and politics which have emerged in the modern West. Most prominent among these, of course, are liberal humanism and Marxism (including its Freudian revisions). By *grand theory* I refer to any attempt to formulate a global or systematic discourse of the historical or social totality in order to legitimate programs and practices as progressive or emancipatory.

One of Foucault's more original moves involved isolating the similarities between the two great theoretical traditions that are more often contrasted. Thus, he claimed, both liberalism and Marxism operate with a juridico-discursive model of power consisting of the following basic assumptions: (1) power is possessed, by the presocial individual, a class, a people; (2) power is centralized, in the law, the economy, the state; and (3) power is primarily repressive. In his own analysis, Foucault represented power as exercised rather than possessed, as decentralized rather than exercised from the top down, and as productive rather than repressive. Equipped with this model of power, Foucault was able to focus on the power relations instead of the subjects related; to show how power relations at the micro level of society make possible global effects of domination such as class or patriarchal power, without taking these theoretical unities as its starting point; and to give an account of how subjects are actually constituted through power relations. Foucault's model of power enabled him to trace the power effects of the theories themselves, power effects obscured by traditional theories of power.

Foucault adopted a skeptical stance toward the emancipatory claims of liberal and Marxist theories insofar as they were based on essentialist, total theories of humanity, its history, economy, and libidinal economy.[4] His genealogy is not a theory of power or history in any traditional sense, but an antitheory. Therefore, it does not tell us what is to be done or offer us a vision of a better society. Instead, the genealogist offers advice about how to look at established theories and a method for analyzing them in terms of power effects. Foucault's genealogies describe how some of our ways of thinking and doing have served to dominate us, how, in his words, "men [sic] govern themselves . . . through the production of truth."[5] They serve less to explain the real than to criticize other attempts to grasp it, particularly insofar as these attempts are reductionist, essentialist, and presentist. Thus, it is misguided to turn to the genealogist for an endorsement of established theory.

When Balbus describes genealogy as an account of what power really is, when he suggests that Foucault offers a theory of history as a succession of power/knowledge regimes, and when he demands that Foucault accept his ahistorical criteria for distinguishing liberatory from authoritarian true discourses, he ignores Foucault's nominalism. Power/knowledge represents a grid of analysis, not a theory of power or history.[6] As such, Foucault's discourse on power attempts not to displace others but, rather, to get us to see them as material events with power effects.

If I am correct in maintaining that Foucaldian genealogy is not a theory but an instrument for criticizing theories, then the basis for an alternative interpretation of the latent Foucault that Balbus uncovers is established. Balbus claims that a Foucaldian can endorse his own humanistic emancipatory theory once he or she recognizes the following: (1) that genealogy is implicitly committed to a distinction between libertarian and authoritarian true discourse, (2) that the totality envisioned by mothering theory is heterogeneous, not homogeneous, and (3) that the founding subject to which mothering theorists appeal is not the disembodied subject of liberalism which Foucault allegedly targeted, but an embodied subject.

In what follows I shall argue that Balbus's effort to reconcile Foucaldian and feminist discourse deradicalizes Foucault's analysis of power and begs some of the most important questions that he raised.

Libertarian Versus Authoritarian True Discourse?

Balbus argues that when Foucault attributes liberatory effects to his own critiques, he implicitly remains within the opposition between truth and power which genealogy opposes. Left without an appeal to truth free of power, genealogy remains groundless.

Here Balbus begs Foucault's question concerning the possibility of providing absolute foundations for any discourse. As David Hiley argues, genealogy need not appeal to a transhistorical ground to avoid the charge of arbitrariness, for the "alternative of 'either grounded or arbitrary' makes sense only within the framework Foucault's work has set aside."[7] Hiley continues:

> The sheer weight of detail and the force of his analysis support his abhorrence of modernity without having to have a meta-story to tell, and without grounding his interpretation. The charge of arbitrariness begs the question. The burden is on those who oppose his analysis to enter the dispute with a contrary vision, rather than pose the dilemma that Foucault must ground his inquiry or produce normative criteria. . . . Foucault could legitimately respond to questions about the correctness of his interpretation of the danger of normalization, not by producing criteria of correctness, but by shifting the burden of proof.[8]

Foucault resists establishing criteria for distinguishing libertarian from authoritarian discourse not because he believes that all true discourses are inevitably authoritarian (here Balbus has erected a straw figure), but because determining the liberatory status of any theoretical discourse is a matter of historical inquiry, not theoretical pronouncement. From a Foucaldian perspective, no discourse is inherently liberating or oppressive. This includes psychoanalytic discourses.

As evidence for this last claim consider Foucault's observation that psychoanalysis played a liberating role in relation to psychiatry insofar as it denounced the complicity of psychiatrists with political regimes.[9] In a lecture from the same period, he suggested that psychoanalysis and Marxism have provided "useful tools for local research."[10]

Of course, Foucault also claimed that as a global theory psychoanalysis hindered research and contributed to forms of social control and normalization. But if we consider all of these statements in conjunction, we can only conclude that for Foucault, the status of psychoanalytic theory is ambiguous, a matter that must be judged by looking at specific instances and not by setting up general criteria. No doubt this is the point Foucault was making in one of his last interviews when he said: "My point is not that everything is bad, but that everything is dangerous."[11]

So rather than seek to legitimate feminist psychoanalytic theory, a Foucaldian looks for its dangers, its normalizing tendencies, how it might hinder research or serve as an instrument of domination despite the intentions of its creators. Whether it serves to dominate or to liberate is irrelevant to judging its truth. Foucaldian genealogy questions the idea that the only truth which is liberating is one which is free of power or untouched by history. Foucault borrows Nietzsche's hypothesis that power makes truth possible. Unlike Marxist ideology criticism, it does not relegate all knowledge claims conditioned by power to the domain of false consciousness. Indeed, Foucault did not question the truth of disciplinary knowledge as much as the particular ways in which it established the division between truth and falsity.[12] He described the historical conditions that made it possible for certain representations, objectifications, and classifications of reality to dictate which kinds of statements come up as candidates for truth or falsity, which sorts of questions and answers were taken seriously. These conditions are not only constraining but also enabling. Presumably they contain possibilities for liberation as well as domination. As one commentator notes, "If we cannot escape from history—and why should we hope to?—this does not entail confinement in prevailing political conditions, for history also includes the divisions and opposition that provide openness to the future."[13]

For example, the disciplinary knowledge brought to bear on the case of the hermaphrodite Herculine Barbin, whose memoirs Foucault unearthed and edited, is criticized not because it is untrue, but because it demanded that she be classified as either male or female and wrenched her from the "happy limbo" of ambiguous sexual identity.[14] It is not the truths about her as much as her being looked at through a particular mode of knowledge, a particular regime of truth which seals her fate. As Judith Butler states: "it is not her anatomy, but the ways in which that anatomy is 'invested' that causes the problem."[15]

What Balbus fails to take seriously is the way that genealogy suspends the identification of power and repression. Foucault rejects the view that liberatory knowledge is only possible where power relations are suspended. He observes: "Where there is power there is resistance; and yet, or rather consequently, this resistance is never in a position of exteriority in relation to power."[16] Thus, Foucault notes that the knowledge which constituted the homosexual as a particular type of individual made possible both medical and legal forms of power over the homosexual and a form of resistance in which homosexuals embrace their identities and demand a right to their sexuality. The sword of knowledge is double-edged.

In other words, power relations are established within a historical field of conflict and struggle which contains within it possibilities of liberation and domination. Foucault denies that his own discourse is free of power relations without despairing about the possibility that it can have a liberatory effect. This is not liberation as transcendence of power or as global transformation, but rather as freeing ourselves from the assumption that prevailing ways of understanding ourselves and others, and of theorizing the conditions for liberation, are necessary, self-evident, and without effects of power.

The Question of Totality

As Balbus points out, Foucault criticized the concept of totality. His emphasis on discontinuity in history was motivated by a skepticism concerning total histories that represented the historical process as linear, cumulative, and progressive. Nevertheless, in rejecting teleological histories of progress, Foucault was not rejecting the concept of continuity altogether. After all, genealogy involves reconstructing generative processes as well as locating discontinuities. Of course, the processes that he described are neither necessary nor inevitably progressive.

Balbus incorrectly assumes that the purpose of genealogy is to *demonstrate* discontinuity. To the contrary, the isolation of discontinuities is the starting point of genealogy, not its aim. For example, in *Discipline and Punish* Foucault locates a discontinuity between premodern and modern practices of punishment. He asks: How did imprisonment come to be accepted as the general form of punishment when it had been continually rejected by past penal reformers? Thus, isolating a discontinuity poses a historical problem. Foucault chose this particular problem because he questioned the value and function of our contemporary practice of imprisonment. He wanted to undercut our tendency to take imprisonment as a given by revealing its historical contingency.

Not only do continuist histories tend to legitimate rather than criticize present practices, they also obscure the conflicts and struggles in history. By pointing to paths that were not taken, unactualized possibilities, and events that do not fit the functionalist schema of the total history, Foucault hoped to effect an "insurrection of subjugated knowledges."[17]

"Subjugated knowledges" refers not only to historical contents that are obscured within functionalist histories but also to those forms of experience which fall below the level of scientificity. The latter include the low-ranking knowledge of the psychiatric patient, the hysteric, the midwife, the housewife, and the mother, to name only a few. Because these disqualified knowledges arise out of the experience of oppression, resurrecting them serves a critical function. Through the retrieval of subjugated knowledge, one establishes a historical knowledge of resistance and struggle.

There is also the question of the social totality. Balbus takes *Discipline and Punish* to be a portrait of the whole of modern society as disciplinary. Although this representation of Foucault's project is defensible—Foucault did resort to holistic rhetoric in this book—there are good reasons to reject it. First, one can argue that Foucault employed a holistic rhetoric of decline in order to counter the Whig historians' holistic rhetoric of progress. Second, Foucault's comments about the book indicate that it was intended not as a portrait of the whole of society but, rather, as a genealogy of the emergence of the ideal of a perfectly administered social system. Referring to his use of Bentham's panopticon, Foucault remarks:

> If I had wanted to describe real "life" in the prisons, I wouldn't indeed have gone to Bentham. But the fact that real life isn't the same as theoretical schemas doesn't entail that these schemas are therefore utopian, imaginary, etc. . . . That would be to have a very impoverished notion of the real.[18]

Bentham's panopticon is not a metaphor for modern society, but an event, a fragment of reality, that Foucault analyzes in terms of its effects.

Contra Balbus, Foucault is not a holist but a particularist. He does not assume that all parts of society are systemically related. Instead, he begins with a particular practice in the present, of the assumed value of which he is skeptical, and traces its lines of descent in Nietzschean fashion. These histories sometimes read like Spenglerian histories of decline because the point in the present toward which they lead is where Foucault locates a malevolent technology of power.

Given this account of Foucault's skepticism concerning the category of totality, we are in a position to evaluate Balbus's claim that the Foucaldian would accept the appeal of mothering theory to a heterogeneous social whole. This question of totality brings us to the heart of Balbus's critique of Foucault and, from a Foucaldian standpoint, to a major difficulty with mothering theory as Balbus characterizes it.

According to Balbus, appeals to continuous history and the social totality are indispensable to feminist theory since it must be able to name the "massive continuity of male domination" which has persisted throughout changes in social and political formations, and has pervaded all hitherto existing societies (p. 141). Mothering theory provides an explanation of the origins of patriarchy which accounts for its depth and pervasiveness. Balbus says: "History has a meaning, and that meaning is the flight from and the repudiation of the mother" (p. 142). This "flight" is allegedly caused by the universal practice of mother-monopolized child rearing. Thus, a necessary condition for the elimination of male domination (and the instrumental mode of rationality associated with it) is coparenting. Balbus concludes:

> So it is that coparenting is essential not only for the overcoming of male domination but also for the supersession of political and technological domination. It is in this sense that the struggle against patriarchy must be understood as a struggle for an entirely new civilization, a civilization without domination. (p. 144)

Balbus's use of mothering theory involves many features of traditional emancipatory theories which Foucault's genealogy criticized. He construes history as a struggle between two groups, locates the origins of male domination within a key institution—mothering—which he takes as explanatorily basic, and on the basis of this reductionist explanation, prescribes and legitimates a particular progressive intervention, namely coparenting. Balbus says, "Coparenting is the key that can unlock the possibility of a society in which the nurturance and caring that have thus far been largely restricted to the arena of the family come to inform the entire field of human interaction" (p. 148).

When Balbus argues that a Foucaldian could and should accept mothering theory as an emancipatory discourse because it appeals to nondevelopmental continuous history and a heterogeneous totality, he misses the point of Foucault's genealogy. It is not the empirical claim that male domination has appeared in many (even all) societies, the naming of patriarchy, which a Foucaldian would resist, but the attempt to deduce it from a general theory and to privilege a single locus of resistance. For a Foucaldian, patriarchy is the name of a global effect of domination made possible by a myriad of power relations at the micro level of society. By eschewing reductionism, the Foucaldian can bring to light the heterogeneous forms that gender embodiment, the practice of mothering, and power relations producing gendered individuals take. Without rejecting mothering theory, the genealogist adopts a critical attitude towards it, specifically, toward the totalistic reductionism that obscures historical contents.

How might a Foucaldian respond to the tactics and categories of mothering theory? First, rather than assume that mothering represents a unitary phenomenon, the genealogist looks for discontinuities between practices and ideologies and practices across cultures. The inquiry might be sparked by numerous questions such as the following: When did the idea of the mother as an emotional nurturer emerge? When did the idea of women's status as reproducer prevail?

As Jean Grimshaw observes in *Philosophy and Feminist Thinking*, the idea of women as emotional nurturers of men was foreign to the Greeks.[19] Another feminist, Ruth Bleir, refers to cross-cultural comparisons that question the idea that "there is such a simple entity as 'women's status' throughout history."[20] Women's work and men's work have varied significantly in different societies. Bleir cites Karen Sacks's appeal to anthropological data which suggest that in some societies women's productive activities and social relationships condition the relations of reproduction. For example, !Kung women, nomadic gatherers who inhabit the Kalahari desert, nurse their babies for three years in order to control the spacing between births and thereby schedule childbearing to fit the demands of their productive activities. The contrary view of reproduction as explanatorily basic to understanding women's position, Bleir argues, "employs a fundamental assumption of biological determinist theories and reflects our own ethnocentric blindness to alternate modes of interpretation."[21] Finally, Foucault's histories of the rise of the life-administering "biopower" suggest that the idea that exploring one's feelings is a key to the good life has emerged only recently, and its emergence has been linked to new mechanisms of social control. Thus, a Foucaldian might criticize mothering theory for its failure to adopt a historical attitude toward the value of feeling, nurturance, and caring. After all, Foucault described his project as a genealogy of modern morals.

In effect, Balbus's tendency to identify mother-monopolized child-rearing as a monolithic and fundamentally invariant phenomenon turns it into a quasi-biological given. The genealogical impulse is to inquire into the conditions of its genesis in order to reveal its historical limits. Despite pretensions to value heterogeneity, mothering theory obscures historical contents and experiential differences related to class, race, ethnic, and other cultural variants. Balbus rightly values a heterogeneous society but has not attended to the methodological prerequisites for bringing diversity to light.

Balbus's reference to a society without domination raises another point of contention between him and Foucault. For Foucault discourses were radical in terms of their effects, not their promises or their claims to get at the root of a phenomenon. As I have argued, when viewed in terms of probable effects, mothering theory turns out to obscure more differences than it promotes. Moreover, a Foucaldian would resist Balbus's appeal to a power-free society. Balbus operates with the repressive hypothesis inasmuch as he claims that the power of the mother under mother-monopolized childrearing functions to repress the femininity of men (their relational capacities), and the masculinity of women (their capacity for autonomy). His assertion that lifting this power through coparenting will lead to an authentic, integrated humanity represents theoretical humanism with a vengeance.

In contrast, the Foucaldian would look for the productive power of mothering theory, the normalizing tendencies as well as other possibilities that it produces in the social field. For example, as some feminists have already observed, mothering theory may unwittingly reinforce heterosexist norms. Moreover, Balbus himself admits (contra Nancy Chodorow) that "the commitment of the mothering theorists to embodied identity perforce entails a commitment to a specifically gendered identity" (p. 160). It is clear that he has only two genders in mind. Yet, as Judith Butler points out, Foucaldian discourse challenges the assumption that sexual difference is irreducible when it rejects the idea that sex is either primary or univocal. The materiality of the body is significant only insofar as it is invested in historically specific ways.[22] Thus, mothering theory may enforce the restriction of gender to a binary division insofar as it assumes that bodily identity is determining.[23]

Finally, the model of liberation as total to which Balbus adheres is incompatible with the Foucaldian understanding of freedom and resistance. Foucault does not hope to transcend power relations but rather to multiply the forms of resistance to the many forms that power relations take. To do this we must first bring the myriad forms into focus by utilizing the productive model of power. Thus, the Foucaldian tries to open up more space for resistance and self-creation by combating the constraining effects of totalistic theories and the juridico-discursive model of power with which they operate.

What makes mothering theory problematic is not its endorsement of coparenting, a worthy aim in itself, but rather its attempt to privilege and legitimate coparenting on the basis of a quasi-essentialist science of gender. This tactic is objectionable because it ignores the many other rationalities within which appeals to the notion of a deep gender identity are found, as well as the myriad relations of power through which gender, and the mother, are constituted.

The Subject of Foucaldian Feminism

This brings us to the question of identity. Postmodern feminists Nancy Fraser and Linda Nicholson have criticized mothering theory for adopting the Freudian premise "that there is a basic sense of self constituted at an early age through the child's interaction with its parents," and for assuming that this gendered deep self continues through adult life and cuts across divisions of race, class, ethnicity, and so forth.[24] A Foucaldian would reject the concept of a deep self for the same reasons that he or she rejects an ahistorical appeal to the theoretical category of mothering. It obscures cultural and historical specificity. Furthermore, inasmuch as mothering theory identifies male domination with a psychologically based male gender identity, it overlooks the complexities of institutional mediation which are surely also a part of the story of male domination. In contrast, a Foucaldian feminist would stress the sheer variety of ways in which effects of male domination are produced and gendered identities constituted.

That Balbus's feminist discourse refers to a material, embodied subject is not sufficient for it to escape the homogenizing theoretical tendencies that a Foucaldian abhors, as I have already argued above. Left without an appeal to an embodied founding subject, must the Foucaldian be left without any creative subjects whatsoever? To assume so is to fail to take seriously Foucault's reasons for rejecting humanism. Indeed, Foucault did suspend the use of humanistic assumptions in order to account for how individuals are produced by disciplinary technologies. He believed that humanist discourses that placed the subject at the center of reality or history had failed to grasp the extent to which the subject is fragmented and decentered in the social field. But to describe the ways in which individuals have been dominated through a rigid attachment to particular modern identities is not equivalent to rejecting identity *tout court*. As Ian Hacking notes: "Foucault said that the concept of Man is a fraud, not that you and I are nothing."[25] To suggest, as Foucault does, that the human is a social and historical construct is not to discredit every attempt to understand ourselves, but merely to discredit those that claim to be universal and to represent the Archimedean leverage point from which society might be moved.

Moreover, what Foucault objected to about psychoanalytic theories of identity was their tendency to represent individual identity as a fixed and unified phenomenon. Ironically, like mothering theorists, Foucault employed a relational model of identity. Rather than privilege any particular relationship as central to identity formation—for example, mother-infant relations—he highlighted the many relationships through which individuals are produced. Thus, the Foucaldian would not exclude mothering theory altogether but simply deny it theoretical privilege.

When Foucault speaks of power producing individuals, he refers not only to the production of individualist rhetoric, as Balbus suggests he does, but also to the production of forms of embodiment, of disciplined bodies. Foucault makes detailed and extensive references to the many techniques such as daily regimens and timetables, methods for distributing and organizing bodies in space, drills, training exercises, examination and surveillance techniques, and so on. In effect, both the soul and the body are produced through disciplinary technologies.

Inspired by Foucault's descriptions of the ways in which modern individuals are produced, Sandra Bartky provides her own compelling descriptions of the disciplinary technologies that produce specifically feminine forms of embodiment, for example, dietary and fitness regimens, expert advice on how to walk, talk, dress, style one's hair, and wear one's make-up. Bartky uses Foucault's model of power to show

how these technologies subjugate by developing competencies, not simply taking power away. She explains that one reason such technologies are so effective is that they involve the acquisition of skills and are associated with a central component of feminine identity, namely, sexuality. The disciplines enhance the power of the subject while simultaneously subjugating her. Hence, women become attached to them and regard feminist critiques of the feminine aesthetic as a threat.

Nevertheless, Bartky also recognizes the ambiguity of these technolgies. They produce possibilities of resistance as well. For example, new images of women are created when some women develop strong, muscular bodies. And as female body builders defy the canons of the feminine aesthetic, building their bodies beyond traditional limits, they destabilize feminine bodily identity and confuse gender.

Again, "where there is power, there is resistance." The Foucaldian views the relationship between the social and the individual not as one of univocal determination but as one of conflict and ambiguity. Individuals are the vehicles as well as the targets of power—a point that Balbus leaves out in his account of Foucault. In Foucault's relational view of identity, identity is fragmented and shifting. Black, lesbian, feminist, mother, and poet, Audre Lorde captures this conflict within the individual when she remarks: "I find I am constantly being encouraged to pluck out some one aspect of myself and present this as the meaningful whole, eclipsing other parts of self."[26] Eschewing the notion of a core identity, the genealogist attempts to mobilize the many sources of resistance made possible by the many ways in which individuals are constituted.

Stripped of its global dimensions, mothering theory might serve as an instrument of resistance to male-centered psychoanalytic theory. Mothering theory could be included as one among a plurality of tactics of resistance to male domination, but it would not be accorded the theoretical privilege that Balbus demands.

Conclusion

In claiming as he does that Foucault robs feminists of conceptual tools that are indispensable to feminist criticism, Balbus begs the most significant questions raised by Foucault's work, namely, questions concerning the nature of radical theory and practice. Foucault consistently questioned the value of global theory, the idea of a power-free society, and the idea of a universal subject of history. As I have shown, Balbus's feminist discourse combines all three ideas. To argue that Foucault implicitly endorses this form of emancipatory theory is to fail to appreciate the limited but nevertheless radical nature of Foucault's project.

Foucault's project is limited because it is not a theory of society, history, or power in any traditional sense, but instead a suggestion about how to look at our theories. Foucault asks us to inquire into the effects of power which theories produce. Foucaldian discourse is radical not because it gets at the roots of domination, but inasmuch as it introduces radically new questions and problems concerning prevailing ways of understanding ourselves which continue to dominate our thinking about radical social transformation. Foucault offers not an alternative emancipatory theory but, rather, tools that might free us from an unquestioning adherence to established ways of thinking. Ultimately, the radical nature of Foucault's discourse, like any other, must be judged on the basis of the effects that it produces.

I have argued that Foucaldian discourse might serve as an effective instrument of criticism for feminists who have experienced the oppressive dimensions of claims to know based on the authority of male-dominated sciences; the inhibiting effects of radical social theories that privilege one form of oppression over another and thereby devalue feminist struggle; and the multiplicity of subtle forms of social control which are found in the micro practices of daily life. In exposing the distortions in Balbus's treatment of Foucault, I hope to have paved the way for an alternative rapprochement between Foucault and feminist discourse which does not require that we abandon either of them.

To the question whether a Foucaldian feminism is a contradiction in terms, a Foucaldian feminist might reply; "No, not a contradiction but a continual contestation." Any self-critical and historically inflected feminism will find Foucaldian genealogy indispensable.

Notes

1. See for example, Barbara Ehrenreich and Deirdre English, *For Her Own Good: 150 Years of the Experts' Advice to Women* (New York: Anchor Press, 1978).

2. Sandra Bartky, "Foucault, Femininity and the Modernization of Patriarchal Power" (Paper read at the meeting of the American Philosophical Association, May 1986), p. 4.

3. See, for example, Jana Sawicki, "Foucault and Feminism: Toward a Politics of Difference," *Hypatia: A Journal of Feminist Philosophy* 1, no. 2 (Fall 1986), pp. 23–36; Jana Sawicki, "Identity Politics and Sexual Freedom: Foucault and Feminism," in *Foucault and Feminism: Paths of Resistance*, ed. Irene Diamond and Lee Quinby, forthcoming; Meaghan Morris, "The Pirate's Fiancée," in *Michel Foucault: Power, Truth, and Strategy*, ed. Meaghan Morris and Paul Patton (Sydney: Feral Publications, 1979); Biddy Martin, "Feminism, Criticism and Foucault," *New German Critique*, no. 27 (1982), pp. 3–30; Judith Butler, "Variations on Sex and Gender: Beauvoir, Wittig, and Foucault," *Praxis International* 5, no. 4 (January 1986), pp. 505–516; Nancy Fraser and Linda Nicholson, "Social Criticism without Philosophy: An Encounter between Feminism and Postmodernism" (Paper read at the meeting of the American Philosophical Association, December 1986); Ruth Bleir, *Science and Gender: A Critique of Biology and Its Theories on Women* (New York: Pergamon Press, 1984); Teresa De Lauretis, *Alice Doesn't: Feminism, Semiotics, Cinema* (Bloomington: Indiana University Press, 1984); Donna Haraway, "A Manifesto for Cyborgs: Science, Technology, and Socialist Feminism in the 1980's," *Socialist Review*, no. 80 (1985).

4. Michel Foucault, "Two Lectures," in *Power/Knowledge: Selected Interviews and Other Writings, 1972–1977*, ed. Colin Gordon, trans. Colin Gordon et al. (New York: Pantheon, 1980), p. 83.

5. Michel Foucault, "Questions of Method: An Interview with Michel Foucault," in *After Philosophy: End or Transformation?*, ed. Kenneth Baynes, James Bohman, and Thomas McCarthy (Cambridge, Mass.: MIT Press, 1987), p. 108.

6. Cf. David Couzens Hoy, "Power, Repression, Progress," in *Foucault: A Critical Reader*, ed. David Couzens Hoy (Oxford: Basil Blackwell, 1986), p. 129.

7. David Hiley, "Foucault and the Analysis of Power: Political Engagement without Liberal Hope or Comfort," *Praxis International* 4, no. 2 (July 1984), pp. 198–199.

8. Ibid., p. 199.

9. Michel Foucault, "Body Power," in *Power/Knowledge: Selected Interviews and Other Writings, 1972–1977*, ed. Colin Gordon, trans. Colin Gordon et al. (New York: Pantheon, 1980), pp. 60–61.

10. Foucault, "Two Lectures," pp. 80–81.

11. Michel Foucault, Afterword to *Michel Foucault: Beyond Structuralism and Hermeneutics*, by Hubert Dreyfus and Paul Rabinow (Chicago: University of Chicago Press, 1982), p. 232.

12. Foucault, "Questions of Method," pp. 111–112.

13. Stephen David Ross, "Foucault's Radical Politics," *Praxis International* 5, no. 2 (July 1985), p. 134.

14. *Herculine Barbin, Being the Recently Discovered Memoirs of a Nineteenth Century Hermaphrodite*, trans. Richard McDougall (New York: Pantheon, 1980).

15. Butler, "Variations on Sex and Gender," p. 515.

16. Michel Foucault, *The History of Sexuality*, trans. Robert Hurley (New York: Pantheon, 1980), 1:95.

17. Foucault, "Two Lectures," p. 81.

18. Foucault, "Questions of Method," p. 110.

19. Jean Grimshaw, *Philosophy and Feminist Thinking* (Minneapolis: University of Minnesota Press, 1986), p. 63.

20. Bleir, *Science and Gender*, p. 140.

21. Ibid., p. 146.

22. "Variations on Sex and Gender," pp. 514–516.

23. Marilyn Frye argues that sexual dimorphism is a culturally enforced phenomenon that constitutes one of the necessary conditions for sexism. She suggests that there is a continuum, not a rigid dichotomy, in the expression of secondary sex characteristics at the anatomical level. Hence, she too could envision the possibility of more than two genders. See Marilyn Frye, "Sexism," in *The Politics of Reality: Essays in Feminist Theory* (New York: Crossing Press, 1983), pp. 17–40.

24. Fraser and Nicholson, "Social Criticism without Philosophy," pp. 20–21.

25. Ian Hacking, "The Archaeology of Foucault," in *Foucault: A Critical Reader*, ed. David Couzens Hoy (London: Basil Blackwell, 1986), p. 39.

26. Audre Lourde, *Sister Outsider* (New York: Crossing Press, 1984), p. 120.

ON THE THEORY AND
PRACTICE OF POWER

Sheldon S. Wolin

Perhaps no writer of the last half of the twentieth century has done more to illuminate the nature of power than Michel Foucault. Almost singlehandedly he moved the discussion of that most elusive and illusive concept from its modern or state-centered understanding to a postmodern or decentered version. Yet for all of its fertility, Foucault's critique left standing some of the bastions of modern power while ignoring its peculiar dynamics. The best that it could produce was an insurrectionary gesture against a corporatized world with no exits. The Foucaldian conception of power remains, therefore, incomplete. This is fortunate because it allows the opportunity to criticize current post-Modern conceptions before they settle in as reigning orthodoxies.

For the purposes of the present discussion I shall take the phrase *postmodern politics* to mean:

(a) Politics conducted with minimal dependence on any principle of legitimacy which justifies the exercise of power by appealing to some myth of origins or by deriving it from some *Grundnorm*, for example, popular sovereignty; the authority of a constitution; natural law; or a social contract. For the postmodern the traditional conceptions of legitimacy are tainted by transcendentalism, foundationalism, myths, or metanarratives.

(b) Accordingly, postmodern politics is content with a minimalist justification for the exercise of power. In this respect it presents a striking historical contrast to modern democratic and liberal conceptions. The modern politics inaugurated by the English revolution of the seventeenth century and the American and French revolutions of the eighteenth century was shaped in important ways by the belief that for power to be legitimate it had to be grounded in a broad public basis. The metaphor of a basis or foundation had concrete and specific referents: to increased popular participation in political processes, to the securing of political rights (voting, rights of association and assembly, and free public communication), and to the establishment of a national forum, a definite focus of attention where political actors would debate matters of public concern. The modern economy of power, especially in its liberal rather than its democratic form, was profoundly if not always self-consciously shaped by revolutionary experiences that were simultaneously wars that attempted to mobilize the energies and resources of entire populations. Consequently, the revolutionary appeals to a broadly public conception of power were the ideological mirroring of a broader, more collectivist actualization of power which would become the hallmark of the modern state.

Postmodern politics preserves the public as an opinion rather than as a set of practices. Postmodern politics solicits approval rather than requires legitimation. Approval is broadly expressed as a rating that registers the opinion of the citizen about the job performance of politicians. It is not tied to periodicity as elections are but can be elicited at whim. This minimalist conception of legitimacy gives to contemporary politics its peculiarly asymmetrical character. The power that modern science has made available to the postmodern state exceeds all previous scales, but the political basis for it has steadily shrunk. We might say that the postmodern attack upon foundationalism has abetted a politics whose simulacrum is a pyramid of power resting on its apex.

(c) That job performance has assumed importance as a principal category of appraisal reflects the elevation of competence to the top rank of political virtues. Postmodern politics fears incompetence more than corruption because it is haunted by fears about the fragile character of postmodern structures. If competence is the first of the virtues for maintaining the system, human error is the cardinal vice that always threatens it.

(d) Competence is one of several entries in the postmodern lexicon which contribute to obliterating the modern distinction between public and private. Others are: management, expert, and cost/benefit. The practices of postmodern politics are illustrated by the revolving door through which executives pass from corporate positions to governmental agencies and vice versa, or by selling governmental functions to private entrepreneurs ("privatization").

Foucault's central preoccupation was with power, and he approached it through a running criticism of some of the distinctive categories of modern political theory. The most important of these were theory, action, and the sovereign state.

Theory and action is a formula as old as Western political theory, but it became the hallmark of modern political thinking, both in Hobbes's conjunction of theory and technology and in Marx's linking of theory to revolution.[1] The differences between the two are, for my purposes, less relevant than that the formula itself represents the kind of conceptual language which Foucault considered suspect: theory signified in his eyes a totalizing system of thought, an all-inclusiveness that was at once authoritarian and ignorant. Theory professed to explain all phenomena when it was merely transposing them to a plane of abstract generality whose terms it controlled. Preoccupied with deep questions of history's meaning, man's fate, and universal truths, theorists, according to Foucault, mostly ignore the relationships and systems of meaning which actually constituted human life. Although Foucault indicated that this conception of theory had its origins in ancient philosophy, the modern representatives, such as Hegel and Marx, were his special targets.

Foucault was equally, if not more, suspicious of the association of theory and action in the formula of theory and praxis made familiar by Marxist writers of this century. "Do not," Foucault urged, "use thought to ground a political practice in Truth; nor political action to discredit, as mere speculation, a line of thought."[2] If the common theme in this injunction is liberation—the liberation of practice from the tyranny of transcendental foundations and of thinking from the leaden and limited horizon of practicality—that theme was produced because Foucault himself had initially theorized a tight and systematic union between thought and action that rivaled anything projected by German idealism or materialism. Foucault identified liberation with resistance rather than revolution, exploiting the interstices that exist because all power formations are incomplete. Action is, however, unable to escape from the formations that constitute, in Foucault's conception, its own necessary and sufficient conditions. There can be no leap from the realm of necessity to the realm of freedom, only an insurrectionary moment before power is reconstituted and action is redomesticated.

Foucault's conception of power seemingly depended on a thoroughgoing rejection of the proudest achievement of modern theory, the conception of the sovereign state as the center of power and authority, the ultimate source of rules, and the final arbiter of social conflicts.

> What we need, however, is a political philosophy that isn't erected around the problem of sovereignty, nor therefore around the problems of law and prohibition. We need to cut off the king's head: in political theory that has still to be done. . . . To pose the problems in terms of the state means to continue posing it in terms of sovereign and sovereignty, that is to say, in terms of law. If one describes all these phenomena of power (discipline, normalization, surveillance) as dependent on the state apparatus, this means grasping them as essentially repressive.[3]

Foucault was protesting against juridical conceptions of the state, arguing that there were innumerable networks of power which were outside state authority and that the state was not an independent source of power but rather "can only operate on the basis of other, already existing power relations. The state is superstructural" (*P/K*, p. 122).

Foucault's conception is flawed by a narrow construction of state power as essentially negative and preventive ("this metapower with its prohibitions"), parasitic rather than grounded ("rooted in a whole series of multiple and indefinite power relations that supply the necessary basis for the great negative forms of power") (*P/K*, p. 122). Still trapped by Marxist metaphors of base and superstructure, Foucault failed to grasp the positive role of the modern state in promoting the modernization of society. Although the state repressed (for example, abolishing local standards of weight and measure in favor of nationally uniform standards), it also created (roads, bridges, schools). What it created was the infrastructure of modernity, most strikingly in the form of modern science whose subsidization by the state over the past three centuries has made possible the phenomenal growth of scientific knowledge and its practical applications.

The modernity of modern power in its state-centered form is captured most tellingly in the phrase *industrial democracy*. Less than a decade ago that phrase was widely employed by social scientists to categorize societies that were highly industrialized, were considered dynamic, and were governed by a representative system of government, responsible officials, the rule of law and free elections. The use of the word *democracy* was intended to signal that state power was legitimated by the citizens who voted its governors in or out. Thus state power was distinguishable from most of the other great types of social power, such as wealth, status, knowledge, ownership of property, and (most) religions.

The second feature of the world of advanced modernizing societies is the remarkable degree to which it is the premeditated product of mind. From weaponry to medicine, from social therapies to administrative organizations we see artifacts that do not merely happen to come into existence but are planned and invented. All of these products are the result of the systematic application of mind. They are also the constraints within which mind must operate. So while mind is demiurge, it is also conscript. Its name is technical knowledge: knowledge that is methodized, administered as a practice.

Third, the imperatives of the modernizing, technical state shape a politics in which policy is the central focus. Politics takes the form of policy making, policy formulation, and policy implementation. The modes of action characteristic of this politics are negotiation, compromise, adjudication, and litigation. Policy signifies the attempt to create a private space in which decisions can be removed from the unpredictable pressures of mass publics. Private space is established by the cult of technical expertise which envelopes policy formulation with the aroma of the sacred. Then everything turns on what powers have access to the various stages of the policy process. The primacy of policy relegates electoral politics to the margins where it functions as a myth of legitimation.

Although much more could be and needs to be said about this version of the political world, it is a world with a central political paradox. The hoariest cliché is that we live in a changing world. The

second hoariest cliché associates change with progress toward freedom, democracy, and the alleviation of mass suffering. The significance of Reaganism and Thatcherism is that change has become a
conservative category. We live in a constantly changing world because change is institutionalized and manufactured. Its institutionalization imposes narrow limits—intensive rather than extensive
—so that rigidity seems to be built into change. As a consequence it
reenforces those forms of power which have managed to oligopolize
the process of change and are best adapted to a technocratic politics.

Those who consider this system of politics to be unjust, inegal-
itarian, repressive of human potentialities, and a threat to the health,
welfare, and future of mankind must contend with the absence of
any point of leverage. For the evils and dangerous tendencies of the
system are interwoven with its material inducements.

Foucault attempted to supply a point of entry into this problem
by developing a notion of power focused upon the interplay of
knowledge and power. He promised entry into the world shaped by
technical knowledge and centralized state power. He rejected the
ideal of theoretical knowledge and sought a conception that would
bridge the gulf between knowledge and its application and thus
would eliminate the traditional problem of the proper relationship
between theory and practice. His solution was contained in the
notion of a discursive formation.

A discursive formation consists of practices and institutions that
produce knowledge claims that the system of power finds useful. A
specific discourse serves a maieutic function: it brings objects into
being by identifying them, delimiting their field, and specifying
them, as when psychiatry declares schizophrenics to exist and to be
the objects of psychiatric therapies.[4] Objects of knowledge are defined in ways that converging practices can use: the practices of the
criminologist, the psychiatrist, the hospital administrator, and the
legislator. Thus a discursive formation unites thought and practice in
a seamless and circular web: Practices set the conditions for discourse
and discourse feeds back statements that will facilitate practice. Discourse appears completely incorporated into practice. It has no autonomous identity or distance.

The concept of a discursive formation represents a sharp break
with state-centered conceptions of power and, by extension, with
revolutionary or radical politics which defined itself by opposition to,

or overthrow of, the state. Foucault proposed a vision that could be called Frondiste: it opposes centralization in favor of localism. It is in these local formations that the element of mind, as I have called it, plays its double role, partly constitutive of power and partly the creature of power. So closely are knowledge and power associated that it is difficult to say whether Foucault's legacy is primarily a politics of discourse rather than a discourse about politics or whether it is a discourse in which each is absorbed into the other and transformed by it: politics becomes discourse and discourse politics.

His notion of genealogy seemed to have been fashioned as a weapon in a political struggle against the dominant form of discourse.[5] But the announced aim of the struggle was to liberate forms of knowledge, not to found a new society. Genealogy, he wrote, is "a kind of attempt to emancipate historical knowledges" from the "hierarchical order of power associated with science" and "to render them capable of opposition and struggle against the coercion of a theoretical, unitary, formal, and scientific discourse"(P/K, p. 85). Although the specific target was Marxism, the criticism reflected Foucault's rejection of any "global systematic theory which holds everything in place" (P/K, p. 145). The critical references scattered throughout his writings to Plato, Hobbes, and Hegel made it clear that his attack was directed at the idea of theory as the representation of political totalities and the idea of the theorist as the creator of political truth, "the sovereign figure of the *oeuvres*," as Foucault called him (AK, p. 139). The theoretical project and the theoretical subject are targets for Foucault because they are the carriers of a state-centered, authority-centered politics that is inherently repressive.

Foucault's discourse about politics was thematized in the following: "The set of relations of force in a given society constitutes the domain of the political. . . . To say that 'everything is political' is to affirm this ubiquity of relations of force and their immanence in a political field" (P/K, p. 189). Foucault took the idea of force literally, insisting that politics was war conducted by different means and that "the mechanisms of power are those of repression" (P/K, pp. 90–91). He also drew certain implications for the relationship between politics and discourse: "Do not use thought to ground a political practice in truth; nor political action to discredit, as mere speculation, a line of thought."[6]

These statements sketch a conception of the political and of the relationship between political theory and political action which sharply challenges received notions. There is a strong sense in which each of the major terms—political, theory, and practice—has been reduced to power. This is not surprising because in all of its manifestations—words, things, beings, institutions, and relationships—Foucault's world is suffused with power. There is no social space undefined by power relationships and no socially significant form of power which is not housed. It is a social world totally dominated by power but not necessarily a totalitarian world.

In a curious way, therefore, Foucault seems to have repeated the same error of totalistic thinking with which he taxed classic theory. Foucault's error may have had its own troubling consequences. Not only does he give us a vision of the world in which humans are caught within imprisoning structures of knowledge and practice, but he offers no hope of escape. Every discourse embodies a power drive and every arrangement is repressive. There is no exit because Foucault has closed off any possibility of a privileged theoretical vantage point that would not be infected by the power/knowledge syndrome and would not itself be the expression of a Nietzschean will-to-power. "[I]t is not possible for us to describe our own archive, since it is from within these rules that we speak" (AK, p. 130).

But for that position to be consistently maintained it would have to confront the fact that for three centuries most Western societies have firmly believed that such a privileged body of knowledge is in their actual possession and they have deliberately banked their social and political future on it. They have believed that this mode of knowledge is not class-biased in its nature, that its progress serves the interests of all humanity, and that it is, so to speak, objectively objective despite being highly theoretical.

Since the seventeenth century the modern ideal of knowledge has been identified with scientific theory. As the writings of Bacon, Hobbes, and Descartes illustrate, the modern understanding was perfectly clear about why scientific knowledge was valuable. It was, according to Bacon, for "the enlarging of the bounds of human Empire, to the effecting of all things possible."[7] It was, after all, Bacon who first proposed a design whereby power and knowledge would "meet in one." Despite the quasi-Nietzschean candor of these early proponents of science, subsequent thinkers helped to create a divided vision of science. While urging kings and parliaments to support science for its practical value, they themselves treated it as though it were a body of truths which might offer itself in the service of power without becoming distorted. The political nature of science was thus concealed in an epistemological myth which taught that because scientific knowledge could be rendered into mathematical formulas it must be innocent knowledge.

Although modern science seems to be the perfect example of a discursive formation of power/knowledge, the exact status of scientific knowledge in Foucault's writings is unsure. There is a sense, but a qualified one, in which science occupies a privileged position. It was the standard presupposed in his description of the various stages or "thresholds" a body of knowledge would pass over on the way from "positivity" to "scientificity" and "formalization." (AK, pp. 186–187). Although he acknowledged the possibility that ideological elements might penetrate science, he seemed to resist, as a working hypothesis, the idea that ideological influence could be detected in the theoretical ("ideal") structure of science and in technological applications of science (AK, p. 185). His denial was part of an unargued distinction between "the contents, methods, or concepts of a science," which are placed outside genealogical suspicions, and "the effects of the centralizing powers which are linked to the institution and functioning of an organized scientific discourse within a society" (P/K, p. 84). Nor did he contest the scientific pretensions of the social sciences. Although he located the social sciences among those archaeological territories where scientific aspirations exceeded scientific achievements, Foucault seemed not to have doubted that they were useful and should be accorded a measure of scientific respect. He dismissed as "a secondary matter" the question of the ideological content of the social sciences and of their place in a system of rule (P/K, p. 112).[8]

This impression of ambivalence is not dispelled by Foucault's criticisms of the role of "organized scientific discourse" in sustaining systems of domination. A careful examination of these criticisms shows that they were directed not against the seamless web of involvements between science, governmental bureaucracies, and business corporations, but against "the power of a discourse considered to be scientific," that is, against Marxism (P/K, pp. 84, 85). The problem, he insisted, was not whether Marxism was truly a science but the determination of Marxists to make it one. The problem was "the politics of the scientific statement" (P/K, p. 112). Wanting Marxism to become a science, Marxists were seeking to invest their discourse with "a power which the West since Medieval times has attributed to science and has reserved for those engaged in scientific discourse" (P/K, pp. 84–85).

There was, however more at stake than what got articulated in Foucault's attack upon Marxist science. It had to do with the precarious status of science within classical Marxism. Like Bacon, classical Marxists exalted the economic power of scientific knowledge and exempted it from being under the sway of various idols whose influence caused thinking to err. While claiming to be a science and, by definition, immune to social distortions, Marxist theorists were also busy discrediting all other forms of discourse as ideological, that is, their truth-value was historically relative, a product of their function in a power formation grounded in control over the material means of production and expressed through rule by a particular class. Clearly the perpetuation of the myth of epistemological innocence left science poised at the edge of the ideological abyss into which all the other discursive constructions—theology, philosophy, ethics, and classical political economy—had already tumbled.

From the middle of the nineteenth century to the 1960s the vulnerability of science to Ideologie-Kritik went unnoticed because most thinkers, from Marxists to conservatives, believed scientific knowledge to be immaculately perceived. Pure theory was the usual name, and the distinction between basic and applied science was the typical way of rephrasing the mythic warning about purity and danger. The modern function of the myth was to make the following question appear silly: How was it conceivable that scientific knowledge was permeated by ideological elements when that knowledge had provided the basis for an endless number of technologies that plainly worked?

Soviet Marxism betrayed the myth not only by openly employing science (psychiatry) to suppress dissent and to buttress the authority of the Stalinist dictatorship (the Lysenko affair in genetics or the linguistics controversy), but by injecting ideological elements into scientific methods and theories. As a consequence of this trauma, the presumption of scientific innocence was shaken. Scientific knowledge became a guilty knowledge. Although Soviet Marxism displayed the crisis of scientific faith in its most brutal form, the crisis ran deeper in the non-Marxist West. Ever since Hobbes bravely declared that human beings could be scientific and at the same time interest-driven and power-obsessed, it had become an article of faith that in scientific method the mind had devised a prophylaxis against interest and bias. Accordingly, in the predominantly bourgeois world of the West where, thanks to the canonical status of political economy, the widespread acceptance of notions of self-interest, class-interest, and national interest testified to the conviction that interest pervaded the entire range of personal, social, and political relationships, the vocation of science alone seemed disinterested. In a corrupt world science seemed the only saving knowledge.

In the non-Marxist West the Vietnam War destroyed the illusion of scientific innocence. Thanks to television, itself a product of applied science, everyone could see that this was a war between a technological power and a prescientific society and that science alone had made possible the terrible devastation loosed upon that society. In addition, the critique of American power developed by American radicals contributed to the end of illusions about science. The attack upon corporate capitalism exposed the role of scientific knowledge, while the rise of the environmental movement and the early opposition of establishment scientists to it helped to deflate the myth of scientific purity. Henceforth the meaning of science included an ineradicable political element.

A postlapsarian science produces a problem for all forms of discourse. In a secular age guilty knowledge suggests ideological taint. The surrender of innocence means that instead of being buoyed by the hope that mankind is about to enter the long-promised era of science triumphant, in which mere modernizing will be succeeded by postmodernity, we find that that hope may be our secret nightmare and that we shall be left with nothing more than scientific man with all of the frailties that a genealogical exposé insinuates.

Foucault did not quite face the circularity that his own analysis implied but proceeded as though a permanent residue of strict scientificity remained. The privileged character of science did not mean that it occupied some absolute sanctuary where it was shielded from the relativism that is inscribed in all Foucaldian formations. In Foucault's discourse science enjoyed the sanctuary of equivocation despite its inconsistency with his basic principle that there is a power element that is constitutive of knowledge and a knowledge element that is constitutive of power. While insisting that the institutionalization of science embedded it in structures of power and rendered it complicit in strategies of domination, Foucault wanted nevertheless to limit the contaminating effects of complicity, "the world's slow stain," by denying that they had seeped into the infrastructure of knowledge itself, into its concepts, data, hypotheses, logical or mathematical proofs, and so on.

If Foucault did not challenge the epistemological myth of science directly, he did so indirectly by showing that science did not hold a monopoly over the generation of social power and that social control was exercised through other forms of knowledge which were just as firmly integrated into the knowledge/power circuit. Disciplines with varying claims to scientificity—psychiatry, medicine, sociology, criminology—were deeply implicated in structures that defined while they disciplined the human being. He accomplished this in a novel way. He did not challenge the fact-value dichotomy on which positivist social science continues to rest, albeit less securely than before, nor did he deny the existence of objective knowledge, only its neutrality. "What is at stake in all these genealogies is the nature of this power which has surged into view in all its violence, aggression, and absurdity in . . . the last forty years. . . . My aim [has been] to expose [the fact of domination in] both its latent nature and its brutality" (P/K, pp. 87, 95).

Foucault's intention was not, however, to expose a general system of domination but to identify the dispersed nature of power formations. One of the curiosities of Foucault's writings is that, despite his fascination with power, nowhere does he systematically analyze its supreme embodiment in modern totalitarianism. He was not directly concerned with great tyranny but with smaller ones. His choice rested on strategic considerations as well as on theoretical (or perhaps countertheoretical) ones. The focus on dispersed power follows consistently from Foucault's attack on the centralized conception of power in classic theory.

Foucault paid a heavy price for his refusal to engage central power structures, for he virtually ignored those social sciences that were most heavily implicated in them, namely, economics, political science, and law.[9] It is as though his notion of politics oscillated between two extremes: on the one hand, carceral institutions and, on the other, the dispersed forms of control which define sexuality.

Foucault's attack on the classic conception of theory seems motivated by two contradictory beliefs. One is that the structure of such theories forms a homology with structures of domination. Theories display the same "unitary," totalizing tendencies as the centralized apparatus of the modern state.

Yet at the same time Foucault appears to dismiss the great theoretical constructs described in histories because they were and are dissociated from systems of power. Thus theory appears both dangerous and impotent. My concern is not to belabor the apparent contradiction but to try and show the consequences that follow from Foucault's dismissal of classic theory and of his belief that classic theory neglected the problem of practice.

In using the (not altogether happy) term *classic theory*, I want it to designate a certain kind of project rather than to identify myself with the contents of any particular theory from the past. I shall try to conceptualize the classic project of theory and especially its understanding of the relation of theory to practice. I intend this not as a plea to resurrect the classic project but to clarify the stakes in Foucault's disavowal of it.

My starting point is Foucault's rejection of the notion of theoretical truth independent of practices. For Foucault truth is not a knowledge claim that has been validated by procedures or conventions recognized by some appropriate community of inquirers. "Truth," for Foucault, is always accompanied by quotation marks to signify that it is being unmasked as it is being described: "'Truth' is to be understood," he writes, "as a system of ordered procedures for the production, regulation, distribution, circulation and operation of statements." It is "linked in a circular relations with systems of power which produce and sustain it" (P/K, p. 133). Truth, then, is literally and ambiguously a fabrication. Truth is to Foucault's discursive formations as the commodity was to Marx's account of capitalist production. It is a product of the practices that make it possible.

The obvious criticism to be made is that Foucault has overstated the coherence and ambiguities of discursive formations. They never attain the monolithic unity ascribed to them, not even in that perfect combination of precept and practice known as the Catholic church, much less in that rancorous and divisive discourse that goes by the deceptively unified name of psychoanalysis. But this answer, while perhaps telling, is too facile. The more important point is that although theoretical discourse has never achieved that perfect symbiosis with practices implied in Foucault's notion of a formation, a good many political theorists wished it had, as any reader of Plato's *Republic* or Hobbes's *Leviathan* can testify. Does this mean that theory has always longed to be swallowed up into practice? Did Plato, for example, want to disappear into the *Republic* and reappear in the philosopher guardians, or into the *Laws* and reappear in the Nocturnal Council?

The answer is, I think, mostly no. I say "mostly" because, undeniably, the temptation was there. But the main reason for my answer lies in the nature of the theoretical project itself. That project as a practice—that is, the activity of theorizing—declares its autonomy from politics, its separate identity from political practices, even while it is prescribing them. The reason why Moses, who was Israel's founder and lawgiver, does not enter the promised land is why Socrates, who is used by Plato to describe the ideal polis, would have been the first political prisoner in Plato's *Republic*. The reason lies with the necessary tension between the objectives of theorizing and the tendencies of political action.

In *The Republic* Socrates asks, "Is it possible for anything to be realized in deed as it is in spoken words, or is it the nature of things that action should partake of exact truth less than speech?"[10] Plato's formulation may be interpreted as a double warning that serves to establish the nature of theoretical discourse. The first is the relationship between critical distance and political failure. If theory is absorbed into the discourse of action so as to become inseparable, it will be impossible for it to perceive when action has fallen short of what it should be. It is the nature of action to fall short of theory and it is the role of theory to declare that. Theory can only perform that critical function if it retains a separate identity. Otherwise theory becomes *techne*, and the theorist becomes indistinguishable from the technician of power. Moses does not enter the promised land and because he does not, theory can return as prophecy and criticize the Canaanizing of the desert religion, the "baalizing" of its religious life.[11] Plato is careful to specify that if a state were to come into being it would be only an approximation to the ideal, but the discrepancy would signify that theory would remain distanced from power (*Republic*, 472E, 473A).

The second warning embodies a form of folk wisdom as old as politics and theoretical discourse. Political practice, like its close companion religion, does not simply apply ideal truths but diminishes them. Practice does not merely use theory as it would technical knowledge but uses it calculatingly. The history of religious discourse is a history that testifies to the experience of betrayal through incorporation and to the need for continual rededication and renewal. Collective life reflects the same experience: of justice systematically applied and individually denied, of revolutionary hopes frozen into a new establishment, of virtue smoothed into realism.

For Foucault there is domination but not betrayal or diminution because theory has been denied integrity. In fact, truth only becomes truth when it is integrated with practice and systems of power. The tensions between theory and practice have disappeared. At best any discrepancies appear as mere slippages, technical problems of ironing out applications of thought to practical realities, not as an ontological predicament.

The disappearance of the critical element is signaled by the focus on what Foucault called "political technologies" represented by such institutions as asylums, hospitals, prisons, barracks, and schools. Each of these is treated as a discrete world in which power and the discourse of experts converge upon the body of the individual who, in isolation, is the perfect object of their ministration, not only because he is enclosed but because he is an inmate without choice.

These carceral institutions signify the perfect melding of discursive-ness and practice into a hermetic whole with no outside. Conse-quently there is no purchase point for criticism because there is no general plane remaining, either in theory or political practice. In Foucault's political world we are oppressed, yet no one is oppressing us and no single system dominates us. We can agree that we feel oppressed solely because Foucaldian discourse is parasitic. It has reso-nance because it presupposes the theoretical forms, especially Marx-ism, that it discredits.

To be sure, in the *History of Sexuality* Foucault appeared to retreat from the emphasis in *Discipline and Punish* on total institu-tions. "Power," he now declared, "is not an institution, and not a structure . . . it is the name that one attributes to a complex strateg-ical relationship in a particular society."[12] Which is to say that the idea of strategical relationships is a more fitting focus for studying sexuality. Whatever else it may be, however, sexuality is not, like the forms of power previously studied by Foucault, a carceral cre-ation. The power relationships of sexuality are, instead, the most localized and rationalistic. Relations are formed, Foucault declares, that are "intentional and non-subjective." He even insists that there is a general level at which power relations are inscribed upon sexual-ity and at which the logic and aims are clear. Yet unlike the local practices, the general power relations are the result of no one's inten-tional thoughts or actions. "No one is there to have invented them, and few can be said to have formulated them" (*Sexuality*, 1:95).

This analysis naturally suggests the question, how does Fou-cault's discourse stand in relation to the discursive formations it ana-lyzes? His answer to the question has two aspects, a disavowal both of the centered and totalistic approach to discourse identified with classic theory, and of the state-centered politics that has been a notable feature of modern theory beginning with Bodin and Hobbes. "One impoverishes the question of power if one poses it . . . in terms solely of the state and the state apparatus" (*P/K*, p. 158). His answers take him to a conception of discursive activity as decentered and of politics as decentralized. That conception will prove to be remarkably and perhaps fatally faithful to the etymological origins of the word *discursive:* the latter derives from the Latin verb *discurrere*, or "to run in different directions."

As we have already noted, Foucault rejects theoretical systems and the idea of a theorist-author. He rejects as well what he characterizes as "the traditional question of political philosophy. . . . How is . . . philosophy as that discourse which par excellence is concerned with truth, able to fix limits to the rights of power?" Foucault insisted that the notion of power could not be usefully investigated independently of discourse because "relations of power cannot themselves be established, consolidated nor implemented without the production, accumulation, circulation and functioning of a discourse" (P/K, p. 93). He proposes, therefore, the humbler notion of a theory as "a toolkit." The tool is described as an "instrument" or "logic" for analyzing "the specificity of mechanisms of power," "power relations," and "the struggles around them" (P/K, p. 145). Or in the fuller formulation that he gave toward the end of his life. His aim, he announced, "is to move less toward a theory of power than toward an analytics of power: that is, toward a definition of a specific domain formed by power relations and toward a determination of the instruments that will make possible its analysis" (Sexuality, 1:82).

Thus society is dissolved into a pluralism of power domains and to these the "analytics of power" will apply appropriate "instruments" of analysis. The political purpose motivating the investigations would be "to build little by little a strategic knowledge [savoir]" (P/K, p. 145). This strategic knowledge, in turn, will link up with "local criticism." There exists, Foucault contended, "an autonomous, non-centralized kind of theoretical production" (P/K, 81). Examples were to be found, he maintained, in prisons and asylums and in the student revolt of May 1968.

Although Foucault did not develop the idea of subjugated knowledges in detail, it clearly formed a piece with his rejection of overarching theoretical systems and state-centered politics. During the heady years of the late sixties and early seventies Foucault testified that "we are witness [to] . . . an insurrection of subjugated knowledges" (P/K, p. 81). This sets the stage for Foucault's conception of the political role of those who pursue knowledge without illusions about its purity or, presumably, the purity of their own motives. In his discussion of "subjugated knowledges," Foucault distinguished between the "knowledges of erudition," which refers to the "exact historical knowledge" of those who, like Foucault himself, expose "blocs" of knowledge which have been suppressed and ignored, and a "particular, local, regional knowledge" that is "popular" in character, disorganized but rich in the memory of historical struggles (P/K, pp. 81–83). An example of the latter is the knowledge of the psychiatric patient. The two knowledges are combined in genealogies that will unite them as antisciences. The union was in preparation for a struggle against "the claims of a unitary body of theory" which would assign them a place in a hierarchy of knowledge or delegitimate them altogether (P/K, p. 83).

In a slightly later formulation Foucault restated the idea. In place of the "knowledges of erudition" he inserted "the specific intellectual." The latter was to replace the "universal intellectual" of the past whom Foucault scornfully described as "the spokesman of the universal . . . the consciousness/conscience of us all" (P/K, p. 126). The specific intellectual, who Foucault thought was ideally embodied in the physicist J. Robert Oppenheimer, is the "expert" who possesses a "competence" valued in the truth-domains of society, but who uses that knowledge for "political struggles." The specific intellectual is identified by Foucault as having acquired his importance from "the extension of techno-scientific structures in the economic and strategic domain" (P/K, p. 129).

But why should the specific intellectual employ his or her knowledge in political struggle and why should he side with the dominated? Unfortunately Foucault is silent on these questions, unfortunate because, as the work of Richard Rorty suggests, there is nothing inconsistent between combining advanced views on the demise of theoretical hegemony with political views that are, at best, complacent, and at worst reactionary. Foucault has come to a deadend, the consequence of having accepted an unqualified Nietzschean conception of knowledge as generated by power drives that leaves no room for conceptions of theoretic vocation and civic commitment.

A fundamental political and theoretical question that used to be asked of a radical thinker was this: has he identified the crucial point of vulnerability in the system(s) of power he seems to be opposing? One thinks, for example, of Habermas's legitimation crisis, Marx's analysis of the downfall of capitalism, or of Machiavelli's conception of civic corruption. Within the context of vulnerability, the peculiarity of Foucault's discourse is exposed: there is no place allowed for notions of decline or crisis. Discursive formations seem to have acquired the occult qualities that the ancients ascribed to circles: they reproduce themselves to infinity. Even if one discursive formation, say, criminology or penology, were captured by the forces of deconstruction, it would become immediately evident that what was captured was merely one element in a linked system of fairly substantial, though not necessarily total, interconnections. In short, the problem of theory presents itself not only as the need to identify those interconnections but also as a problem of action. For the practical problem is not simply what to do about the discourse that encompasses prisons and asylums, but how to deal with the practical pressures emanating from an apparently nondiscursive formation, such as an elected legislature that annually votes appropriations for asylums.

The futility that emerges as the key characteristic of Foucault's politics is, I would suggest, not the consequence of an endlessly changing world constituted by mind, but its reflection. Foucault insisted that in adopting a genealogical method he was deliberately choosing to remain at the surface of things, a strategy that was universally applauded by sympathetic interpreters fatigued by the traditional talk about essence and logos. But Foucaldian genealogies— unlike, for example, the logical positivist attack on "metaphysics"— do not puncture linguistic illusions; they simply reduce metaphysical chatter to a historical instance of power/knowledge discourse, more feckless than psychiatry perhaps, but not necessarily its intellectual inferior.

Foucault could not, of course, appeal to a privileged form of discourse without reinstating the heresy of a hierarchy of knowledge. As a result all discourse is reduced to the level of positivity at which power and thought reproduce each other. This means that henceforth knowledge lacks the legitimating quality that in earlier centuries had been associated variously with sacred, divine, or ontological origins. In fact its status is virtually indistinguishable from practices because both are rooted in power. Which is to say that interpreters of Foucault who claim that his discourse is ungrounded are wide of the mark. It is grounded in precisely what ancient conceptions of knowledge were always grounded in, namely, power. One need only recall that Yahweh was a god who was not only omnipotent but omniscient.

What is different is the nature of power: for Foucault the emphasis is upon the repressive, dominating quality of power. Even when he tries to suggest the idea that the objects of power come to serve as its bearers, not simply as its focus, he clearly implies their passivity. Ancient understandings, whether, for example, biblical or Aristotelian, conceive of power as a political relationship in which the object must be receptive without being passive, that is, he possesses a being or structure with its own integrity. He responds to power by learning what it exacts of him, but he tries to connect that exaction with practices designed to make power work on his behalf. Thus in the medieval and early modern institution of kingship the coronation rites had the king pledging to promote the true religion. That promise also tried, however, to connect God's blessing with the practices of monarchy. God was supposed to support the king's military ventures, inspire his judges, and quicken his counsellors. But Foucaldian power operates in a world where things do not have a nature, only a discursive definition shaped by the needs of power. It is not enough to say, as Foucault does, that in the notion of insurgent discourses he has supplied a conception of a subject who, as it were, fights back and resists discursive formations. The Old Testament shows how a people can resist the discourse of Yahweh but also gain his favor and in the end help to shape the terms of the covenant. Or a more humble, contemporary example: consider the "welfare cheat" (in the language of Ronald Reagan) who chisels a system of power by using it while being used by it.

These options were not open to Foucault because he consistently confused politics with the political. Foucault's identification of politics with power has a genealogy of its own extending back to Thucydides and to Plato's portraits of Thrasymachus and Callicles.

The problem of the political is not to deny the ubiquity of power but to deny power uses that destroy common ends. The political signifies the attempt to constitute the terms of politics so that struggles for power can be contained and so that it is possible to direct it for common ends, such as justice, equality, and cultural values. Commonality is what the political is about. Whatever the pretentiousness and vanities of theorists may have been, it was the recollection of commonality and the restatement of its terms which defined the point of theoretical discourse.

Foucault has posited an untrue antagonism between theory and decentralized politics. The result is to leave us with an unlocated self who is denied the critical vantage point that theory allows. The vantage of theory is interconnected with its proclivity toward superiority and quasi-domination. What follows is not that we should renounce theory to avoid its dominating discourse; rather, we should find forms of theory that will be consistent with a localizing—or better—participatory, community-oriented politics. As a starting point: most people don't live in carceral institutions and are only episodically subject to distinct discursive formations. They are instead, located in a certain place. Place is geography and vocations. (Vocations: what we do in and to the world.) This means that subjectivity and historicity are connected. Our place in the double sense of geography and vocations is known only by its history, so, therefore, is our identity.

Locality is the ground that has to be defended against state-centered politics. Which bring us to the crucial role of theory.

The preferred form, I would argue, was prefigured by those writers whom, ironically, Foucault singled out as the most horrendous examples of totalizing: Plato, Hegel, and Marx. And although each was a totalizer, each also held to a conception of theory in which, as it were, theory self-destructs. Thus Plato's dialogue is always incomplete and the issue is never closed. Hegel and Marx both understood theory dialectically, and it was only an urge toward premature—though not logically demonstrable—closure that undid this element.

Self-consuming theory—to use Stanley Fish's term—preserves the playful, self-derisive mien of theory without surrendering its potential contribution to decentered politics. Theory locates the self and the local grouping in relation to the more encompassing structures of power which are the hallmark of state-centered politics. But theory is valuable not only for being able to locate movements but also for helping to overcome the autistic tendencies of localism and the self-centered preoccupation of the postmodern individual. Theory has been a civic discourse. It has called the self out of the self, beckoned it to a plane of generality which reminds the self in its locality that other beings and other life forms inhabit public space and are bent on establishing their own collective identities.

This conception of theory also liberates action from being

200
SHELDON S. WOLIN

haunted by theory and absorbed into the notion of practice. Foucault has no place for action, only for practice. Action is not identical with practice. Practice signifies doing things competently according to the appropriate received canons. Action is often role-breaking or custom-defying, for frequently it seeks to defend the collectivity against evils that are sanctioned by rules and traditions. Action can only play this role if it is free to respond to experience and is guided by theory only to a limited extent. By this formulation discourse is denied the pretensions illicitly gained by its incest with practice.

But this conception of theory makes no claim to the power that discourse enjoys in the discursive formation. The irony of Foucault's attack on the pretensions of totalizing theory is that his own notion of the production of truth represents a power-laden conception of theory which is the equal of the claims made by any theory-intoxicated totalizer of the past. A return to a critical conception of theory, one that can intimate but not prescribe practice, can preserve the means of thinking that can both grasp state-centeredness and point to ways out of it.

Notes

1. For a general survey see Nicholas Lobkowicz, *Theory and Practice: History of a Concept from Aristotle to Marx* (Notre Dame: University of Notre Dame Press, 1967).

2. Michel Foucault, Preface to Gilles Deleuze and Felix Guattari, *Anti-Oedipus: Capitalism and Schizophrenia*, trans. Robert Hurley, Mark Seem, and Helen R. Lane (Minneapolis: University of Minnesota Press, 1983), p. xiv.

3. Michel Foucault, *Power/Knowledge: Selected Interviews and Other Writings, 1972–1977*, ed. Colin Gordon, trans. Colin Gordon et al. (New York: Pantheon, 1980), pp. 121, 122. Hereafter cited as *P/K*.

4. Michel Foucault, *The Archaeology of Knowledge*, trans. A. M. Sheridan Smith (New York: Pantheon, 1972), pp. 41–48. Hereafter cited as *AK*.

5. Michel Foucault, *Language, Counter-Memory, Practice: Selected Essays and Interviews*, ed. Donald F. Bouchard, trans. Donald F. Bouchard and Sherry Simon (Ithaca, N.Y.: Cornell University Press, 1977). See especially the essay "Nietzsche, Genealogy, History," pp. 139–164.

6. "Preface" to *Anti-Oedipus*, p. xiv.

7. H. G. Dick, ed., *Francis Bacon, Selected Writings* (New York: Random House, 1955), p. 574.

8. See the discussion in Hubert L. Dreyfus and Paul Rabinow, *Michel Foucault: Beyond Structuralism and Hermeneutics* (Chicago: University of Chicago Press, 1982), pp. 197ff. See also Foucault's ambiguous remarks about the relationship between the Panopticon formation and the emergence of social science in *Discipline and Punish: The Birth of the Prison*, trans. A. M. Sheridan Smith (New York: Pantheon, 1977), p. 305.

9. Although Foucault attended to economics in *The Archaeology of Knowledge*, he was wholly concerned with the emergence of political economy as a mode of discourse, not as an element in a power/knowledge formation. In the *Archaeology* there is a glaring gap between geneaology and power.

10. Plato, *Republic*, trans. Paul Shorey (London: Heinemann, 1930–1935), 473A. Hereafter cited as *Republic*.

11. On this point see F. W. Albright, *Yahweh and the Gods of Canaan* (London: Athlone, 1968).

12. Michel Foucault, *History of Sexuality*, trans. Robert Hurley (New York: Pantheon, 1978), 1:93. Hereafter cited as *Sexuality*.

CONTRIBUTORS

JONATHAN ARAC is Professor of English and Comparative Literature at Columbia University. Author of *Commissioned Spirits* (1979), one of the first works of literary history to use Foucault, and of *Critical Genealogies* (1987), he co-edited *The Yale Critics* (1983) and edited *Postmodernism and Politics* (1986).

ISAAC D. BALBUS was awarded the C. Wright Mills Prize for *The Dialectics of Legal Repression* (1973) and is also author of *Marxism and Domination* (1982). He is currently completing a book on gender struggle and the transformation of Western child-rearing, 1500–1950. He is Professor of Political Science at the University of Illinois at Chicago.

PAUL P. BOVÉ is Professor of English at the University of Pittsburgh. Associate editor of *boundary 2: a journal of postmodern literature and culture* and co-editor of *The Question of Textuality* (1982), he authored *Destructive Poetics* (1980) and *Intellectuals in Power: A Genealogy of Critical Humanism* (1986).

H. D. HAROOTUNIAN is Palevsky Professor of Civilizations, University of Chicago, where he chairs the Department of History. He is author of *Toward Restoration: The Growth of Political Consciousness in Tokugawa Japan* (1970) and *Things Seen and Unseen* (1988); co-editor of *Japan in Crisis* (1974); and contributor to several volumes of the *Cambridge History of Japan*.

DAVID COUZENS HOY, author of *The Critical Circle: Literature and History in Contemporary Hermeneutics* (1978) and of several articles on

Foucault, edited *Foucault: A Critical Reader* (1986). He is Professor of Philosophy at the University of California, Santa Cruz.

MARIE-ROSE LOGAN is Associate Professor of French and Italian and of Humanities at Rice University. She edited two special issues of *Yale French Studies: Graphesis* (1976) and *Rethinking History* (1980); and has published several essays illuminating topics in the Renaissance through Foucault's work.

DANIEL T. O'HARA is Professor of English at Temple University. His books include *Tragic Knowledge* (1981), *The Romance of Interpretation* (1985), and a forthcoming study of Lionel Trilling. He also edited *Why Nietzsche Now?* (1985).

EDWARD W. SAID has used and criticized Foucault extensively in *Beginnings* (1975), *Orientalism* (1978), and *The World, the Text, and the Critic* (1983). He is Parr Professor of English and Comparative Literature at Columbia University.

JANA SAWICKI is Associate Professor of Philosophy at the University of Maine at Orono. She has published essays on Foucault and Heidegger and on Foucault and feminism, as well as on the ethics of medical information systems.

SHELDON S. WOLIN, Professor Emeritus of Politics, Princeton University, and founding editor of *democracy* (1981–1983) is author of the classic *Politics and Vision* (1960) and has been a leading commentator on American political life in *The New York Review of Books* and elsewhere.

INDEX

208

INDEX